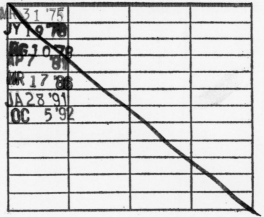

BURT FRANKLIN: RESEARCH & SOURCE WORKS SERIES
American Classics in History and Social Science 239

THE PRESIDENT'S CABINET

THE PRESIDENT'S CABINET

STUDIES IN THE ORIGIN, FORMATION AND STRUCTURE OF AN AMERICAN INSTITUTION

By
HENRY BARRETT LEARNED

BURT FRANKLIN
New York, N. Y.

Published by LENOX HILL Pub. & Dist. Co. (Burt Franklin)
235 East 44th St., New York, N.Y. 10017
Originally Published: 1912
Reprinted: 1972
Printed in the U.S.A.

S.B.N.: 8337-46448
Library of Congress Card Catalog No.: 72-80393
Burt Franklin: Research and Source Works Series
American Classics in History and Social Science 239

Reprinted from the original edition in the Wesleyan
University Library.

PREFACE

THE following Studies are designed to reveal those factors in the history of the President's Cabinet which explain the origin and formation of the council as well as the establishment of the structural offices which form the institution. They are complete in themselves. Only incidentally are they concerned with cabinet practices and personnel. The study of cabinet practices and personnel is a large and difficult subject. At another time, when I have succeeded in compassing scattered and refractory materials, I propose to set it forth in accordance with the plan projected in the Introduction. The limited task has yielded results which admit now of the presentation of a book which will throw light, I hope, on a subject concerning which there has been hitherto no satisfactory record.

I have felt obliged to give much attention to political debates. "Few forms of literature or history are so dull," says John Morley, "as the narrative of political debates. With a few exceptions, a political speech like the manna in the wilderness loses its savour on the second day." On the other hand, the truths of my subject were not to be extracted at many points from any other sources. These sources, too, afforded frequent glimpses of men of marked distinction, and accordingly helped to relieve the structural aspects of the theme by supplying warmth and life. I cannot resist paying tribute in this connection to Charles Pinckney, the brilliant statesman from South Carolina, whose work in the Philadelphia Convention of 1787 has been better appreciated of late years than ever before. The longer I studied the materials which have entered into my third chapter on the "Development of the Idea of a President's Council: 1787-1788," the stronger became my interest in Pinckney. If I have succeeded in setting in truer perspective such a well-known figure as Robert J. Walker of Mississippi; and if I have drawn forth into the light from their dim recesses two such comparatively unknown men as Judge Augustus B. Woodward of Virginia and Charles B. Calvert of Maryland, I shall have done only what the truth of history seemed to warrant.

Portions of the matter in several of these Studies have been printed already in such periodicals as the *American Historical Review* (April, 1905, and July, 1911), the *Yale Review* (August, 1906, and October, 1911), the *American Political Science Review* (August, 1909), and the *Political Science Quarterly* (September, 1909). While I have drawn freely upon such printed matter, the book is the product of a renewed effort to reconsider, to elaborate, and to extend to the point of great fullness a collection of notes on the basis of which it has been written.

To many persons I am under obligations for encouragement or assistance at different stages of the work. The task was originally suggested by Professor A. B. Hart. It was begun under the guidance of Professors Hart and Edward Channing, my teachers at Harvard University. It developed in interest and gained proportion as a result of many conversations on the subject of method with my friend, the late Professor E. G. Bourne. His discerning criticism first aroused me to the possibilities of the theme, notwithstanding his characteristically frank admission that he cared little about the sort of task in which I had become involved. On many points of law I have had the helpful counsel of Governor S. E. Baldwin of New Haven, Connecticut; Professor W. R. Vance of the Yale Law School; Mr. Middleton Beaman, until recently Librarian of the Law Library of Congress and the Supreme Court; and Mr. Henry E. Colton, Special Assistant to the Attorney-General. Professor J. Franklin Jameson, Director of the Department of Historical Research of the Carnegie Institution of Washington, was kind enough to read the first rough draft of the manuscript; he made several suggestions by means of which I was enabled to improve the book. Professor William A. Dunning of Columbia University aided me in similar fashion by reading several of the early chapters. Others to whom I am grateful for encouragement are: President Lowell of Harvard University, ex-Secretary of War Jacob M. Dickinson, Hon. James R. Mann of Chicago, Illinois, Professors Franklin B. Dexter and Charles M. Andrews of Yale University, Mr. Charles H. Adams of the *Hartford Courant,* Mr. George L. Fox of New Haven, and Mr. Robert Brent Mosher, formerly Chief of the Bureau of Appointments in the State Department at Washington and now Consul at Plauen in Saxony. For her painstaking care in examining under my direction certain historic materials which have entered into the body of the book I am indebted to the late Miss E. G. Fowler of Hartford, Connecticut. To no one, however, do I acknowledge with greater readiness my gratitude for inspiration and assistance than to my friend, Professor Max Farrand of Yale University. He has spared much time in allowing me to discuss with him many problems all along the way.

The book can hardly be free from errors of fact and judgment. For these errors I am alone responsible. The publishers have taken the utmost care to have the volume meet my wishes in every respect. Mr. E. Byrne Hackett in particular has given time and thought to the selection of type and to oversight of all the mechanical details.

H. B. L.

New Haven, Connecticut,
    October 15, 1911.

CONTENTS

THE PRESIDENT'S CABINET

INTRODUCTION

NO man can rule a people alone. However primitive a government may be, the chief, called by whatever name, is bound to rely for his successful direction of it on aid outside himself. From the distant beginnings of historic polity, whether these beginnings are studied in the Homeric poems, in the traditions that lay behind the Roman Commonwealth and the succeeding Empire or in the slender records of the German tribes—so far at least as these tribes had a common permanent head—kings had their groups or councils of intimate advisers. When Moses complained that he was not able to "bear this people alone, because it was too heavy for him," the Lord had him gather seventy men of the elders of Israel and "bring them into the tabernacle of the congregation" to stand there and bear with him the burden of the people.

Essential factors of kingly influence and power these councils were in any system of government. The simplest form of council was one composed of assistants selected by the chief from among his immediate friends and following, such as his household servants and officers. These intimate assistants were at their leader's beck and call. Helping him to formulate plans and then to carry them out, they sustained his sway. Some such body characteristic of force and efficiency stood at the very beginnings of successful

government. But it marked not only primitive organization, for it appeared under many and varying guises
and forms all through the course of the historic ages.
The ancient empires of the East knew it. Roman
administrators utilized it. Diocletian developed it.
Charlemagne would have been helpless without it. In
the progressive organization of the medieval Church
it found a place. By means of it the Capetians laid
those firm foundations on which monarchs of a later
time established absolutism in France during the sixteenth and seventeenth centuries. In England the
course and development of the royal council have been
traced with exceptional clearness through various
stages until in Lancastrian days it became known as
the Privy Council. In time an inner body differentiated itself from the Privy Council. This inner
council, attracting attention, was occasionally termed
the Cabinet Council early in the seventeenth century.
This was the precursor of the Cabinet Committee over
which after many difficulties Parliament was destined
at length to gain a controlling grasp—the committee
around which the working government of England is
organized, and by means of which that government is
directed.

Into the manifold and subtle intricacies of these
many historic councils it is not the plan to enter.
Whatever is true regarding the origin of the American
President's Cabinet Council, that institution was in no
sense a conscious imitation of any organization in
existence at the epoch of its creation. Nevertheless it
was certainly the expression of a need quite as old as

government—the need, in brief, of a corps of closely associated assistants qualified to aid an executive chief magistrate in whom leadership and directive force were intended to be vigorous and really effective.

Such officers as at first constituted the President's Cabinet—three Secretaries known as heads of departments and an Attorney-General—were similar to administrative officers found not only in the government of England but elsewhere in western Europe. Indeed they were foreshadowed by somewhat similar officials in the various American colonies, although not by exact prototypes.

The term *cabinet* or *cabinet council* is English. There was just a sufficient analogy between the group of officials which formed the English Cabinet late in the eighteenth century and the American President's intimate advisers at the same time to make the application of the English term to the American group appear to be reasonably significant. It should, however, be remembered that the English Cabinet Committee had developed in the course of a complicated evolution of party practices and peculiar circumstances into a parliamentary committee which was largely responsible even at that time to the House of Commons. Historic processes were pressing it forward to its goal, a place of such influence that it was to become the deciding factor in matters of government policy long before the close of the nineteenth century. Its spokesman and director was already customarily known as the Prime Minister. The President's Cabinet, in contrast to the English institution, was essentially and simply an advisory council quite independent of the Legislature. The President summoned it if he wished to do so. To the President alone its members were responsible. It had at the start no pivotal place in the structure of the American government, certainly no place that was so recognized outside of its immediate membership. Indeed the principle of the Cabinet's distinct association with the executive chief alone was not determined until early practices under Washington and his immediate successors had developed the principle into clearness, and given it authority. Moreover, the responsibility imposed upon the President by the Constitution has always tended to keep the Cabinet a subordinate element in our government. As an advisory body it has been an interesting addition to the executive, at times helping much to make or mar the reputation of a President, for the Cabinet must often be utilized to create if not to direct a President's policy, and to shape his attitude toward various problems of moment to the national welfare. Unseen in its workings, but presumably supporting him in his plans, the Cabinet is a combination of qualified experts that has stood behind every chief magistrate. The President may of course ignore the advice of his council, but—as Alexander Hamilton cogently observed in 1800[1]—no President can as a rule afford to do so. If one were to seek identity of type for the President's Cabinet, one could probably discover it more easily in the organization of the French monarchy before 1789 than in the

[1] *Works* (ed. H. C. Lodge), VI, 419.

government of England, for the Cabinet is a veritable *conseil du roi.*

From a time soon after the formation of the Constitution down to the present day the associates of the President who compose the Cabinet have been freely termed "constitutional advisers." Hamilton thus characterized them.[2] Such usage, although loose, rests partly on the fact that the Constitution as well as the statute law helped to predetermine a council.

The Constitution referred to the "principal officer in each of the executive Departments," and again to the "Heads of Departments": the President might require their opinions "in writing" upon any subject relating to the duties of their respective offices. Although not expressly enjoining executive departments, the Constitution thus clearly contemplated principal officers. In accordance with this view the first Congress under the new government in 1789 proceeded among its earliest acts to draw up laws for the establishment of three Secretaryships, and to provide for the office of Attorney-General. By 1792, or perhaps a little earlier, the practice of President Washington brought these four officers together as an advisory council. In 1793 the body was popularly termed the Cabinet. In the course of time Washington's practice, persisted in by his successors, became an established custom.

Five other officials with duties clearly defined in the laws have since been added to the original four, making to-day a council of nine regular advisers about

[2] For a discussion of this usage see chapter XIII, pp. 389 ff.

the President. Although the laws which from time to time have provided for the creation of these nine officials have taken no account of their combination into a body of counsellors, it should be observed, nevertheless, that the Secretary of the Navy (1798), the Secretary of the Interior (1849), the Secretary of Agriculture (1889), and the Secretary of Commerce and Labor (1903) were regularly conceived of as "cabinet" associates of the chief magistrate at the different times at which the bills creating these respective offices were discussed, passed, and sanctioned. In fact it is assumed to-day simply as a matter of course that the "Secretary" of a new department will become as such an intimate adviser and associate of the President, and that by mere custom he is entitled to cabinet place and rank. Yet there has never been either constitutional or legal provision requiring the President to consult or to summon the Cabinet. Once only has the term *Cabinet* been allowed thus far to slip into a federal statute, the word appearing for the first time in a law signed by President Roosevelt on February 26, 1907. The Cabinet, in brief, remains to-day what it was at the beginning, a customary body of advisers.

No thoroughly complete history of such a customary institution as the President's Cabinet can, I think, be written. Here and there for lack of evidence its story must ever remain unknown—concealed by impenetrable darkness. Research and discovery, however, aided by inference and reflection, should yield much in the way of reliable information on the following subjects:

I. Origin, Formation, and Structure.

II. Practices and Personnel.

The present—and first—series of Studies has been written chiefly from such historic materials as throw light especially on the origin and structural offices of the institution. This series is consequently limited to setting forth the anatomy in contrast to the functions of the Cabinet. It seemed essential to discover and present those factors and influences which could account for the early summoning under President Washington of the council, and for the council's natural enlargement by the gradual addition of chief offices. The historic development of administrative work, which not only brought heavy tasks to the shoulders of the secretariat but also increased the responsibility of the President, has had to be observed and frequently commented on. While under this first phase of the subject I have refrained from venturing far into the domain of political practices, and have avoided the entanglements of personal factors, at very few points in the narrative could I forget how important practices and personnel must always have been to the vitality of the institution as an element in the workings of the national government.

In order to complete my plan I have in process of construction a second series of Studies which are concerned with the whole subject of Cabinet Practices and Personnel. This second series is designed to consider such subjects as cabinet appointments and resignations, the qualifications of cabinet officers, the influence of the Cabinet on executive policy and on legislation, the history of the cabinet meeting; and to set forth some of the curious episodes that have occasionally marked the history of the institution.

CHAPTER I

HISTORIC SIGNIFICANCE OF THE TERM "CABINET" IN ENGLAND

I

THE period of three centuries following the Norman Conquest was a formative one for English institutions. The circumstances of the Conquest brought immense authority to the Crown. This authority was certain to be controlled and limited as English liberties were secured.

The original nucleus of royal power was the *curia regis*. The early history of this body would involve an account of the gradual and complicated process by which judicial, executive, legislative and political functions were separated, one from another, and assigned to different organs. Out of the *curia regis* there developed the King's Council.[1] "At no time," says a recent writer,[2] "did English kings fail to have particular counsellors, known as *consiliarii, consultores, familiares, domestici,* or *aulici,* including men of the household, of the curia, and of the exchequer. In this they were like other kings (most notably the King of France), other princes, and even bishops and barons who possessed councils of uncertain composition."

[1] A. V. Dicey, *The Privy Council* (1887), pp. 2, 6-7.
[2] James F. Baldwin, "The Beginnings of the King's Council" in *Transactions of the Royal Historical Society* (1905), XIX, n. s. 29 ff.

Just when the King's personal advisers began to have a recognized position as a distinct and organized body it is not easy to say. The view of Bishop Stubbs that this council can be traced only from the minority of Henry III can no longer be accepted because of the discovery of good evidence that the King's Council was already distinct and organized in the reign of John. It seems possible that it may yet be distinguished as early as Henry II's reign. But there is no positive proof.[3] We know that the Common Council of the realm claimed under Henry III the right to nominate as well as to confirm great officers,[4] and thus to force the King to choose worthy associates as his personal advisers. But the problem presented numberless practical difficulties, especially as there was at the time no developed or clearly defined legislative power apart from the King—no Parliament with acknowledged prerogatives.

The historic process of the thirteenth and fourteenth centuries brought the King's Council to its maturity by the close of the Plantagenet period. It was then the one sworn council of the King. Not large in numbers, it possessed, nevertheless, real power and efficiency as well as great dignity. Devoted to the work of legislation as well as administration, touching at times on the domain of a jealous and watchful Parliament, it was the mainspring of government. The powerful status to which it had attained was the result

---

[3] Stubbs, *Constitutional History of England*, 4th ed. II, 40 ff. For the more recent view, Baldwin in *Trans. of the Royal Hist. Soc.*, op. cit., p. 32.

[4] Stubbs, *Constitutional History*, II, 41.

of the cumulative effect of custom rather than of statutory regulation.[5]

In the fifteenth century under the house of Lancaster the Council, now coming to be known as the Privy Council, reached its greatest power. Through force of many circumstances it was able to overshadow alike the Crown, Parliament, and the people. It had fallen from its great traditions and its prestige by the time of Henry VII's accession; but it afforded the later Tudors, intent upon building up a great system of centralization, a royal instrument by means of which they were enabled to establish organized and efficient rule throughout the kingdom. Under their sway the Privy Council gathered together and held all the threads of administration and diplomacy.[6] In its effectiveness as a Tudor organ, it has been characterized as "practically the predecessor of the modern Cabinet of Ministers."[7]

Soon after the coming to the throne of the obstinate and injudicious line of the Stuarts, the problem of the relations of the King to his personal associates and close political advisers began to assume a foremost

[5] Baldwin, "Early Records of the King's Council" in *American Historical Review* (October, 1905), XI, 1-15. "Antiquities of the King's Council" in *English Historical Review* (January, 1906), XXI, 1-20. "The King's Council from Edward I to Edward III" in *Eng. Hist. Rev.* (January, 1908), XXIII, 1-14. "The Privy Council of the Time of Richard II" in *Amer. Hist. Rev.* (October, 1906), XII, 1-14.

[6] Dicey, *Privy Council;* J. F. Baldwin, as previously cited; Lord Eustace Percy, *The Privy Council under the Tudors* (Stanhope Prize Essay, 1907), pp. 1-2.

[7] *Acts of the Privy Council of England* (1542-1547). J. R. Dasent, ed., I, Preface, viii.

place. By the beginning of the reign of Charles I it was clearly defined. What its solution would be was determined as a result of the political upheaval which followed. In the seventeenth century parliamentary government germinated. It developed markedly in the eighteenth century. The maturity of the system is one of the characteristic features of English government in the nineteenth century.

The personal monarchy of Charles I, with all that it implied in the way of restriction of popular rights and widespread oppression, was more than a progressive people could endure. At the very outset of the reign the claims of the Crown and Parliament were felt to be incompatible. The Commons demanded supremacy in the state and attempted to extract from the King a promise that he would change his ministers whenever the Commons were displeased with them. Parliament really was striving to make the government dependent upon itself. In other words the idea of parliamentary leadership was assuming a positive and aggressive maturity. At the time, as perhaps never before, English popular opinion won not only expression but very capable direction. It was inevitably an epoch of experiment, but of experiment which often was made along conservative and older lines.

The demand that the King submit to the guidance of such worthy counsellors as Parliament could trust was so frequently reiterated after 1640 that its reiteration is strong evidence that it had assumed the aspect of a very vital political principle. Among numerous instances it was clearly formulated in the petition preceding the Grand Remonstrance (1641), in a document according to which the King's subjects beg—

That your Majesty will . . . . be pleased to remove from your council all such as persist to favour and promote any of those pressures and corruptions wherewith your people have been grieved, and that for the future your Majesty will vouchsafe to employ such persons in your great and public affairs, and to take such to be near you in places of trust, as your Parliament may have cause to confide in . . . .[8]

Such a demand, when put into practical shape, meant a government residing in a body of men acting under the control of Parliament.

It is not necessary to analyze the steps taken or projected by the Long Parliament from 1640 onwards for the purpose of wresting from Charles certain special powers and thereby gaining control over administrative, financial, judicial, and military affairs. It is enough to say that by 1644 Parliament was fully determined in its purpose to control such matters. In the first half of that year, in view of the indefinite continuance of the war, two ordinances were passed, dated respectively February 16 and May 22, which provided for the so-called Committee of Both Kingdoms. This Committee, composed of seven Peers,

---

[8] S. R. Gardiner, *Constitutional Documents of the Puritan Revolution* (1889), p. 129. Gardiner prints his volume for everyday use, and consequently he omits old-fashioned italics and numerous capital letters and some superfluous commas. The same passage may be found in J. Rushworth, *Historical Collections*, IV, 438. Cf. the similar demand of the Grand Remonstrance, Gardiner's *Documents*, pp. 131, 153, 154. See also the demand in the Ten Propositions of June 24, 1641. *Ibid.*, p. 92. Cf. pp. 125, 171 (Nineteen Propositions), 246, 340 (Humble Petition and Advice of 1657).

fourteen Commoners, and four Commissioners of the
Scottish Parliament, was to "order and direct whatsoever doth or may concern the managing of the war
. . . . and whatsoever may concern the peace of
his Majesty's dominions." By Mr. Gardiner it is
regarded as "the first attempt to give practical shape
to the idea of a government residing in a body of men
acting under the control of Parliament."[9] Here,
according to the same writer, the student of English
institutions comes upon "the first germ of the modern
Cabinet system." The Committee exercised "general
executive powers under responsibility to Parliament.
. . . . Though it was not, like a modern Cabinet, composed of persons of only one shade of political opinion,
the opinion that the war ought to be carried on with
vigour was decidedly preponderant in it." "That
the Committee thus instituted," he adds, "could never
be more than an interesting experiment was the natural result of the fact that the Parliament from which
it sprung had no claim to be regarded as a national
body."[10]

The Committee of Both Kingdoms disappeared in
1648, within about four years of its creation. What
the reader should observe is this: that the demand

[9] S. R. Gardiner, *Constitutional Documents*, Introd., pp. xliii-xliv, 190,
192. The first Ordinance, it will be observed, was limited to three
months. Cf. C. H. Firth, *The House of Lords during the Civil War*
(1910), pp. 138-141.

[10] Gardiner, *History of the Great Civil War*, I, 357 ff. As yet Gardiner
is the only historian who has given these Ordinances any careful attention, although Mr. Firth touches upon them in his most recent book, *The
House of Lords during the Civil War*. Cf. D. Masson, *The Life of
John Milton*, III (ed. 1896), 41, 331, 579, 585.

which called it into existence represented a sound and fundamental principle, which was repeatedly voiced or formulated during the epoch, and was never afterwards surrendered, at least by the more liberal leaders. In brief, the later and matured English Cabinet Committee was the consummate and practical achievement of this persistent demand.

II

As the seventeenth century in England witnessed the crude beginnings of parliamentary government, so that century first began to attach political significance to the term *cabinet*. The term had originally appeared in the language of the sixteenth century. Francis Bacon was among the earliest writers to reflect in his *Essays*[11] its political sense. From Bacon's time it may be traced with many varieties of shadings through Speed, Walter Yonge, Massinger, Clarendon, Selden, Pepys, Sir John Reresby and Evelyn to Bolingbroke, Swift, Roger North, and other memoir writers of Queen Anne's and the Georgian epoch.[12]

An extract from the *State Papers* dated at London, June 8, 1622, reads as follows: "Chamberlain to Carleton. A Cabinet Council is talked of, to which the most secret and important business may be committed. . . . ."[13] This is the earliest usage of the term

[11] Ed. S. H. Reynolds (Oxford: 1891), p. 148, foot note a.
[12] See Note 1 at the end of this chapter.
[13] *Calendars of State Papers—Domestic* (1619-1623), p. 404. Cf. also *Ibid.* (1623-1625), pp. 156, 203. On April 23, 1625: "There is talk of

that I can discover in these valuable and miscellaneous sources. By the last decade of the century, however, the term is frequently found in them.

The varied and often vague applications of the term it is needless to dwell upon. For much of the seventeenth century it signified a body of royal counsellors or ministers which met in private, a committee of state apt to be concerned with such secret and informal measures as Parliament could not easily fathom or control. It was seldom used without opprobrium even well into the eighteenth century. There is no better illustration of this than in two discussions of the term as it cropped up in Parliament in the years 1692 and 1711 respectively.

" 'Cabinet-Council' [retorted an angry member in the House of Commons in November, 1692] is not a word to be found in our Law-books. We knew it not before; we took it for a nick-name. Nothing can fall out more unhappily than to have a distinction made of the 'Cabinet' and 'Privy Council.' . . . . If some of the Privy Council must be trusted, and some not, to whom must any gentleman apply? Must he ask, 'Who is a Cabinet-Counsellor?' This creates mis-

a selected or Cabinet Council, whereto none are admitted but the Duke of Buckingham, the Lords Treasurer and Chamberlain, Lord Brooke, and Lord Conway.'' Walter Yonge probably refers to the same matter when he records in June, 1625, this entry in his *Diary* (p. 83, Camden Society, 1848): ''The King made choice of six of the nobility for his *Council of the Cabinet.''* On July 14, 1630, Sir Thomas Roe referred to Sir Henry Vane—as Mr. Gardiner long since (1886) pointed out—as one ''who is of the Cabinet.'' *Cal. of St. Papers—Domestic* (1629-1631), p. 306. According to Clarendon (*History*, I, 263, ed. of 1826), within a few years the terms ''Committee of State,'' ''Junto,'' and ''Cabinet Council'' were used synonymously when a group of royal advisers was referred to.

trust in the people. . . . ."[14] "The method of the cabinet [declared another member on the same occasion] is not the method nor the practice of England . . . . things are concerted in the Cabinet, and then brought to the council. . . . . If this method be, you will never know who gives advice. . . . ."[15]

In January, 1711, discussion arose in the House of Lords over the question of using the term *cabinet council*—as at first it was proposed to do—or *ministers* in a resolution of censure. It was objected that both terms were ambiguous. Both terms, moreover, were unknown to the law. Of the two, *ministers* or *ministry* was called "too copious" in its meaning, for the Cabinet Council, it was observed, did not take in all the ministers. The discussion became strenuous and was delaying really important and pressing business, when the Earl of Peterborough gave it an amusing turn by reminding his colleagues of a distinction with which he was familiar. He had heard, he said, that "the Privy Counsellors were such as were thought to know every thing and knew nothing; and . . . . those of the Cabinet Council thought nobody knew any thing but themselves. . . . ."[16]

However reproachful the reflections cast on the term by members of Parliament might be, "cabinet" or "cabinet council" was well recognized and in frequent use by the last decade of the seventeenth century.

[14] *Parliamentary History*, V, 731.
[15] *Ibid.*, V, 733.
[16] *Ibid.*, VI, 971 ff.

Thus on June 16, 1690, the Marquis of Carmarthen, writing to King William III, says: "The Lords of the Cabinet think. . . . . ."[17] A week later: "Her Majesty is very diligent at cabinet councils. . . . . The Queen hereupon called the cabinet council and gave several orders. . . . . ."[18] On September 5, 1694, there was recorded the draft of a summons "to the Cabinet Council to meet this day at 5 p.m. . . . . ."[19]

III

Behind the term, which it has been comparatively easy to trace, was the thing—the Committee or Council of the Cabinet. It would certainly be vain to seek any precise beginnings for such a committee; the search for these would lead inevitably into a maze of practices which are found far back in history. But two matters are tolerably clear: in the first place some such committee began to attract enough attention to be noted in the records of the first quarter of the seventeenth century; and writers of authority in that century regarded the Cabinet Committee as an offshoot of the Privy Council, itself the traditional organ of executive power. Roger North, for example, basing his statements on records left by his brother, Francis North, the Lord Keeper Guilford, intimately associated with the government of Charles II, could say of the Cabinet Council this: "as offices of the law, out of clerkships, spawn other offices, so this council was

17 *Calendars of State Papers—Domestic* (1690-1691), p. 33.
18 *Ibid.,* p. 38.
19 *Ibid.* (1694-1695), p. 295.

derived from the Privy Council, which, originally, was the same thing. . . . . Assemblies, at first, reasonably constituted of a due number and temper for dispatch of affairs committed to them, by improvident increase, came to be formal and troublesome, the certain consequence of multitude, and thereby a new institution becomes necessary: whereupon it is found easier and safer to substitute than to dissolve. Thus the cabinet council, which, at first, was but in the nature of a private conversation, came to be a formal council, and had the direction of most transactions of the Government, foreign and domestic."[20] Although this well-known passage may have been descriptive of what took place under Charles II near the opening of the reign, it can reasonably be interpreted as having had, in its author's mind, a more general and wider application. In the wider sense it affords a statement close to historic truth.

Institutions have a way of appearing before they are named. And this postulate would tend to turn the student on the trail of the Cabinet Committee into the Tudor epoch. Knowledge of the workings of the Privy Council within the epoch is still very incomplete, but it is larger than that of the Stuart epoch, for as yet the acts of the Council after 1604 have not been printed.[21] Under the Tudors the mass of admin-

[20] R. North, *Lives of the Norths* (London: 1826, 3 vols.), II, 50-51. Cf. John Trenchard, *A Short History of Standing Armies in England* (1698), for a similar view.

[21] Lord Eustace Percy, *op. cit.*, pp. 35-39, 68 ff. G. W. Prothero, Introd. to *Statutes and Constitutional Documents* (1559-1625), pp. xcviii ff.

istrative, judicial and executive business in the hands
of the Privy Council was enormous.   The size of the
Council increased, especially under Edward VI and
Mary.   With larger tasks than ever to perform, it was
inevitable that it should delegate some of its jurisdiction if not its authority.   Under Edward VI and his
successor the work of the Privy Council was divided
among sundry committees, the most notable of which
was probably the Committee of State of 1553.   From
this point Sir William R. Anson dates the permanency
of the practice of discussing important business in an
interior council.   This committee may be regarded,
according to the same writer, as the precursor of the
Committee of State of 1640 which Clarendon described
as being termed by way of reproach a ''Cabinet
Council.''   ''It seems,'' says Anson, ''almost inevitable that unless the entire Privy Council was often
reconstituted the treatment of important matters must
pass into the hands of a few.   The Council would
always contain men qualified for one cause or another
to be Councillors of the Crown but not possessed of
the practical sagacity, promptitude of judgment, and
force of character which come into play when some
crisis calls for immediate action and nothing that can
be done is free from risk.   The men who possess these
qualities would be the men to form the 'Committee of
State,' the 'junto,' the 'Cabinet.' ''[22]

[22] Anson, *The Law and Custom of the Constitution*, Pt. II, The
Crown (2d ed., 1896), pp. 92-93.   Anson draws his conclusion from Bur-
net's *History of the Reformation*, V, 119, from the minutes of a cabinet
council of August 16, 1640 (*The Hardwicke Papers*, II, 147), and from
Clarendon's comments in his *History*, Bk. II, ss. 61, 99.   Lord Eustace

This truly notable conclusion which places the establishment of the practice of interior councils—in other
words the beginnings of the Cabinet Committee—back
in the Tudor epoch is plausible. It rests upon insuffi-
cient evidence to make it altogether convincing. What
it helps to explain is this: the appearance under
James I of a new political phrase; the apparent
decline of the Privy Council in position and power
under the Stuarts.

The practice of advising with an inner ring of councillors or of going even outside the Privy Council for
advice was certain to arouse the suspicions of a watchful Parliament. It would seem, moreover, to give
special point to Clarendon's observation regarding
Charles I, that the King's failure properly to estimate
the importance of the Privy Council as an institution
and to maintain its authority was one of the chief
causes which help to explain the fall of the monarchy.[23]
There is no doubt, however, that the practice of inner
councils was continued under Charles II, but with certain modifications that reveal some growing deference
on the part of the monarch toward Parliament. Once
back in England in 1660, the circumstances of the
political situation forced upon Charles a large and
unmanageable Privy Council. It was soon found
expedient to divide it into various committees. Conspicuous among these was the so-called Committee of
Foreign Affairs. There was another committee, which

Percy detects in some of the Marian and Elizabethan committees of the
Privy Council elements of permanency. *Op. cit.*, p. 39.

[23] C. H. Firth in *English Historical Review*, January, 1904, pp. 42 ff.
(Art.: ''Clarendon's 'History of the Rebellion.' '')

Clarendon describes in this way. The King, he
wrote—

appointed the chancellor and some others to have frequent
consultations with such members of the parliament who were
most able and willing to serve him; and to concert all the
ways and means by which the transactions in the houses
might be carried with the more expedition, and attended with
the best success.[24]

This latter measure is suggestive of Temple's well-
known plan of 1679, which proved to be a vain
endeavor to establish a sort of mechanism by which
Parliament and the King's Council could work
together. But the complaint of the time was that
some Cabinet Council "takes things out of the hands
of the Privy Council"[25]—a complaint that was based
on the conviction that so long as any inner committee
of the Privy Council, called by whatever name,
remained under royal control, such a committee must
be only a variation of a time-worn means of sustaining
the King's arbitrary power.

The King's arbitrary power was precisely the traditional feature of government which the more liberal
English statesmen of the seventeenth century endeavored to find means to control. Inasmuch as the future
liberties of the nation were felt to depend on the
success or the failure of their efforts in this direction,
the issue became the most vital one of the century.
As it matured, it was destined to give form and

[24] *The Life of Edward Earl of Clarendon.* By Himself (Oxford:
1857), I, 308. T. H. Lister, *Life and Administration of Edward, First
Earl of Clarendon,* II, 6 ff.
[25] Grey's *Debates,* VI, 313. December, 1678.

impetus to numerous ideas and practices. Among ideas was the conception of the importance and growing need of some sort of parliamentary control over the King's advisers, especially over those inner councils which were too apt to direct and sway his policy. Among practices may be noted those which prevailed during the period of the Long Parliament—the appointing of parliamentary committees for executive purposes.[26] Taken together, this conception and the practice of parliamentary executive committees may be regarded as the most important contributions of the seventeenth century toward the formation of England's future government.

IV

The eighteenth century was marked by a steady but rather unconscious development of parliamentary or committee government in England. The process had certainly begun long before that period, but it was invigorated by and rested upon ideals that were largely the outcome of the seventeenth-century struggles between King and Parliament. From the epoch of the Revolution which brought William and Mary to the throne, the problem was essentially this: the arrangement of political mechanism in a way such as

[26] "The practice of appointing committees is almost as old as Parliament itself, but the appointment of committees for executive purposes was the invention of the seventeenth century . . . . it remains certain that it was the one method of the Long Parliament." Edward Jenks, *The Constitutional Experiments of the Commonwealth* (Cambridge Hist. Essays, No. III), p. 12.

would allow Parliament or more especially the House of Commons to gain control of the small and informal group of intimate royal advisers sometimes termed the Cabinet Committee. It was particularly to the credit of Robert Spencer, second Earl of Sunderland, perhaps the most influential director of William's internal policy, that he pointed out to the King the importance of securing parliamentary support by giving the great offices to parliamentary leaders and making these his ministers. Moreover, he perceived the advantages to be gained if the monarch could be induced to prefer one or the other of the two parties, Whigs and Tories.[27] Sunderland's advice was along these lines in the last decade of the seventeenth century, and helped toward the solution of the problem which proved to mean in the long run that Parliament would ultimately contain, nominate, guide and control its own executive.[28]

Near the beginning of the eighteenth century within the reign of Anne there was an informal Cabinet Committee, councillors and administrative officers who were exercising functions in the state that can be traced in part from those of the old Tudor office of Principal Secretary of State. There was no clear evidence that the individuals composing this committee recognized their responsibility for the conduct of affairs. They owed as yet no special allegiance to any one of their number. And they were still unaware that their continuance in office would depend on the

[27] *Dictionary of National Biography*, LIII, 368 ff.
[28] John Morley, *Walpole* (English Statesmen ser.), p. 139.

continuance of the support of a majority of the House of Commons.[29] In unforeseen ways both circumstances and personnel kept affecting the practices of government. But neither the meaning of circumstances nor the force of personality could be determined easily or quickly in respect to their influence on the process of the development of committee government.

Two conservative clauses in the Act of Settlement were summarily nullified in the early part of Anne's reign by being repealed.[30] As originally passed, they raised a barrier directly in the way of parliamentary control over the ministry. Yet neither when they were first incorporated into the law nor when they were repealed, could men have understood their full bearing on the future of governmental mechanism. The Tories, eager to check the practices of interior councils by reviving the authority of the Privy Council, were responsible for a provision of the Act of Settlement which declared that all matters properly cognizable in the Privy Council by the laws and customs of the realm were to be transacted there, and furthermore that all Privy Councillors advising and consenting to any resolution must sign such resolution. Another provision excluded all servants of the Crown from the House of Commons. The restriction on a stateman's liberty in the first provision was against the sentiment of the time. The second provision would have destroyed close relations between the executive and the legislature, and by withdrawing ministers from the

[29] Anson, *Law and Custom*, Pt. II, p. 105.
[30] 4 *Anne*, c. 8, ss. 24, 25.

House of Commons would have weakened completely its influence.

The directive forces of the century, the forces which carried parliamentary government well along towards maturity, were with the Whigs. And Walpole probably did more than any single man within the century to establish what has been called the bias of the system. Many circumstances and many men aided in the process. The harmony of policy that existed between the Whig leaders and two such foreigners as George I and George II was a circumstance of paramount importance. The reactionary effort of George III, nourished as a youth on the conservative philosophy of Bolingbroke's *Idea of a Patriot King,* failed miserably.[31] Yet the fact of its failure was not to be foretold much before the close of the American Revolution. The Whigs had inherited the liberal traditions of government from the seventeenth century. Their ideas molded the Cabinet into a vital institution.

There was no writer in the eighteenth century who attempted to make an exposition of the place of the Cabinet Committee in the English system of government.

Montesquieu's *Esprit des Lois,* which appeared in 1748, set forth an idealized view of the British Constitution which influenced a number of conspicuous writers on law and government. The French author

[31] Bolingbroke's famous essay was written at a time (1738) when parliamentary government was at a low ebb. The attempt, says Mr. G. W. Alger, ''to put this philosophy into effect was among the causes of the Revolution which separated us from Great Britain.'' *Atlantic Monthly,* November, 1908, pp. 581-582.

perceived some of the great principles which had been at work and were making for the advancement of English political liberties. He was convinced that the secret of the Constitution lay in the clear separation of the executive, the legislative, and the judicial powers. But he failed to see or to appreciate those subtle features of parliamentary custom and practice, on the basis of which the Cabinet was assuming the guise of a working and organic institution.[32]

Blackstone was the first legal writer in England over whom Montesquieu had a marked influence. The *Commentaries* were published between 1765 and 1769. Concerned primarily with the law of the Constitution, the work took no account of such a customary institution as the Cabinet. From the more general realm of history Blackstone ventured to draw the ordinary distinctions between the various parts of the mechanism of government, and presented the optimistic conclusion that the British Constitution afforded the best of all possible governments. However unsound such views might be, they were not likely to detract much from the essential merits of the great treatise in which they were to be found, or to attract general attention. Yet it was just these views that furnished the means of bringing a young student of law and philosophy into his first prominence as a writer.[33]

Moved by his recollections of Blackstone's lectures at Oxford, with which at the time he heard them (1763) he was inclined to disagree, and convinced of

[32] Especially Bk. XI, chap. 6.
[33] Paul Janet, *Histoire de la Science Politique* (1887), II, 399 ff.

the unhistoric and misleading nature of certain passages in Blackstone's first volume, Jeremy Bentham
published anonymously in 1776 *A Fragment on Government*. In this pamphlet Bentham took Blackstone
to task for his optimism, and discussed at some length
his view of the British Constitution, dwelling upon
the great lawyer's failure (as he conceived it) to dis-
tinguish clearly or adequately the executive from the
legislative power. To Bentham the work of the Swiss
writer, De Lolme, appealed as far more thoughtful and
historically sound than Blackstone's. While Bentham's criticism was amply justified, it rested on no
intimate knowledge either of English history or of
parliamentary practice, and was accordingly chiefly
destructive. It is notable, however, as Bentham's first
effort to apply the scientific method to problems of
legislation.[34]

The original edition of De Lolme's *Constitution de
l'Angleterre* was published in 1771.[35] Revised by
its author several times and considerably elaborated,
it assumed final form in 1784, and then included eleven
chapters in addition to those it originally had contained, making a total of thirty-five chapters besides
a brief Introduction and a bibliographical note. Trans-
lated into English a few years after its first appearance, it attracted many readers, among them
"Junius," Bentham, Alexander Hamilton and some
other American statesmen. The work was no doubt

[34] *A Fragment on Government* (London: 1776). Chapter III, British
Constitution, pp. 92-123. Leslie Stephen, *The English Utilitarians*
(New York: 1900), I, 181 ff.
[35] Amsterdam, pp. 308.

suggested by Montesquieu's well-known views on the British Constitution, but in comparison with Montesquieu it afforded a more systematic and detailed study of English governmental institutions, particularly of the English kingship and its supposed functions in the actual government of the kingdom. Unlike the work of Montesquieu, which took its final form on its first appearance in print, De Lolme's treatise was gradually developed from the original essay of 1771 over a period of thirteen momentous years. Yet it is true that its original form was set largely by impressions gathered by the author about the end of the first decade of George III's rule.

"The first peculiarity of the English government as a free government," wrote De Lolme, "is its having a king—its having thrown into one place the whole mass . . . . of the executive power, and having invariably and forever fixed it there."[36] This postulate, expressed in some variety of ways, sounded a keynote of the treatise. The Constitution "placed all the executive authority in the state out of the hands of those in whom the people trust."[37] "The English government will be no more . . . . when the representatives of the people shall begin to share in the executive authority."[38]

In discussing the legislative power De Lolme stated clearly that the representatives of the people in Par-

[36] *The Constitution of England;* or, an account of the English Government. By J. L. De Lolme. A new ed. with Life and notes by John MacGregor, M. P. (London: Bohn, 1853), p. 143.
[37] *Ibid.,* p. 257.
[38] *Ibid.,* p. 316. Cf. pp. 147, 252, 309.

liament possessed the right of initiative in all matters of legislation.[39] From the nation, he said, the Crown "receives the force with which it governs the nation. Its resources are official energy, and not compulsion— free action, and not fear.'"[40] He was careful to admit near the close of his work that in England there had never been "more than one assembly that could supply the wants of the sovereign. This has always kept him in a state, not of a seeming, but of a real dependence on the representatives of the people for his necessary supplies; and how low soever the liberty of the subject may at particular times have sunk, they have always found themselves possessed of the most effectual means of restoring it, whenever they thought proper so to do.'"[41] Among his most matured considerations on the legislative power is the following passage taken from the concluding chapter of the work in its final form. "Two circumstances more I shall mention here," he wrote, "as peculiar to England: namely, the constant attention of the legislature in providing for the interests and welfare of the people, and the indulgence shown by them to their very prejudices: advantages these which are, no doubt, the consequence of the general spirit that animates the whole English government, but are also particularly owing to the circumstance peculiar to it, of having lodged the active part of legislation in the hands of the representatives of the nation, and committed the care of alleviating

[39] *Constitution of England*, pp. 164, 167, 307.
[40] *Ibid.*, p. 300.
[41] *Ibid.*, pp. 327-328.

the grievances of the people to persons who either feel them, or see them nearly, and whose surest path to advancement and fame is to be active in finding remedies for them.'"[42]

Quotations can give only the barest glimpse of De Lolme's views. He had a remarkable appreciation of that flexibility of the English Constitution in general, and certain factors in particular which afforded a balance among the different parts of the mechanism. But he could neither fully abandon nor forget his postulate as to the indivisibility of the executive, impressed as he was by his conviction of the fixed and dominant place of the King in the English scheme of government. He was consequently quite unable to give any really adequate account of the functions of the Ministry or the Cabinet. He did not understand the secret of their relations to Parliament on the one hand or to the King on the other. The conception of the Prime Minister, as to-day we understand it, dates only from the epoch of the younger Pitt.[43] De Lolme could not of course have had it. Nor did he have any notion of the functions of party government in operating the machine. Yet it must be admitted that he was not simply an alert student of history and law, but that he was likewise an observer of political practices. His treatise was not profound, but it was clever

[42] *Ibid.*, p. 338. MacGregor, editor of De Lolme in 1853, was moved to give in connection with this passage a note on the Cabinet as a very essential element in the government. Pp. 364-367.

[43] Sir William R. Anson, *Autobiography and Political Correspondence of Augustus Henry Third Duke of Grafton, K. G.* (London: 1898), Introd., p. xxx.

and inclusive of much that was of interest to statesmen. Altogether it remains as quite the most remarkable exposition of the English government which was written during the last thirty years of the eighteenth century.[44]

It remained for a statesman peculiarly accomplished in the theory as well as in the practices of government to throw light on the true functions of the Ministry in the eighteenth century. "There are but very few," wrote Edmund Burke, "who are capable of comparing and digesting what passes before their eyes at different times and occasions, so as to form the whole into a distinct system."[45] Of these few Burke may certainly be reckoned among his contemporaries as the most distinguished one. In his well-known defence of the Whig system of party government, a pamphlet entitled *Thoughts on the Cause of the Present Discontents* (1770), Burke discerned some of the secrets of ministerial functions. While the pamphlet was primarily an attack on the corrupt system of aristocratic and court influence, a system which

___

[44] No writer, so far as I know, has ever attended to the fact that De Lolme's book was re-shaped during the years from 1771 to 1784. The author could hardly have changed his original views without essentially recasting the whole work. Yet the final revision indicates that De Lolme's views had changed in some respects. He was inclined, I believe, in his last edition to assign a more vital place in the governmental machine to the House of Commons. One is tempted to conjecture that, had he re-written his book in the light of the younger Pitt's long ministry (1783-1801), De Lolme might have produced a treatise in which the crucial position of the Cabinet Committee would have been suggested for the first time. De Lolme died in 1806 or 1807. The best brief sketch of his work and career is to be found in the *Dictionary of National Biography*, XIV, 325 ff.

[45] *Works* (Boston: 1866), I, 442.

George III and the adherents of the ideal of a restored absolutism tried to build up during the decade after 1760 and for some years following, it penetrated beneath the mere surface of history, for it afforded a sketch of political tendencies and practices since the revolution of 1688.

Briefly summarized, the objects which the King and his followers sought were these: A court separated from the Ministry; a powerful body of adherents dependent on the King's personal favor; and a House of Commons alienated from the Ministry. As means to these ends it was necessary to exclude men of commanding influence from the regular Cabinet of Ministers; furthermore it was essential to nullify as far as possible the regular Cabinet by limiting Ministers to the confines of their regular departments and to discredit them in the eyes of the nation either for their character or through the odium which they might incur for approving unpopular acts; finally, by means of patronage and corruption, to put the majority of the House of Commons at the disposal of the court's agents. The nucleus of the system was an inner cabinet of "King's Friends."[46]

Such objects and the means adopted to attain such objects were entirely out of accord with the progressive tendencies which had been active since the Revolution. By slow degrees the burden of public affairs had come to rest on the Ministers. The Ministry,

[46] Edward Jenks has summarized these points clearly in his volume on the evolution of the cabinet system entitled *Parliamentary England* (1903), p. 194.

having relieved the Crown of its cares, had somewhat unconsciously appropriated much of the Crown's authority, and was being held responsible by the House of Commons for acts which formed the basis of a national policy. "It must be remembered," wrote Burke, "that since the Revolution . . . . the influence of the Crown had been always employed in supporting the ministers of state, and in carrying on the public business according to their opinions."[47] George III had endeavored to change all this. "The power of the Crown, almost dead and rotten as Prerogative, has grown up anew with much more strength, and far less odium, under the name of Influence."[48] To this influence, especially as it had been asserted in the House of Commons, Burke was firmly opposed. "The House of Commons," he declared, "can never be a control on other parts of the government unless they are controlled themselves by their constituents; and unless these constituents possess some right in the choice of that House, which it is not in the power of the House to take away."[49] In any event there must be, according to Burke, "but one administration; and that one composed of those who recommend themselves to their sovereign through the opinion of their country, and not by their obsequiousness to a favorite."[50] In brief, the Cabinet must be trusted by the nation as well as by the King.

Burke was writing no treatise on the British Con-

[47] *Works*, I, 460.
[48] *Ibid.*, p. 444.
[49] *Ibid.*, p. 503.
[50] *Ibid.*, p. 537.

stitution such as De Lolme had tried to make. His pamphlet was no text-book from which men of the day could draw precise statements about the workings or the structure of ministerial government. He was imbued with the passion of a conservative reformer, and was bent upon calling attention to the attempt of the King to put the false and—as Burke conceived it— the dangerous philosophy of Bolingbroke's *Patriot King* into effect. Such an attempt was wholly out of accord with the progressive tendencies that had prevailed since the Silent Revolution, and was likely to interfere with the political life of the entire state. What Burke understood better perhaps than any man of his time was this—that no formal organization as set forth in a constitution or in the law can ever quite adequately represent the political life of the state. "The laws reach but a very little way," he wrote. "Constitute government how you please, infinitely the greater part of it must depend upon the exercise of the powers which are left at large to the prudence and uprightness of ministers of State. Even all the use and potency of the laws depend upon them."[51] Such a sentiment, taken into account with the reasoning revealed throughout the pamphlet, may be taken to indicate some perception in Burke's mind of the change that was in course of accomplishment throughout the eighteenth century. The change amounted to a slow revolution. Its accomplishment through the custom rather than the law of the Constitution centered on the Cabinet Committee. Although

[51] *Ibid.*, p. 470.

no one in the eighteenth century expressed the fact—
indeed, probably no one could have expressed it—the
chief function of that committee was to bring about
a co-operation among the different forces of the state
without interfering with the legal independence of
those forces.[52]

V

At the beginning of the nineteenth century party
government by means of a Cabinet Committee drawn
from the two Houses of Parliament for the conduct of
the business of the state was an accomplished fact.
It is true that through the Prime Minister the Crown
was to exercise some influence. But the life of the
Cabinet had come to be dependent on the maintenance
of the confidence of the House of Commons. The
Cabinet had drawn to itself not only the royal power
over legislation, but also many of the most important
legislative powers of Parliament.[53] It was in fact the
mainspring of government. The time was nearly at
hand when the historic processes of its subtle evolution could be expounded and set forth with some
degree of detail and clarity.

In Hallam's *Constitutional History of England
from the Accession of Henry VII to the Death of
George II*—a work first published in 1827—there is to
be found a brief sketch of the seventeenth-century

[52] A. Lawrence Lowell, *The Government of England*, I, 53. Cf. Morley, *Burke*, pp. 48 ff. Lecky, *History of the Eighteenth Century* (London: 2d ed., 1883), III, 181 ff.

[53] J. Redlich, *The Procedure of the House of Commons* (Eng. trans.,
1908), I, 71 ff.

process of cleavage between the Privy Council and the Cabinet Committee.[54] As far as it goes, this sketch is penetrating and careful. It was not written, however, with the maturity of the cabinet system in view. Hallam dealt summarily with the reigns of Anne and the first two Georges. It was clearly not in his plan to forecast the results of the evolution of ministerial government, although some of the essential features in the process were presented in his account of William III and his three successors. In truth the system of party government as well as the significance of the historic evolution of the Cabinet were likely to attract more attention after the reform measures of 1832 than before.

Macaulay was the first historian who wrote appreciatively of the English Cabinet. In the first volume of *The History of England from the Accession of James the Second,* which appeared in 1848, he wrote: "Few things in our history are more curious than the origin and growth of the power now possessed by the Cabinet. . . . . During many years old-fashioned politicians continued to regard the Cabinet as an unconstitutional and dangerous board. Nevertheless, it constantly became more and more important. It at length drew to itself the chief executive power, and has now been regarded, during several generations, as an essential part of our polity."[55] This passage was sufficiently explicit to promise well for a careful study of cabinet development when parliamentary affairs in

[54] Paris: 1827, III, 466 ff.
[55] *History* (Boston: Houghton, Mifflin, 1901), I, 207-208.

the latter part of 1693 came under consideration. And just before entering upon the intricate circumstances of 1693-1696—the period in which Macaulay discovered the first definite clue to a ministry united and leading in good order a majority of the House of Commons—he remarked: ''No writer has yet attempted to trace the progress of the institution, an institution indispensable to the harmonious working of our other institutions.''[56] Had he been able to carry out the extensive plan of his work as originally he had contemplated it, Macaulay might have left a valuable record of the historic evolution of the cabinet system of government from its seventeenth-century beginnings to its nineteenth-century maturity. As it was, however, his work remained an illuminating narrative of English history only to the death of William III in 1702. So far as he concerned himself with the Cabinet, he differentiated skilfully the beginnings of the institution from the complicated elements of the seventeenth-century process. These beginnings he set forth in the light of the maturity of the system—a maturity so fully appreciated by him, that the reader to-day will find it difficult to discover a better statement of the theory of cabinet government than was written by Macaulay in the twentieth chapter of his *History*.[57]

The year 1867 witnessed the appearance of three notable contributions to the literature of cabinet

[56] *History*, IV, 543.

[57] *Ibid.*, IV, 542 ff. Sir Courtenay Ilbert cites the passage in the preface which he wrote for the English translation of Redlich, *op. cit.*, pp. xiii-xiv.

history and to the elucidation of the practices of parliamentary government. These contributions came from three writers living far apart, but all of them residents of the British Empire. The writers were Walter Bagehot, editor of the *Economist* (London); William E. Hearn, Professor of Modern History, Logic, and Political Economy in the University of Melbourne; and Alpheus Todd, Librarian of the Parliament of Canada. Although Bagehot's *The English Constitution* was published in 1867, it had first appeared, it should be said, in instalments in the pages of the *Fortnightly Review,* beginning in the first issue of that periodical of May 15, 1865. Hearn's volume was entitled *The Government of England: its Structure and its Development.*[58] Todd, eager to help toward the formation of the confederation of the Canadian provinces, hurried into print early in 1867 with a first volume entitled, *On Parliamentary Government in England: its Origin, Development, and Practical Operation.* He was obliged to leave as part of a second volume the history of the origin, organization, and functions of the Cabinet. This second volume appeared in 1869.

Taken together, these three works elucidated both the history and the intricate workings of cabinet government as well probably as it was possible at the time to do. They indicated, moreover, how widespread and vital was the interest that had been aroused in an understanding of the matured system of the Eng-

[58] Second edition. Longmans, Green, London: 1886. Hearn died in 1888.

lish form of government. Behind this interest was the pressure of the agitation for the reform of Parliament in England—an agitation which had achieved its first success in 1832 and was just on the eve of its second; and the new governmental problems which were pushing for solution in Canada, Australia, and other British colonies.

Bagehot was not interested to any extent in the history of the Cabinet or in the history of cabinet government. He was bent rather upon presenting vividly the workings of the English parliamentary system as actually it existed. Hearn was something more of a historian—inclined to sketch or to trace the course of practices from more or less distant origins, and ever ready to observe comparisons or contrasts as he discovered them in different systems of polity. Yet he too was primarily concerned with the actual structure and activities of government. Todd, in contrast to Bagehot and Hearn, was possessed by the instinct of the antiquarian; while by no means ignoring the field of current practices, he amassed a deal of historic lore, and so, in historical matter, he supplemented to a great extent the work of his two contemporaries. Versed as he was in the older aspects of his theme, he lacked the judgment of the trained scholar. His work was consequently prolix and overburdened with details. But it has since lent itself readily to re-arrangement and condensation under the guiding hand of the late Sir Spencer Walpole.[59]

The real significance of Bagehot and Hearn has been

[59] Longmans, Green, 2 vols. London: 1892.

so well estimated by Mr. A. V. Dicey, late Vinerian
Professor of Law at Oxford, that I venture to quote
from him as follows:

No author of modern times . . . . has done so much to elucidate the intricate workings of English government as Bagehot. His *English Constitution* is so full of brightness, origi-
nality, and wit, that few students notice how full it is also
of knowledge, of wisdom, and of insight. The slight touches,
for example, by which Bagehot paints the reality of Cabinet
government, are so amusing as to make a reader forget that
Bagehot was the first author who explained in accordance
with actual fact the true nature of the Cabinet and its real
relation to the Crown and to Parliament. He is, in short,
one of those rare teachers who have explained intricate
matters with such complete clearness, as to make the public
forget that what is now so clear ever needed explanation.

To Hearn he pays the following tribute:

Professor Hearn . . . . has approached English institutions
from a new point of view, and has looked at them in a fresh
light; he would be universally recognized among us as one
of the most distinguished and ingenious exponents of the
mysteries of the English constitution, had it not been for
the fact that he made his fame as a professor, not in any
of the seats of learning in the United Kingdom, but in the
University of Melbourne.

"From both these writers," adds Dicey, "we expect to
learn, and do learn much, but . . . . we do not learn
precisely what as lawyers we are in search of. The
truth is that both Bagehot and Professor Hearn deal
and mean to deal mainly with political understandings
or conventions and not with rules of law."[60]

[60] *Introduction to the Study of the Law of the Constitution* (5th ed.,
1897), pp. 19-20.

In this last sentiment Dicey suggests a remarkable peculiarity which confronts any student of cabinet history. The Cabinet Council finds no recognition in the English statute book. It is the most characteristic feature in a system of government that developed out of many practical exigencies—exigencies which had to be met by a series of conventions or political understandings. It may fairly be asked whether an institution so evolved could be described completely or thoroughly in any work? Probably not. At any rate, as Mr. Edward Jenks points out,[61] there is no complete exposition of cabinet government in existence. Among scholars who have written since Bagehot, Hearn, and Todd wrote, Sir William R. Anson, in his *Law and Custom of the Constitution,* has presented a clear survey of the field of lore on the Cabinet and has given a judicious account of cabinet organization and functions in the working government of England.[62]

It is no part of my aim to enter into the details of cabinet government or history in the nineteenth century. It is enough to have pointed out that not until the nineteenth century was the system of cabinet government sufficiently well understood to be interpreted. American statesmen in the last quarter of the eighteenth century had, it may be assumed, few clear notions regarding the English Cabinet Committee. Had cabinet government, as we term it to-day, been far enough along in its development to have been

---

[61] *Parliamentary England,* p. 399.

[62] Anson issued the first edition of this work in two volumes between 1886-1892.

interpreted lucidly in the writings of English statesmen, it is conceivable that the system might have
exerted an influence on the formation of the structure
of the American government. But among American
writers of that day it is difficult to find any explicit
references to the functions of the English Cabinet. In
a general way it was known to be an important factor
in government. But the peculiar circumstances of its
development and its practical workings were beyond
most minds of the eighteenth century.

NOTES

1. BIBLIOGRAPHICAL:

The most available guide to the historic usages of the term "cabinet" is the *New English Dictionary* (Oxford: 1888 ff.) *s. v.* cabinet. In the first edition of Johnson's *Dictionary* (1755) the phrase "Cabinet-council" is defined as—

A council held in a private manner, with unusual privacy and confidence.

In the fourth edition (1773), revised by the author, Johnson differentiates another definition as follows:

2. A select number of privy counsellors supposed to be particularly trusted.

This he bases upon a quotation from the poet, Gay, which was printed in the edition of 1755 as illustrative of the original definition.

Before setting down the first usage of the phrase "cabinet-council" which I could find in the *State Papers* as under date of June 8, 1622, I examined some twenty-two volumes of the *Calendars of State Papers—Domestic* (London: 1858 ff.), which cover the period from 1603-1641. Among printed sources of particular value to the student of usage are: *The Clarke Papers,* 4 vols., edited by C. H. Firth and found in the Publications of the Camden Society (1891 ff.). *The Memoirs of Sir John Reresby....* Written by Himself. Edited by James J. Cartwright (London: 1875). Miss H. C. Foxcroft's *The Life and Letters of Sir George*

Savile (2 vols., London: 1898) gives numerous extracts from hitherto unprinted sources, and contains a long chapter (VI) on Temple's scheme of a Privy Council. Anson's *Law and Custom of the Constitution* (3d ed., vol. II). The Crown, Pts. I and II [1907-1908] is an available and excellent guide to the sources, if one is studying historic usage. My chapter was written before Anson's third edition was printed, hence I have referred to the second edition only, although the third edition, it should be said, has some new materials on the historic evolution of the Cabinet.

2.   FROM MACAULAY TO BAGEHOT: 1848-1865:

Two writers during these years helped to prepare the way for a better appreciation of Bagehot, Hearn, and Todd.   Hearn in particular acknowledged his indebtedness to both of them.   In 1858 there appeared an essay entitled *Parliamentary Government considered with reference to a reform of Parliament* (London: Bentley), written by the third Earl Grey (1802-1894). This essay contained several illuminating passages on the historic development of the Cabinet and the practical significance of the ministerial organization.   A London barrister, Homersham Cox, printed in 1854 a work entitled *The British Commonwealth: or a commentary on the Institutions and Principles of British Government* (London: Longmans).   This touched on the Cabinet and gave a brief account of the secretariat.   It was followed by a much more comprehensive and important work by the same author in 1863, *The Institutions of the English Government,* etc.

Book I contained a chapter on "The Privy Council and the Cabinet Council" (pp. 222-259); Book III comprised a series of chapters on "Administrative Government" (pp. 589 ff.).

CHAPTER II

WHEN Congress in 1789 provided by law for the establishment of three administrative Secretaryships and an officer to be known as the Attorney-General, it was arranging machinery by means of which the chief magistrate might surround himself with four expert assistants, men qualified in foreign affairs, in finance, in army organization, and in the law. Such speakers as Fisher Ames, Madison, Vining, Sedgwick, and Boudinot voiced this truth in the debates on the organization of departments.[1] But no man of the time put the thought more directly than Washington when, in the course of a letter to the Count de Moustier under date of May 25, 1789, he wrote: "The impossibility that one man should be able to perform all the great business of the state I take to have been the reason for instituting the great departments, and appointing officers therein, to assist the supreme magistrate in discharging the duties of his trust."[2] A similar thought was long afterward expressed by Jefferson when, in 1823, he said to a friend that we had "fallen on the happiest of all modes of constituting the executive, that of easing and aiding

[1] The debates on the subject of the organization of the departments opened in the House of Representatives on May 19, 1789. *Annals of Congress*, I, 383 ff. For the idea that the principal officers were intended to be the President's assistants, see especially *Annals*, I, 492, 516, 531, 542, 548, 549.

[2] *The Writings of George Washington*, ed. W. C. Ford, XI, 397-398.

our President, by permitting him to choose Secretaries of State, of finance, of war, and of the navy, with whom he may advise, either separately or all together, and remedy their decisions by adopting or controlling their opinions at his discretion.''[3] The advisory function of the principal officers was prominent in Jefferson's thought.

An examination of historic processes that had been at work for some years before 1789 may help to explain the establishments arranged for and will make the association of the principal officers with the President seem not only natural but in some degree to have been foreordained.

I

While John Adams was on his way to Philadelphia as a delegate in 1774 to the Continental Congress, he heard certain apprehensive comments over the probable deficiency of power in the coming Congress. The Congress, it was said, ''will be like a legislative without an executive.''[4] It would be wanting in adequate means to enforce obedience to its laws or to direct a policy. And this in fact proved to be the case.

There was no plan of executive organization that met the approval of Congress when the Articles of Confederation were under consideration. These Articles contained no provision, consequently, for an executive. There was, to be sure, a presiding officer during regular sessions, president in name

---

[3] *The Writings of Thomas Jefferson,* ed. H. A. Washington, VII, 321.
[4] *Works of John Adams,* ed. C. F. Adams, II, 344.

alone. There was also an anomalous Committee of the States which was to act during the recess of Congress.[5] An attempt to get the Committee to work in the summer of 1784 proved a complete failure.[6] Shortly before this significant experience, Thomas Jefferson left Congress, having been appointed plenipotentiary to France. He liked to recall several years later that he "often proposed," when in the Continental Congress, that all executive business be placed in the hands either of the Committee of the States or of another similar committee specially appointed by the Congress. He felt sure that one of the most fundamental needs of the government of the Confederation was the separation of the executive from the two other departments, legislative and judiciary. Jefferson's theory was no doubt sound. He watched with distinct satisfaction any evidence that he could obtain during 1786-1787, while he was still residing in France, of its recognition in the United States, and particularly of its recognition by the men influential in altering the methods and form of government.[7]

Without doubt the Articles reflected a pretty widespread fear, prevalent especially near the opening of the Revolution, of the single executive placed over continental concerns. The nation was resolved that it would submit on no account to a despot, called by whatever name. A single-chambered body of delegates might, after the manner of an estates-general, serve

[5] Articles of Confederation, ix, x.

[6] Journals of Congress, IX, 1-29 following the Index.

[7] Documentary History of the Constitution, IV, 43, 217, 243, 249-250, 278, 303, 314, 348, 369, 411.

the purposes of a central form of government. The enforcement and administration of laws could be safely left to the states and to the state governors or presidents.

The administrative history of the government from 1775 to 1789 was one long commentary upon the weakness of a national organization with only a single-chambered Congress at its head. The Congress attempted to control an organization that proved altogether difficult to manage. Lack of power at the head made the organization inefficient—so much so that at times it was on the point of disintegration. The exigencies of the war tended inevitably to develop a series of committees, boards, and other agencies— an administrative organization that amounted to an executive department co-ordinate with the legislative. These exigencies forced into the foreground the importance and necessity, if not the general trustworthiness, of individual leadership, an idea that Robert Morris laid particular stress upon very early in the period of the Revolution.[8]

In August, 1780, a meeting at Boston attended by delegates from the New England states voiced a view that was becoming general. At this meeting it was urged that the "national Concerns of the United States be under the Superintendency and Direction of one supreme Head."[9] On January 29, 1781, James

[8] December 16, 1776. P. Force, *American Archives*, 5th series, III, 1241.

[9] *Proceedings of a Convention of Delegates from several of the New-England States, Held at Boston, August 3-9, 1780.* Ed. F. B. Hough (Albany: 1867), p. 50.

Duane wrote to Washington, saying that "the people
. . . . perceive the want of a common head to draw
forth in some just proportion the resources of the
several branches of the federal union."[10] Congress
was coming to be regarded, especially by the army, as
a very impotent body. And the impression occasionally gained utterance that George Washington might
wisely be made king.[11] Indeed, one bold observer proposed in a private letter a plan looking toward some
such consummation: he regarded as desirable such a
change of government as would result in—

two distinct and well-organized bodies: legislative and executive; whose powers and capacities shall be equal to the task
of managing the unruly affairs of America. To effect this
. . . . at the head of the last branch there must be a great
and fearful executive officer to do anything; the power of
that officer must be greater than that which is hereditary in
the house of Orange, and as nearly like the head of that power
we are contending with as can well be imagined, the name
only excepted. . . . . [12]

This view which was conceived and written early in
1783 was no doubt somewhat extremely expressed, for
it was not intended for publication. Yet the general
truth is there—a truth which Noah Webster stated
fairly in his way not many months later. "Let the
power of the whole," he said, "be brought to a single

[10] Bancroft, *History of the Formation of the Constitution* (4th ed.,
1884), I, 283.
[11] L. C. Hatch, *The Administration of the American Revolutionary
Army* (1904), pp. 161 ff.
[12] Bancroft, *op. cit.*, I, 299.

point and vested in a single person, and the execution of laws will be vigorous and decisive. . . . . '[13]

It was not difficult for the Philadelphia Convention in 1787 to determine at least on the form of executive. It should be a single one such as had been already widely advocated and was here and there forcibly illustrated in the state governor and his predecessor, the colonial governor.

II

Meantime the principle of one-man power had already won its way to significant results in the practices of government, for early in 1781 Congress passed several ordinances for the purpose of establishing four heads of departments, single officers who should assume direction over the organizations of foreign affairs, war, finance, and marine.[14]

For months there had been discussions in and out of Congress with reference to some such arrangement. On August 29, 1780, Congress approved the appointment of a committee of five, Robert R. Livingston chairman, "to report a plan for the revision and new arrangement of the civil executive departments." Early in September, Hamilton formulated his now famous plan of administrative organization which he communicated to James Duane.[15] The subject of the proper administration of the finances was most fre-

[13] *Sketches of American Policy* (Hartford: 1785), p. 7.
[14] *Journals of Congress*, January 10, 1781; February 7, etc.
[15] *Works of Alexander Hamilton* (ed. Lodge), I, 226 ff.

quently in view. By November even Congress was convinced that there must be "a single officer accountable to Congress"[16] for the finances. There can be no doubt that the principle of holding one man responsible for the great administrative tasks was approved by most of the more liberal and constructive statesmen, such men for examples as Jay, Washington, the two Morrises, and Alexander Hamilton. And long before February, 1781, when Congress passed the ordinances, men were considering the problem of selecting persons fitted for the headships. Just after the first choice had been made, Washington received word from one of the interested workers on behalf of the new project to this effect: "We are," declared his correspondent, "about appointing the officers who are to be at the head of our great departments. Yesterday [February 20] Mr. Morris, without a vote against him . . . . was chosen financier. I cannot say he will accept, but have some hopes he will. Our finances want a Necker to arrange and reform them. Morris is, I believe, the best qualified of any our country affords for the arduous undertaking. We shall in a day or two appoint the officers for the foreign affairs and the marine. I wish we had men in these offices as well qualified to execute them as Morris in the Treasury."[17]

The titles of the proposed new officials were to be Secretary for Foreign Affairs—altered in 1782 to

16 *Journals*, November 24, 1780.

17 *Letters of Joseph Jones.* 1777-1787. Ed. W. C. Ford (1889), pp. 69-70. Letter dated Philadelphia, February 21.

Secretary to the United States of America for the Department of Foreign Affairs[18]—Superintendent of Finance, Secretary at War, and Secretary of Marine. Morris accepted the Superintendency in May, 1781. Before the year was out two Secretaries had likewise been appointed, Robert R. Livingston taking the headship of foreign affairs in September, and Benjamin Lincoln that of the war organization somewhat later in the autumn.[19]

The plan of placing administrative work under the responsibility of single heads marked the basis of administrative organization as we know it to-day. It is true, however, that the plan was not consistently maintained in practice through the trying years of the Confederation, nor was it altogether successful, for it was partly dependent upon a plodding and limping Congress, and partly upon diverse personalities, only two of whom proved to be men of first-rate administrative ability. Congress appointed Major-General McDougall to the Marine Secretaryship on February 27, but McDougall made certain conditions to the appointment which Congress was disinclined to accept, and accordingly the appointment was not arranged for. The work of the Marine Department was merged in the following September in that of the department

[18] *Secret Journals of Congress,* II, 580.

[19] Morris accepted his appointment on May 14, taking the oath of office late in the following June. H. B. Learned in *American Historical Review,* April, 1905, p. 565. Livingston was appointed by Congress on August 10 and accepted the following September 23. G. Hunt in *American Journal of International Law* (October, 1907), p. 876. Lincoln was appointed late in October. Jameson's *Essays,* p. 153.

directed by Robert Morris.[20] The finances themselves after Morris's resignation and retirement in the autumn of 1784 were soon directed by a board of three commissioners, a recurrence to Revolutionary practices. Only the two Departments of Foreign Affairs and War remained to 1789 under single heads.[21] There is no evidence that any official analogous to the later federal Attorney-General was contemplated at this time.

The new organization was a natural and for the most part an indigenous development out of the circumstances of the Revolution. We were creating rather than copying an administrative system. In the arrangements of 1781 there is no clear evidence of colonial precedents. Yet it seems only fair to assume that the statesmen of the Revolution could not have escaped the influence of British traditions and forms, for the British secretariat had been maturing since the later days of the Tudors. The very titles of some of the offices suggest foreign influence. ''Secretary at War'' was a title that went back at least to the period of Charles II.[22] ''Superintendent of Finance'' was almost certainly adapted from the old French title of the Duc de Sully, *superintendant des finances*.[23] It seems likely that French influence before 1781 aided

[20] *Journals of Congress,* February 27, March 30, 1781. C. O. Paullin, *The Navy of the American Revolution* (1906), pp. 218-226.

[21] *Journals of Congress,* VII-XIII, *passim,* where the whole trend of changes may be easily followed by reliance on the indexes.

[22] Anson, *Law and Custom,* Pt. II, 378.

[23] ''Origin of the Title Superintendent of Finance'' by H. B. Learned in *American Historical Review,* April, 1905, X, 565-573.

us in the general direction toward which we were tending, for the principle of one-man power was probably more satisfactorily matured in the administrative organization of France than in that of any country. Hamilton, who took a pronounced interest in advocating the principle in America, remarked regarding the proposed heads of departments that "these officers should have nearly the same powers and functions as those in France analogous to them." [24] It should not be forgotten in this connection that Congress had not only been willing, but had actually taken steps to look abroad for suggestions at a time when it was most puzzled about proper and effective methods of administration. The very year of the French alliance (1778) they made a direct appeal to Dr. Richard Price, the well-known English writer on finance and a warm friend to the Revolutionary cause, to come to America and help to reorganize the continental finances.[25] Early in the following year Congress resolved to urge its European agents to inquire into any methods known abroad of administering departments of war, treasury, naval and other offices.[26]

The personnel of the new administrative system afforded during the years from 1781 to 1789 at least two very impressive examples of men of marked executive abilities.[27] While Robert Morris and John

[24] *Works* (ed. H. C. Lodge), I, 226.

[25] Wharton, *Revolutionary Diplomatic Correspondence*, II, 474, 756, 853.

[26] *Secret Journals of Congress*, II, 130 (January 25, 1779).

[27] R. R. Livingston at the head of foreign affairs (1781-1783) was an able man. As first incumbent of the position, he had much to do in es-

Jay were technically subject to Congress, in fact were the administrative officials of that body, they probably exercised large if not directive influence over it. Robert Morris was all but alone in his knowledge of the problems of national finance. It was easy to characterize him as a "pecuniary dictator"[28] with reference to Congress as early as the autumn of 1781. Although he faced bitter opposition both in and outside that body, there is no doubt that through his energy, tact, and careful planning the final triumph of the Revolutionary cause was largely due.[29] Morris retired from office on November 1, 1784. In the following December, rather more than a month after Morris's retirement, John Jay undertook the task of Secretary of Foreign Affairs. He raised the office from what it had been, a clerkship under congressional direction, to the most dignified and influential post in the Confederation. Jay, like his predecessor Livingston, was privileged to appear on the floor of Congress, and occasionally spoke before Congress in an advisory capacity.[30] About a year after Jay's accession to the post, Otto, French *chargé d'affaires,* remarked in a letter to Vergennes that "Mr. Jay especially has

tablishing practices and was much hampered by an overwatchful Congress. Madison considered him indifferent to the place. Madison's *Writings* (ed. Hunt), I, 141. For estimates of Livingston see Hunt, *American Journal of International Law* (October, 1907), pp. 876 ff. Wharton, *op. cit.,* I, 596-597.

[28] W. B. Reed, *Life and Correspondence of Joseph Reed,* II, 296.

[29] Wharton, *op. cit.,* I, 289, 600.

[30] *Secret Journals,* IV, 109, 110. W. Jay, *The Life of John Jay,* I, 186, 202, 236-237, 241-242. J. S. Jenkins, *Lives of the Governors* (1851), p. 114. Jameson, *Essays,* pp. 164 ff.

acquired a peculiar ascendency over the members of Congress. All important business passes through his hands."[31] Early in 1786 Otto spoke once more of the increasing political importance of the American Secretary, saying: "Congress seems to me to be guided only by his directions. . . . . Congress . . . . does not perceive that it ceases to be anything more than the organ of its chief minister. . . . . He inspires the majority of the resolutions of Congress."[32]

Otto expressed some admiration for the whole system of administration as he had observed it. He went so far as to say in February, 1787, that "a regular system has been introduced into all the branches of the general administration. . . . . The departments of foreign affairs, of war, of finances, are in the hands of trusty and capable men, whose integrity, wisdom, and circumspection will stand every test. Secrecy is much better observed than during the war. . . . . But this fine structure," he concluded, "is, unfortunately, useless on account of the exhaustion of the treasury."[33]

Whatever the theory of the secretarial positions was at the time of their creation in 1781, the conditions as time elapsed, notably the fact that Congress was an inefficient and diminishing body, inevitably forced the direction of affairs on the capable administrative officers. And it seems fair to assume, although the evidence is scanty, that John Jay became really what may be called the chief executive of the Confederation.

[31] Bancroft, *Formation of the Constitution*, I, 474. December 25, 1785.
[32] *Ibid.*, I, 479. January 10, 1786.
[33] *Ibid.*, II, 411. February 10, 1787.

Indeed, with Robert Morris as director of the continental finances from June, 1781, to November, 1784, succeeded in the following December by Jay as head of the country's foreign affairs until March, 1790, the idea of an executive chief supported by administrative assistants untrammeled by too intimate and controlling a connection with Congress must, it would seem, have gained strength, for that idea had received in the almost continuous services of Morris and Jay clear and effective illustration. When arrangements for a change of government under the new Constitution were under way in 1788 and 1789, Jay, Morris, and Knox—the latter Secretary at War since March, 1785 —were naturally considered for high places in the administrative work.[34]

III

Side by side with the practice of administration under great officers or heads of departments and apt to be associated with the expression of a conviction of the need of an executive chief, there appeared from 1781 onwards various suggestions for combining principal officers of administration into a council.

As early as February 10, 1781, just three days after Congress had arranged by ordinances for the new secretariat, an anonymous writer in the *Pennsylvania Packet,* expressing satisfaction that management by boards was to be superseded, commented on the new

[34] Madison, *Writings* (ed. Hunt), V, 303. Letter of November 5, 1788. Elbridge Gerry in *Annals of Congress,* May 20, 1789.

plan as follows: "Congress," he said in his quaint
fashion, "hath determined on a measure which will
give life and energy to our proceedings, both in civil
and military line . . . . that of putting a man at the
head of each of the great departments. . . . . As the
persons who shall fill those offices have the fullest
information respecting all our affairs, they may render
the public essential services and facilitate the business
of Congress, if they were frequently to meet together
to deliberate on them, and then to lay their opinions
and plans before Congress. Much therefore will
depend on their having a good understanding and
friendly intercourse among themselves. . . . ." Two
months later, on April 11, a similar suggestion was
thrown out by a nameless writer in the *Pennsylvania
Gazette.* Remarking on the importance of the new
system, aware of the large administrative duties likely
to devolve upon the occupants of the new positions,
the writer was convinced that these officers "might,
if they should be men of general knowledge beyond the
line in which they act, be extremely useful in another
capacity; for, possessing among themselves ample
knowledge of everything relative to public affairs, they
might meet frequently together, consult what ought
to be done, and submit their sentiment to Congress.
By this means much time and labor would be saved to
Congress; and the public business would be carried
on with regularity, vigor and expedition. . . . ."

For the first time in American history a combination of department heads as an advisory council to
Congress could be suggested as a possibility in the

spring of 1781. The two foregoing plans were probably made casually and without any reference to precedent, colonial or British. They came naturally from the circumstances of the American continental situation. Both writers perceived that a council of well-informed and sagacious administrative officers could do something toward vitalizing and perhaps enforcing a congressional policy. The weakness or strength of any such body would depend upon the degree of its subordination to Congress and the mutual relations existing between it and Congress. To have given such a body of administrators a status around an executive chief, himself relatively free from congressional control, would have resulted in a combination very much akin to the later President and Cabinet.

The maturing of thought is evident in a more definite proposal that was formulated about two years later. Pelatiah Webster, a merchant, resident in Philadelphia and a writer of some influence, printed a small pamphlet early in 1783 which was in substance a series of suggestions rather than a consistent plan for the alteration and improvement of the form of government of the Confederation. Webster believed in a bi-cameral Congress which should consist of a Senate and a Commons. He assumed that there would be several heads of departments which he termed "great ministers of state." With these ministers he would have associated certain judicial officers. "These ministers," he remarked, "will of course have the best information, and most perfect knowledge, of the state of the Nation, as far as it relates to their several

departments, and will of course be able to give the best
information to Congress. . . . .''[35] He was inclined to
recommend that the ministers give their information
"in writing," but he perceived that Congress might
choose to admit the ministers into their sessions for
the purpose of granting them a hearing in debate,
though not the right of voting. Herein the plan was
clearly suggestive of British practices. That the ministers should form a distinctive council was made plain
in the following passage:

The aforesaid great ministers of state shall compose a
Council of State, to whose number Congress may add three
others, viz., one from New-England, one from the middle
States, and one from the southern States, one of which to be
appointed President by Congress; to all of whom shall be
committed the supreme executive authority of the States
. . . . who shall superintend all the executive departments,
and appoint all executive officers.[36]

Webster was groping not without skill and regard
to the existing government towards an improved form
of executive organization. His President could not
have been independent in any true sense, for he was
too intimately associated with Congress. In fact he
was the creation of Congress.[37] The Council likewise
must have been controlled and trammeled by Congress.
But the real significance of the plan should be clearly
borne in mind. In proposing to combine President

[35] *A Dissertation on the Political Union and Constitution of the Thirteen United States of North-America*, etc. I quote from the reprint which
is to be found in Webster's *Political Essays* (Philadelphia: 1791), omit-
ting the old-fashioned italics, p. 213.

[36] *Ibid.*, p. 221.

[37] *Ibid.*, pp. 220, 221.

and heads of departments into a "Council of State" (employing a well-known phrase) and keeping in view the character of the body as representing the geographical sections of the country, Pelatiah Webster hit upon the clearest prototype that probably can be discovered for the later Cabinet Council. To Webster's President and Council was to be committed "the supreme executive authority of the States."

The further maturing of the conciliar idea in relation to the formation of the Constitution and the establishment of the laws which provided for the creation of the chief administrative positions about the President can be traced during the years from 1787 to 1789. The consideration of the subject is sufficiently important to warrant the space of a separate chapter.

NOTE

HISTORY OF ADMINISTRATION: 1775-1789:

The most careful discussion of administrative development and ideals during the period is to be found in Francis Wharton's introductory chapters to *The Revolutionary Diplomatic Correspondence of the United States*, I, 251-666. J. C. Guggenheimer's essay, "The Development of the Executive Departments, 1775-1789" in J. Franklin Jameson's *Essays in the Constitutional History of the United States in the Formative Period, 1775-1789* (Boston: 1889) remains a clear study of the main facts and tendencies of administrative history. Gaillard Hunt has contributed something to our knowledge of the administration of foreign affairs from 1775 to 1789 in his first paper printed as part of a History of the Department of State in *The American Journal of International Law* (October, 1907), I, pt. ii, 867 ff. Naval administration has found a very competent historian in Dr. Charles O. Paullin, *The Navy of the American Revolution: its Administration, its Policy, and its Achievements* (Cleveland: 1906). This work should be supplemented by an article by Dr. Paullin, "Early Naval Administration under the Constitution," in the *Proceedings of the United States Naval Institute* for September, 1906, XXXII, 1001-1030, and by Dr. Gardner W. Allen's *Our Navy and the Barbary Corsairs* (Boston: 1905). Such books as W. G. Sumner's *The Financier and the Finances of the American Revolution* (New York: 2 vols., 1891), and

A. S. Bolles's *Financial History of the United States,*
I (New York: 1879), give the facts regarding financial
administration. There is no special work of moment
on either the war administration or that of the Post-
Office during this period.

CHAPTER III

DEVELOPMENT OF THE IDEA OF A PRESIDENT'S COUNCIL:
1787–1788

B Y 1787 the conception of the pressing need of a
form of continental executive endowed with
power and some degree of independence had gained
consideration if not general acceptance among statesmen in the United States. The practical failure of
the government of the Confederation under congressional direction must have done much to enforce it.
About this time John Adams probably expressed a
rather general view regarding executive power when
he declared that the "attention of the whole nation
should be fixed upon one point, and the blame and
censure, as well as the impeachment and vengeance
for abuse of this power, should be directed solely to
the ministers of one man." [1] In view of the growing
strength of the conception, it is hardly surprising to
discover that not a single plan of government was presented to the Convention at Philadelphia which did not
embody as a prominent feature some form of executive.

Two leading theories regarding the executive came
before the Convention for discussion. In advocating

[1] "A Defence of the Constitutions of Government of the United
States of America," etc., in *Works*, IV, 586. Elsewhere in the same treatise Adams comments approvingly on the single executive. *Ibid.*, pp. 290,
379, 398, 585. Preface dated in London, "Grosvenor Square, January 1,
1787." On June 6 following, Madison referred to this work in a letter
to Jefferson, and said that it "has excited a good deal of attention.
. . . . It will . . . . become a powerful engine in forming the public
opinion." *Documentary History of the Constitution*, IV, 183, 264-265,
314, 333, 369.

one of these Roger Sherman of Connecticut took rather the most conspicuous place, though he was seconded by Charles Pinckney, John Rutledge and Colonel George Mason. Madison, James Wilson and Gouverneur Morris argued ably for the other theory. According to Sherman the executive power was nothing more than an institution for carrying the will of the legislature into effect, hence such power should be confided to one or more officials appointed by the legislature and removable by the same body. Madison and his following, on the other hand, insisted that the executive power should be representative of the people. The President should be president of the whole Union, and elected in such manner as to be justly styled the man of the people. It was a point of view that became especially familiar in the time of Andrew Jackson and his immediate successors, and was very impressively set forth in the last annual message of President Polk in December, 1848.[2] Madison insisted that the functions of the executive, moreover, should be united in one person who could be held responsible for his acts to the people alone. According to the latter theory, the executive must be independent of the legislature for the sake of acting at times as a check upon it.

[2] *Messages and Papers of the Presidents*, ed. J. D. Richardson, II, 447 ff., 518, 591, 648, 652, 655. III, 18, 90, 176. IV, 664 ff. Observe in this connection the statements of Senator W. C. Preston of South Carolina on January 24, 1842, in the U. S. Senate: ''In truth, there was only one department of the Government that was truly Democratic, and that was the Executive . . . . he [the President] was the only officer that came in on the broad basis of the whole Union, and was therefore the proper exponent of the popular will. . . . . The Executive was elected by the people of the United States.'' *Globe*, 27 Cong., 2 sess, p. 167.

Madison's view met finally with the approbation of the Convention. The result of Sherman's position, had it gained the day, would have been something much akin to the parliamentary system that is characterized nowadays as cabinet government. The chief magistrate would inevitably have been subordinated to the legislative will.[3]

I

It was apparent from an early date in 1787 that some place was likely to be found in any useful scheme of national government for the "great ministerial officers." The question as to the mode of relating such officers to the parts—executive, legislative, judicial— of the new or altered structure afforded a minor, though difficult, problem. Perhaps it was his appreciation of just this problem before the assembling of the Convention that moved Madison to remark in a letter to Washington that the "National supremacy in the Executive departments is liable to some difficulty, unless the officers administering them could be made appointable by the supreme Government."[4] Before he left the Convention in June, Hamilton was sure that the executive should "have the sole appointment of the heads or chief-officers of the Departments

---

[3] For Sherman's position, Elliot, *Debates* (1845), V, 140, 142, 192, 322, 508. The views of Madison, Wilson and others may be followed in Elliot, V, 142, 143, 144, 322, 324, 337, 360, 362-367 (*passim*), 395, 472, 473, 516. Governor Simeon E. Baldwin has summarized clearly the two positions in his essay entitled "Absolute Power an American Institution," in his volume, *Modern Political Institutions* (1898), pp. 87-89.

[4] *Writings of James Madison* (ed. Hunt), II, 347.

of Finance, War, and Foreign Affairs.''[5] The appointment of such officers would be the first duty of an executive, according to Gouverneur Morris's view which he expressed about a month later, on July 19. Such officers, he thought, ''will exercise their functions in subordination to the executive. . . . . Without these ministers, the executive can do nothing of consequence.''

Early in the previous April Madison, having conceived the plan of associating the ministerial officers with the executive in a council of revision, communicated his idea to Randolph.[6] But the suggestion was not involved in the Randolph resolutions of the following May 29; the council of revision was there made to include ''a convenient number of the national judiciary''[7] in place of the ministerial officers. And throughout the course of the debates, from June 4 to about the middle of August, Madison argued vigorously at intervals for the union of judicial officers with the chief magistrate in the business of revision. In this matter he was seconded by such capable men as Wilson, Mason and Ellsworth.[8]

Like Madison, Charles Pinckney had at first favored the plan of joining the heads of the principal departments in a council of revision, but apparently he

[5] Elliot, V, 205. I use the capitalization of the *Madison Papers* (ed. Gilpin), p. 891.

[6] April 8. Elliot, V, 108.

[7] *Ibid.*, V, 128. Jay had expressed this same thought to Washington as early as January 7, 1787. *Documentary History of the Constitution*, IV, 56.

[8] *Ibid.*, V, 152, 153, 164-166 (*passim*), 328, 344-349 (*passim*), 378, 428-431 (*passim*). Kate M. Rowland, *The Life of George Mason*, II, 113 ff.

relinquished the idea "from a consideration that these could be called on by the executive magistrate whenever he pleased to consult them. . . . ." At no time does he seem to have favored the view of admitting the judges into the business of revision. Rutledge followed closely in the track of his young colleague from South Carolina.[9]

Out of the discussions over this subject there developed the plan of the qualified veto. And this veto the Convention decided finally to lodge in the hands of the President alone.

A second plan for a council appeared in connection with the problem of arranging for the power of appointment. When Randolph referred to this power as formidable, whether lodged in the hands of the executive or the legislature,[10] he probably expressed a very common apprehension. At all events Colonel Mason, fearful of a possible coalition between the President and the Senate in the business of appointments, recommended urgently the establishment of a distinct council of appointment, the body to be composed of six members appointed by vote of the states in the House of Representatives, with the same duration and rotation of office as the Senate, two selected from the eastern, two from the middle, and two from the southern states.[11] The Convention, however, did

9 *American Historical Review*, IX, 743. Elliot, V, 165, 349, 429.

10 August 24. Elliot, V, 475.

11 I give the plan as set forth in Mason's "Objections" written soon after the Convention had adjourned. K. M. Rowland, *Life of George Mason*, II, 388. Mason expressed himself in a slightly different and less mature way before the Convention. Elliot, V, 522, 525. In the Virginia

not favor the plan, agreeing that the President alone should nominate, but that he should be obliged to ask the advice and consent of the Senate before appointments could be completed. The appointing power was thus shared. "From this fatal defect," declared Mason, "has arisen the improper power of the Senate in the appointment of public officers, and the alarming dependence and connection between that branch of the legislature and the supreme Executive." [12]

Although leaders such as Wilson, Dickinson and Madison acknowledged some force in Mason's view, the weight of authority was against the plan and probably more in accord with the reasonings of Rufus King. To King it seemed that most of the inconveniences charged on the Senate would be incident to a separate council. King did not believe that "all the minute officers were to be appointed by the Senate, or any other original source, but by the higher officers of the departments to which they belong." He was convinced, moreover, that the people would be alarmed at the unnecessary creation of a new and separate body "which must increase the expense as well as influence of the government." [13]

The idea of a council of appointment was neither peculiar to nor original with Colonel Mason, although he was the leading exponent of it in the Philadelphia Convention. In various ways the colonial legislatures

ratifying convention, on June 18, 1788, Mason "apprehended a council would arise out of the Senate, which . . . . he thought dangerous." Elliot, III, 496.

[12] Rowland, *op. cit.*, II, 388.

[13] Elliot, V, 523 ff.

were wont to exercise control over appointments. In New York State after 1777 there was a special council of appointment—a group of senators annually named by the Assembly and representing districts.[14] In 1783 Pelatiah Webster conceived of a council of state for the national government as partly concerned with the business of appointments; and this council, it will be recalled, was composed chiefly of the administrative heads of departments, and included also representatives from the three great sections of the country.[15]

Within a month after the adjournment of the Convention Richard Henry Lee expressed regret that a privy council of eleven members had not been provided, this council to be chosen by the President and to be joined with that officer in civil and military appointments.[16] John Adams in London sent a letter to Jefferson in Paris, under date of December 6, and remarked:

The Nomination and Appointment to all offices I would have given to the President, assisted only by a Privy Council of his own Creation, but not a vote or voice would I have given to the Senate or any Senator, unless he were of the Privy Council. . . . [17]

At about this time one of the reasons given by the dissenting minority of the Pennsylvania state con-

[14] *Charters and Constitutions*, 2d ed. (1878), edited by B. P. Poore, p. 1336.

[15] *Supra*, chap. II, p. 62.

[16] Letter dated New York, October 16, and addressed to Governor Randolph. *American Museum*, December, 1787, II, 557.

[17] *Documentary History of the Constitution*, IV, 390.

vention for their opposition to the Constitution was that the "president general is dangerously connected with the senate." Furthermore, it was their conviction that "the supreme executive powers ought to have been placed in the president, with a small independent council, made permanently responsible for every appointment to office . . . . by having their opinion recorded." [18] In the New York state convention, on July 5, 1788, Melancton Smith, on behalf of a committee, recommended a very similar plan.[19] Even as late as July, 1789, when the subject was merely of speculative interest, in view of the fact that the new government was in operation, John Adams once more expressed himself to Roger Sherman on the same general topic, Adams arguing for a council of appointment "selected by the President himself, at his pleasure, from among the senators, representatives, and nation at large," while Sherman was inclined to accept the arrangement for appointments which the Convention had provided.[20]

Thus efforts to establish two councils, a council of revision and a council of appointment separate from the Senate, had failed. It will be well at this point to examine a third effort—that of establishing a council which had as its most striking characteristic the combination of the heads of departments as an advisory body to the chief magistrate.

[18] *Pennsylvania Packet and Daily Advertiser* of December 18, 1787. The "Reasons" were dated December 12.

[19] Elliot, *Debates* (2d ed., 1836), II, 408.

[20] *Works of John Adams*, VI, 427 ff. Letter written about July 18.

II

In the recently discovered "Outline" of Charles Pinckney's draft of a constitution—a draft that was presented to the Convention on May 29—the President was to "have a Right to advise with the Heads of the different Departments as his Council." [21] This was the first and single project for an advisory council which was offered at the very beginning of the business of the Philadelphia gathering. It is remarkably interesting as a clue to what was probably one of Pinckney's favorite projects.

The thought of some such body was occasionally in the minds of certain members during the months of June and July. As early as June 1 Madison approved a single executive "when aided by a Council, who should have the right to advise and record their proceedings, but not to control his authority." [22] Gerry likewise was in favor of annexing a council to the executive "in order to give weight and inspire confidence." The references are not explicit enough to indicate (at least in Gerry's case) anything more than a vague and general notion. Somewhat clearer was Sherman's idea expressed three days later—on June 4—when he remarked that "in all the states there was a council of advice, without which the first magistrate could not act. A council he thought necessary to make the establishment acceptable to the people. Even in Great Britain the King has a coun-

[21] *American Historical Review*, July, 1904, IX, 742.
[22] *Ibid.*, January, 1898, III, 320. Notes of Major William Pierce.

cil; and though he appoints it himself, its advice has its weight with him, and attracts the confidence of the people.'' Almost immediately after this suggestion the Convention was inclined to approve of the single executive.[23] And they proceeded at once to grapple with the Randolph project of a council of revision. In connection with the discussions of it both Pinckney and Rutledge saw how easy it would be for the chief magistrate to advise with the principal officers or heads of departments and to obtain from them not only sound information on possible laws, but also helpful opinions on various other matters. Accordingly Pinckney and Rutledge refused, partly, it would seem, from their quick recognition of its needlessness, to agree to the council of revision.[24]

It was well along in the month of August before the Convention listened to any elaborated plan for an advisory council to the President. But on August 18 Ellsworth, wishing that a council might be provided, suggested that it should be composed of the president of the Senate, the chief justice, and the ministers of foreign and domestic affairs, of war, of finance, and of marine. The project was sufficiently definite to bring Charles Pinckney to his feet with the reminder that Gouverneur Morris, then absent, had already given notice that he would present a plan for such a body. As for Pinckney, he indicated his own thought in the matter by asserting that ''the President should be authorized to call for advice, or not, as he might

[23] Elliot, V, 141, 150, 151.
[24] Ibid., V, 165, 349.

choose. Give him an able council,'' continued Pinckney, ''and it will thwart him; a weak one, and he will
shelter himself under their sanction.''[25]   Two days
later—on August 20—Gouverneur Morris introduced
an elaborated scheme for an advisory council. Pinckney's original project as well as his occasional references to the subject would seem to imply that he may
have had a hand in the scheme. It should be observed,
at any rate, that he seconded Morris's motion to bring
it before the Convention just after having asserted
his conviction (in writing) that no principal officer
''shall be capable of holding, at the same time, any
other office of trust or emolument, under the United
States, or an individual state.''[26]

Morris's Council of State—such was its first title—
was to be composed of seven members, all of whom,
excepting the Chief-Justice of the Supreme Court,
were to be appointed by the President. Besides the
Chief-Justice and a ''Secretary of State,'' the latter
apparently nothing more than a chief-clerk or scribe
to the council and a ''public secretary'' to the President, there were five secretaries of departments—
domestic affairs, commerce and finance, foreign
affairs, war, and marine. As thus composed, the
council was designed to assist the President in conducting public affairs. It was furthermore provided
that the President ''may from time to time submit
any matter to the discussion of the council of state,
and he may require the written opinion of any one or

[25] Elliot, V, 442.
[26] *Ibid.*, V, 445, 446.

more of the members. But he shall in all cases exercise his own judgment, and either conform to such opinions, or not, as he may think proper.''

The plan went immediately to the Committee of Detail, of which John Rutledge was chairman, and appeared two days later, on August 22, slightly modified.[27] In its modified form there were to be eight members. The Committee, while retaining the Chief-Justice, had discarded the rather unnecessary Secretary of State, and had added to the five secretaries of departments the president of the Senate and the speaker of the House. They had thus combined in a "privy council"—as it was newly termed—representatives of the legislative and the judiciary along with the great administrative officers. This privy council was to advise the President. Its advice, however, should—the Committee employing Ellsworth's language—"not conclude" him. The President must be alone responsible for any measures or opinions that he might adopt.

There is no evidence to show that this scheme of an executive council was ever discussed by the whole Convention. Among other postponed subjects it went at the end of August into the hands of a large committee of eleven of which Morris himself was a member.[28] Here we know from Morris's own state-

[27] *Ibid.*, V, 462.

[28] *Ibid.*, V, 503. Besides Morris on the committee, there were Nicholas Gilman of New Hampshire, Rufus King of Massachusetts, Sherman of Connecticut, David Brearley of New Jersey, John Dickinson of Delaware, Daniel Carroll of Maryland, Madison of Virginia, Hugh Williamson of North Carolina, Pierce Butler of South Carolina, and Abraham Baldwin of Georgia—all of whom signed the Constitution.

ment that the question of a council was considered,[29] but it was decided that the President, by persuading his council to concur in wrong measures, would require its protection for them. On September 4 the barest suggestion of the original phraseology was agreed to: the President might ''require the opinion in writing of the principal officer in each of the executive departments, upon any subject relating to the duties of their respective offices.''[30] This language was all that survived of an elaborate plan for a council. It proved to be the basis in the Constitution which helped to predetermine the President's Cabinet Council.

It takes no very close scrutiny of the development of Morris's project, as thus far revealed in the sources, to conclude that it was first formulated about August 20 in response to a natural feeling that the chief magistrate, however well endowed he might be, would require aid—some such council might *assist* him. That assistance could best be given in the shape or mode of *advice*—an idea that was emphasized in the project as it re-appeared on August 22. It was finally determined on September 4 that advice should be restricted to opinions *in writing*. But aside from the important consideration that it left its stamp upon the Constitution, this plan for an advisory council revealed a historic background which, so far as it can be discovered, should not be overlooked.

The very titles, whether *council of state* or *privy*

29 Elliot, V, 525.
30 *Ibid.*, V, 507.

council, reflected phrases that had been familiar to Americans for generations. The governor's council in its advisory capacity was referred to in colonial days often as the council of state,[31] and rarely as the privy council.[32] In the state constitutions of the Revolutionary epoch (1776-1789) both phrases appear, but the phrase privy council is no longer unusual.[33] In the constitution of Virginia of 1776 the two phrases were used interchangeably. And there can be little doubt that they generally implied the same sort of political organ—as a rule they probably implied a body of men designed to stand in close relationship with the state governor as his assistants and advisers.

Passing beyond the usage of terms, the state governors after 1775 as well as their councils of advisers were markedly dependent on the General Assemblies, by which as a rule they were chosen. In fact, neither governor nor council of state could have been intended to have much real freedom of action. It was a time

[31] Hening, *Statutes,* I, 371, 515, 531, 537. E. I. Miller, *The Legislature of the Province of Virginia* (Columbia University Studies, XXVIII, 1907), pp. 22, 27. N. D. Mereness, *Maryland as a Proprietary Province* (1901), pp. 106-107, 153, 160, 174 ff. E. B. Greene, *The Provincial Governor* (Harvard Historical Studies, VII, 1898), p. 75. W. H. Fry, *New Hampshire as a Royal Province* (Columbia University Studies, XXIX, 1908), pp. 132, 134.

[32] H. L. Osgood, *American Colonies in the Seventeenth Century* (1904), II, 65-66. Mereness, *Maryland,* p. 369. See Note at the end of this chapter.

[33] See the constitutions of Delaware, New Jersey, Virginia, and the two constitutions—1776 and 1778—of South Carolina. Conclusions in this and succeeding paragraphs have been based on a comparative study of the eighteen constitutions which were formulated between 1775 and 1789. The texts used are those which are readily accessible in Poore's *Charters and Constitutions* (2 vols., 2d ed., 1878).

when there was widespread fear of one-man power. Most of the advisory bodies of the epoch appear to have been elected by ballot: ordinarily by joint ballot of the two houses, but occasionally by the two houses balloting separately for portions of the membership. In a few instances members of the advisory council were taken in part from the people at large.[34] The usual practice, however, was to compose the advisory council of men selected from the upper and lower houses. The privy council of New Jersey, with its "three or more" members, was simply a selected group within the legislative council or upper house, a group intended to stand in an especially close relation to the chief magistrate.[35] In a few of the states members of the advisory council retained seats in the legislature after their election as advisers.[36] In other states the advisory council formed a separate body. Occasional statements in these early state constitutions, to the effect that records of advice given to the governors must be carefully kept, and that from time to time such records must be submitted to the inspection of the legislatures, afford proof that the advisory councils were watched and that they were presumably considered as responsible, not to the governors, but to the popular bodies.[37] The truth was well expressed by Madison when he said[38] to the Convention that

[34] South Carolina (1778); Virginia; Massachusetts.

[35] Poore, op. cit., p. 1312.

[36] Maryland; South Carolina (1778).

[37] The Massachusetts constitution of 1780, Article V, will serve as an example.

[38] July 17. Elliot, V, 327. July 21. Ibid., p. 345.

"Experience had proved a tendency in our government to throw all power into the legislative vortex. The executives of the states are in general little more than ciphers; the legislatures omnipotent.''

Whether the state governor's advisory council contained administrative officers, it is impossible to say. The subject is a peculiarly difficult one for the investigator, and still awaits treatment at the hands of some industrious and competent scholar. While it may be noted in passing that the constitution of North Carolina of 1776 expressly prohibited any secretary or attorney-general of that state from holding a seat in the council of state, it is certain that in pre-Revolutionary days the governor's council often included some variety of administrative officials—such, for examples, as the surveyor-general of customs, the colony treasurer, the superintendent of Indian affairs, the secretary of the province, the attorney-general, and others not so easy to specify.[39]

It was no doubt natural for Americans of the Revolutionary epoch still to think of the English institution when the phrase privy council was spoken. In the very height of the quarrel with Great Britain, remarked James Iredell in 1788, "so wedded were our ideas to the institution of a Council, that the practice was generally if not universally followed at the formation of our governments, though we instituted Coun-

[39] Mereness, *Maryland*, pp. 176 ff. W. Roy Smith, *South Carolina as a Royal Province, 1719-1776* (1903), pp. 54, 86. Miller, *Legislature of Virginia*, p. 140. E. P. Tanner, *The Province of New Jersey, 1664-1738* (Columbia University Studies, XXX, 1908), pp. 277, 282, 295.

cils of a quite different nature. . . . .''[40] The statement from such a source is enough to warn us away from the view that there was any very definite or close analogy between the old English institution and the governor's council for advisory purposes, whether such a council was found in colonial times or during the period of the early state constitutions.

The tradition of a council for advice and assistance was probably carried over from colonial days into the period of the Revolution and the years immediately following by the phrases ''council of state'' and ''privy council.'' It is possible that Morris and those interested with him in the project of an advisory council for the President may have been aware of certain colonial or state combinations in the shape of executive councils that served in some respects for examples. But in the absence of any specific evidence, it seems probable that the plan repeated or reflected suggestions made in connection with the central government only as far back as 1781 or perhaps a little earlier. From about that time the evidence is clear that men were considering the desirability of co-operation among administrative officials for the purpose of assisting Congress. Any one ordinarily familiar in that day with English constitutional traditions would naturally think of an executive as consulting with the great officers of state. The really crucial question in 1787 was: What officers, with due regard

---

[40] ''Answers to Mr. Mason's Objections to the New Constitution,'' etc. Reprinted in P. L. Ford, *Pamphlets on the Constitution of the United States* (1888), p. 345.

to the theory of a proper separation of powers, should be brought into such close relations with the American President as to be easily consulted by him for the purpose of assisting him in his tasks? This question Morris attempted to answer when he formulated his plan of a council.

As assistant to Robert Morris, Superintendent of Finance, Gouverneur Morris had had some opportunity to test in practice any theories of administration which he might have preconceived. Like Pelatiah Webster, Morris included in his council a representative of the judicial power. Webster had recommended that Congress obtain the opinions of the ministerial officers ''in writing,'' for the purpose, no doubt, of holding them strictly and individually responsible for their advice. Presumably with similar intent Morris declared that the President ''may require the written opinions'' of members of his council.[41] He was, however, unwilling to shackle the President by such advice—it need not ''conclude'' him.

Brought forward by one of the most daring and brilliant among the younger members of the Convention,[42] the plan was sure to attract attention, especially as it remained the single careful attempt during the entire course of proceedings to enforce the idea of an advisory council. It came from the hands of the Committee of Detail on August 22 in less simple form than that in which it was given to them, and accord-

[41] August 20.

[42] Born at Morrisania, N. Y., on January 31, 1752, but a resident of Pennsylvania in 1787 and a delegate from that state.

ingly tended to hamper the President by forcing into combination certain legislative and judicial factors which must in practice have defied the working of an executive that was meant to be largely independent of those factors and alone responsible. It was quite too complicated a problem, we may conclude, for any committee to re-adjust the plan in a way that would meet the wishes of a wearied Convention. But it is probable that it was neither hastily nor thoughtlessly dismissed.[43]

III

It should be clear from the preceding considerations that there were offered to the Convention at one time or another more or less definite projects for three councils with somewhat distinctive aims—a council of revision, a council of appointment, and a council of state or privy council for the purpose of assisting and advising the President. The Convention disposed first of the possible need of a revisionary council by giving a carefully qualified veto power to the President.

[43] "The question of a council," declared Morris on September 7, 1787, "was considered in the committee, where it was judged that the President, by persuading his council to concur in his wrong measures, would acquire their protection for them." Elliot, V, 525. It is worth noting that some years later Morris drew up, in French, a plan for a council of state in France. Section iii provided for a council composed of the following nine officials: Chancellor or minister of justice, a president of the council, and ministers of the interior, finance, commerce, foreign affairs, war, marine, besides a secretary of state entrusted "with general charge of affairs." J. Sparks, *The Life of Gouverneur Morris* (1832), III, 481, 485, 486.

Toward the end of its labors it determined to divide the appointing power between President and Senate. It declined, finally, to accept the elaborated plan of an advisory council which Morris and others were interested in arranging, and consequently left no word of such a body in the final draft of the Constitution.

In the discussions of the period there are frequent scattered references to the Senate as a ''council to the President,'' ''an advising body to the executive,'' a ''council of appointment,'' or as a body associated with the President ''to manage all our concerns with foreign nations.''[44] These and others of a similar nature represent a plausible and common assumption that the Senate, composed at the start of no more than twenty-six members and closely associated with the President by the letter of the Constitution in the making of treaties and in appointments, would serve as a council to the President. Some of the President's work must be accomplished by and with the advice and consent of the Senate. The unforeseen truth was that experience alone would prove—as it did—that there were essential difficulties in the way of any real intimacy between the chief magistrate and the upper legislative house.

From the establishment of principal officers in 1781 through the proceedings of the Convention to Septem-

[44] Elliot, II, 47, 287, 306. III, 220, 221, 489, 491, 493, 494, 496. V, 549. In an essay entitled ''The Senate of the United States,'' reprinted in his volume, *A Frontier Town and other Essays* (1906), Senator Henry Cabot Lodge has developed clearly the historic facts regarding the Senators as true constitutional advisers of the President, pp. 70 ff.

ber 17, 1787, there had been occasional but quite definite recognition, as we have seen, that these officers
were considered as assistants either to Congress or,
later, to the proposed executive magistrate. As early
as 1783 Pelatiah Webster regarded them as fitted to
have a share or voice in the business of appointment.
It was Madison's first thought—as it was likewise
Charles Pinckney's[45]—that they should be factors in a
council for the revision of legislation. But in view of
another project before the Convention Madison surrendered his first opinion. And Pinckney and his
colleague, Rutledge, took the position that the President, even without constitutional provision for such
a council, could seek the advice and assistance of the
principal officers in case he felt inclined to do so.
Although the Convention failed to force them definitely, by the law of the Constitution, into either a
council of revision or of appointment, it left no word
in the text which would prevent the President from
calling on the principal officers for advice and aid in
the matter of a proposed veto or a proposed nomination. In truth, viewed freely as assistants in accordance with the prevalent thought of the epoch, the
principal officers might be asked for advice on a great
many sorts of business with which the President would
inevitably be concerned.

It was this recognition of the principal officers as
assistants that again may be traced in the autumn of
1787. It was Ellsworth's idea, expressed in December,
that "if any information is wanted, the heads of the

[45] American Historical Review, IX, 743.

departments who are always at hand can best give it, and from the manner of their appointment will be trustworthy.''[46] At about the same time James Wilson reminded his hearers in the Pennsylvania state convention that the President "will have before him the fullest information . . . . he will avail himself not only of records and official communications . . . . but he will have also the advice of the executive officers in the different departments.''[47]

The clause in the Constitution[48] which asserted that the President might require the opinion in writing of the principal officers did not fail to call forth some comment. To Hamilton it appeared "as a mere redundancy . . . . as the right for which it provides would result of itself from the office.''[49] To James Iredell, who fortunately elaborated his view in addressing the North Carolina state convention, the clause seemed to be "in some degree substituted for a council.'' Referring to the principal officers, he said that "the necessity of their opinions being in writing, will render them more cautious in giving them, and make them responsible should they give advice manifestly improper.'' Inasmuch as the President would have extensive and important business to perform, argued Iredell, he "should have the means of some assist-

---

[46] December 10. Reprinted from *The Connecticut Courant* of that date by P. L. Ford, *Essays on the Constitution of the United States* . . . . (1892), p. 163.

[47] Elliot, II, 448. December 1.

[48] Article II, sec. 2.

[49] March 25, 1788. P. L. Ford's edition of *The Federalist* (1898), p. 497.

ance to enable him to discharge his arduous employment. . . . . He can at no time want advice, if he desires it, as the principal officers will always be on the spot.'' He concluded that ''every good that can be derived from the institution of a council may be expected from the advice of these officers.''[50]

The fact that there was some complaint, particularly in the autumn of 1787, because the Convention had left the chief magistrate unprovided with a council must not mislead us. Writing from Paris, Jefferson expressed this complaint to several of his American friends after he had had an opportunity to read the text of the new Constitution.[51] Richard Henry Lee wished ''that a council of state, or privy council should be appointed to advise and assist in the arduous business assigned to the executive powers.''[52] And there were others who expressed the same point of view. Notwithstanding these opinions, it can be shown, I believe, that there were a few minds sufficiently sagacious and able to penetrate into the probable workings of the new system of government to see that a council of advisers was likely to come into existence so soon as the governmental machinery was well started. Only those, however, were capable of predicting the future institution who had known all the difficulties of adjustment by which the Convention had been con-

[50] Elliot, IV, 108, 109, 110. July 28, 1788.
[51] Jefferson to John Adams, November 13, 1787. Jefferson to Carmichael, December 15. *Documentary History of the Constitution*, IV, 377, 408.
[52] Letter of October 16, 1787, in *American Museum* for December, II, 557. Cf. *Documentary History*, IV, 387, 416.

fronted in its considerations over the problem of an executive council when that problem had been definitely presented to it by the matured plan for a council of state which Morris and his accomplices had offered.

Although very unwilling to accept Morris's plan, Colonel Mason was probably in favor of an advisory executive council.[53] But Mason formulated a crude plan that could have satisfied no large number of members of the Convention. And when he published his "Objections" in the early autumn of 1787, he declared explicitly and truly that the "President of the United States has no Constitutional Council." He went on to say, however, almost in the same breath, that "a Council of State will grow out of the principal officers of the great departments; the worst and most dangerous of all ingredients," he added, "for such a Council in a free country."[54] In the following November Governor Clinton of New York reiterated Mason's words, apparently foreseeing, like

[53] September 7, 1787. Mason moved to postpone consideration of the clause "and may require the opinion in writing of the principal officer in each of the Executive Departments," etc., in order to take up the following: " 'That it be an instruction to the committee of the states to prepare a clause or clauses for establishing an executive council, as a council of state for the President of the United States; to consist of six members, two of which from the Eastern, two from the Middle, and two from the Southern States; with a rotation and duration of office similar to those of the Senate; such council to be appointed by the legislature, or by the Senate.' " Elliot, V, 525.

[54] K. M. Rowland, *Life of George Mason*, II, 388. Cf. *Ibid.*, p. 113. It should be noted that in the Virginia state convention, on June 18, 1788, Mason there remarked that "he did not disapprove of the President's consultation with the principal officers." Elliot, III, 496.

Mason, the possible development of a council of state out of the great officers.[55]

Very much more notable are certain remarks which can be found in the pamphlet by Charles Pinckney entitled *Observations on the Plan of Government Submitted to the Federal Convention, in Philadelphia, on the 28th of May, 1787.*[56] This pamphlet was probably printed soon after the adjournment of the Convention, for it was in Madison's hands on October 14, 1787.[57] There is no direct evidence as to the time when it was written. Although its statements are not always consistent with the records of Pinckney's positions as taken during the debates of the Convention,[58] the document would seem to afford good evidence of its author's matured convictions, particularly on the subject of an advisory council to the President.

Near the opening of the Convention Pinckney proposed, as we have seen, that the President should be given the right to advise with the heads of the different departments "as his Council." On August 20 he

[55] "Letters of Cato," reprinted from the *New York Journal* by P. L. Ford in his *Essays on the Constitution*, pp. 262, 265. The original references appeared on November 8 and 22, 1787.

[56] *New York:*—Printed by Francis Childs. No date. Pp. 27. The copy I have used belongs to the Yale Library. It bears on the title-page this statement: "By the Hon. Charles Pinckney, Esq., L. L. D.," etc. Another print with the same pagination reads: "By Mr. Charles Pinckney," etc. See *Nation*, XCIII, 164. August 24, 1911.

[57] *Writings of James Madison*, V, 9.

[58] For example, Pinckney first favored joining the heads of departments in a council of revision, but he gave this up, according to his reported statement on June 6. Elliot, V, 165. The plan of a council of revision of principal officers appears in the *Observations*, pp. 8-9. See for a careful study of the remnants of the original Pinckney Plan and the *Observations, American Historical Review*, IX, 735 ff.

seconded and probably approved of Morris's plan for a council to assist the President. Yet certain casual statements made by Pinckney in the Convention might be taken to indicate that he appreciated the difficulties of having any such combination as the heads of departments formally recognized in the Constitution for a very specific purpose.[59] However, referring in his pamphlet to four departments—foreign affairs, war, treasury, and admiralty "when instituted"—he said of the President: "He will have a right to consider the principals of these Departments as his Council, and to require their advice and assistance, whenever the duties of his office shall render it necessary. By this means," added Pinckney, "our Government will possess what it has always wanted, but never yet had, a Cabinet Council. An institution," he concluded, "essential in all Governments, whose situation or connections oblige them to have an intercourse with other powers. . . . "[60]

This remarkable characterization of an institution unrecognized by the Constitution, an institution which has become a familiar feature of American government, can hardly have been a mere suggestion or chance prophecy on Pinckney's part. Although among the youngest members of the Convention, he[61] had been active in the Continental Congress in 1786. He took

[59] Elliot, V, 165, 349, 442.
[60] *Observations*, p. 10.
[61] Pinckney was born in 1758. J. B. O'Neall, *Biographical Sketches of the Bench and Bar of South Carolina* (1859), II, 138 ff. John Francis Mercer of Maryland was born May 17, 1759. James Mercer Garnett, *Biographical Sketch of Hon. James Mercer Garnett . . . . with Mercer-*

part at that time in the consideration of certain deficiencies of the government of the Confederation. Moreover, his interest in the particular problem of sustaining the central government must then have been stimulated; and his ingenuity in helping to solve the problem was put to the test, for he acted as chairman of an important committee which worked over the whole matter and made a report of it.[62] After this notable experience and his work as a member of the Convention, Pinckney's clear and confident characterization may reasonably be taken to indicate not only that he appreciated the necessity of such a body in aid of the President, but also that he regarded it as almost assured by the common—and constitutional—assumption that there would be principal officers over the great departments.

Pinckney's application of the English phrase ''cabinet council'' to the combination of officers that he foresaw in the new scheme of government is probably the first that can be found.[63] The phrase may be the casual feature in the passage. On the other hand, it probably indicates Pinckney's familiarity with the workings of the British Constitution.[64] At any rate at a time when most men were probably accustomed to term such a council either ''council of state'' or ''privy council,''

Garnett and Mercer Genealogies (1910), p. 53. Jonathan Dayton of New Jersey was born on October 16, 1760. *Cyclopaedia of American Biography*, II, 113.

62 *American Historical Review*, IX, 738.

63 Paul Leicester Ford calls this ''the first suggestion of the body unrecognized by the Constitution.'' *Nation*, LX, 459. June 13, 1895.

64 Pinckney's longest recorded speech in the Convention shows rather unusual knowledge of the English government. Elliot, V, 233 ff. June 25.

it is extraordinary and notable that the young South Carolina statesman should have ventured to employ the phrase which became in the course of years permanently attached to the advisory body of the American President.[65] Yet in this very connection it should be observed that when, in January, 1788, James Iredell of North Carolina attempted to answer Colonel Mason's particular objection to a possible council of state developing out of the principal officers in combination, he reminded his readers that the single truly efficient council in the English government was "one formed of their great officers." "Notwithstanding their important *Constitutional Council*," he added, "every body knows that the whole movements of their government, where a council is consulted at all, are directed by their *Cabinet Council*, composed entirely of the principal officers of the great departments."[66] Iredell certainly would seem to have had no special fear of a body so composed. He was, moreover, clearly appreciative of these two facts: first, that the English Privy Council was at the time rather a belated survival; second, that the English Cabinet Council was already understood by well-informed men to be the important source of directive power in the English state.

---

[65] An English correspondent of Washington, writing from Avignon, on August 20, 1787, enclosed a plan of government for the new nation. This plan reflects many peculiarities of the British system, and particularly recommends a "cabinet council," to be composed of the chief magistrate and "any four of the great officers of State." *Documentary History*, IV, 264.

[66] P. L. Ford, *Pamphlets*, p. 348.

From such evidence, then, as can be assembled, we may conclude that George Mason of Virginia and perhaps Governor Clinton of New York perceived with some degree of clearness in the autumn of 1787 the probability that a council to the future President would arise in a combination of the principal officers. Charles Pinckney was convinced that there would be such a body: he characterized it adequately and named it—as it proved—with startling accuracy. Yet the importance as well as the workings of such a council, were it to take shape, would depend inevitably upon numerous future contingencies all but quite indeterminable—the laws creating the departments, the number of principal officers that Congress might decide upon, and the unknown human factors involved.

NOTE

It is almost impossible to find references in print to the usage of "Privy Council" as applied to an American body in colonial times. Professor Herbert L. Osgood cites from the sources one usage of the phrase as applied to the Governor's Council in Maryland. This council, he writes, "stood toward the governor in a relation analogous to that occupied by the privy council toward the king in England. In 1642 the council received for the first time a commission distinct from that of the governor. In this it was called 'our privie Councell within our said Province of Maryland,' and its members were empowered to meet with the governor when and where he should direct, 'to treate, consult, deliberate and advise of all matters, causes and things which shall be discovered unto you. . . . .' The peculiar function of the council, therefore, was to advise the governor and through him the proprietor, and without that advice the governor should not act." *The American Colonies in the Seventeenth Century,* II, 65-66.

Quite the best description that I can discover of the colonial council of state has been given by Dr. N. D. Mereness in his *Maryland as a Proprietary Province,* pp. 174-184. Mr. Clarence P. Gould of Johns Hopkins University has been kind enough to furnish me with additional information from the Maryland archives as follows:

The privy council as used in Mereness means only the ordinary council of the colony—the same body as the Upper House, but sitting with the governor as a council of state. . . . . The term "privy council" is sometimes applied to this body, but merely "the council" and "the council of state" are more common. "Privy council" was used more frequently in the early days of the colony. Early commissions always read "to be of our Privy Council" or "to be of our Privy Council of State" (*Archives,* I, 114, 131, 201, 240, 242, 251, etc.). In 1669 was framed an "Oathe of a Councellor of State," but in the oath the members of the council were referred to as "privy Councellors" (*Arch.,* V, 41). Again, a revenue act of 1671 provides for "the Privy Council of the Lord and Proprietary of this Province" (Quoted L. H. J., May 21, 1739). Later on councillors' commissions cease to be entered in full, and I have not been able to find what the proprietor himself continued to call the council. Proclamations, however, read "with the Advice of his Lordship's Council of State," and the two Houses usually spoke of it as the "council" or the "council of state" (L. H. J., 1739, May 4, May 24, etc.). *Private Letter of November 7, 1910.*

From this it will be clear that the Privy Council and the Council of State were identical in Maryland.

CHAPTER IV

THE PRINCIPAL OFFICES IN 1789

ALTHOUGH it did not expressly enjoin executive departments, the Constitution clearly contemplated principal officers or heads of departments. Accordingly the first Congress organized under the new system took into consideration early in its first session the subject of departmental arrangements.

I

The congressional debates on the establishment of departments which were opened in the House of Representatives on May 19, 1789, revealed tendencies making toward administrative unity and hence real executive efficiency on the part of the President. The discussions over the places and functions of the Secretaries served to bring the administrative power of the President for the first time distinctly into view. Hence the large historic import of these discussions. In them the guiding influence of James Madison on the course of the debates is particularly apparent. Several matters became clear.

In the first place, the tenure of office of the Secretaries, quite unprovided for by the Constitution, was settled as being at the pleasure of the appointing power. Again, the appointing power was interpreted, after much discussion, as including the power of removal, the Senate having merely a negative over appointments. With the power of removal in his hands it was felt that the President was likely to be a stronger director and more efficient supervisor of the national administration, for the power of removal helped to give the chief magistrate that control over the Secretaries and certain other officers, without which he could have been in no effective way responsible, as he was intended to be by the makers of the Constitution, for the entire executive department.[1] And finally confidence between President and principal officers was seen by a few men to be essential to successful administration.

The evidence on this last point is peculiarly pertinent to our inquiry. "Without a confidence in the executive department," remarked Egbert Benson of New York, "its operation would be subject to perpetual discord." Speaking of the place of the President, Fisher Ames of Massachusetts said: "The only bond between him and those he employs is the confidence he has in their integrity and talents; when that confidence ceases, the principal ought to have power to remove those whom he can no longer trust with safety." Others spoke in a similar strain. Elbridge Gerry of Massachusetts, watchful of the rights of the states and dreading executive prerogative and any-

[1] *Annals of Congress*, I, 394 ff. Madison to E. Randolph (May 31, 1789) in *Writings of James Madison*, V, 373. The debate has been carefully analyzed with special reference to the appointing power by Professor Lucy M. Salmon in her *History of the Appointing Power of the President* in the *Papers of the American Historical Association*, I, 305-313.

thing suggesting possible absolutism in the federal headship, was peculiarly prophetic. He reminded his colleagues in the House that, not satisfied with having made the Secretaries "the creatures of the law," they were "making them the mere creatures of the President." He was himself satisfied that the Secretaries would become "a set of ministers . . . . to hold the reins of government." To the people he felt sure that the principal officers would appear as "consequential persons." "These officers," declared Gerry, "bearing the titles of minister at war, minister of state, minister for the finances, minister of foreign affairs, and how many more ministers I cannot say, will be made necessary to the President." He concluded that in fact the President "will be inclined to place more confidence in them than in the Senate." [2] In this last sentiment Gerry was really close to the view of his former colleague in the Philadelphia Convention, George Mason, when, in September, 1787, Mason had expressed his fear lest a council of state would grow out of the principal officers of the great departments. [3]

Although neither Gerry nor any one else who took part in the long debates of 1789 said directly that the President and heads of departments were likely to form a council, yet the stray evidence just assembled would seem to give ground for inferring that the thought of such a combination as no remote possibility was occasionally near the surface of the debates.

As ideas matured under Madison's able guidance,

[2] *Annals of Congress,* I, 403, 492, 493, 527.
[3] See chapter III, *supra,* p. 89.

the House of Representatives proved to be willing to arrange for the organization of three separate departments—foreign affairs (or state), war, treasury— exactly the number that there had been under the old government of the Confederation since 1781. Over every one of these departments it was finally decided to place a single chief officer. Naval affairs, it should be said, were transferred from the old Treasury Board, in whose charge they had been since 1785, to the care of the Secretary of War.[4] An unsuccessful effort under the lead of John Vining of Delaware, one of the younger members of the House, was made to establish a fourth department of domestic or home affairs.[5]

II

The statutes[6] which established the three departments revealed certain differences that should not be overlooked. Only the Departments of State and War were termed "executive." Their Secretaries were apparently intended to be solely responsible and subordinate to the President. The Department of the Treasury, on the other hand, may have been intended to be within easy reach or control of the legislature. The point is worth a moment's consideration.

According to the express language of the law, the Secretary of the Treasury was to "make report and give information to either branch of the legislature,

[4] Paullin, "Early Naval Administration under the Constitution" in *Proceedings of the U. S. Naval Institute,* September, 1906, XXXII, 1001 ff.

[5] *Annals of Congress,* I, 385, 386, 412, 692-695 (*passim*).

[6] 1 *Statutes at Large,* pp. 28, 49, 65, 68.

in person or in writing, as he may be required, respecting all matters referred to him by the Senate or House of Representatives, or which shall appertain to his office.'' There was not a word in the statute concerning the President's power of direction, although the President must appoint the Secretary to the headship of a department in accordance with the Constitution. While, then, the Secretary of the Treasury, like the two other Secretaries, was certainly responsible to the President, he was apparently intended to be held in some sort of restraint by the legislature, for he was subject at any moment to the legislature's call.

In the absence of direct evidence, there cannot be much doubt that the peculiar position in which the law of September 2, 1789, left the Secretary of the Treasury, was largely due to general recognition of the force of popular tradition and colonial precedent in the matter of financial administration. Heretofore, both in the colonies and in the states of the Revolutionary epoch, financial administration had been all but completely within control of the popular bodies. One of the best-informed students of colonial practices has written that ''by the close of Anne's reign, the colonial assemblies were, with few exceptions, enforcing their claim not merely to lay taxes and determine expenditures, but also to appoint the chief financial officer of the province.'' [7] In the two mature plans[8] for a consti-

---

[7] E. B. Greene, *Provincial America, 1690-1740* (Amer. Nation Series, vol. 6), p. 77. Cf. E. P. Tanner, *The Province of New Jersey*, pp. 393, 397, 400, 430, 433.

[8] Those of August 6 and September 12. *Documentary History*, III, 449, 724.

tution which marked the later stages of the work of the Philadelphia Convention, it was proposed that Congress should have the appointment of a treasurer of the United States. "The people," urged King and Gorham of Massachusetts, "are accustomed and attached to that mode of appointing treasurers."[9] But at the last moment it was decided to allow the President to appoint the nation's treasurer—an innovation, asserted King and his colleague, which "will multiply objections to the system." Perhaps the arrangement of the Secretary of the Treasury's position in 1789 under the restraint of Congress was partly owing to the action of the Convention in allowing the President to name the national treasurer.

For many years after 1789 the peculiar place of the Secretary of the Treasury was a subject of occasional comment. As early as April 2, 1792, Jefferson alluded to it in his "Anas," casting a characteristic slur in this connection upon Alexander Hamilton, his unbeloved colleague.[10] In one way or another the subject came to the attention of every President before Jackson. The law, which allowed the head of the financial department to report annually and at other times to Congress, was sure to interfere with real unity of administration, especially when Congress desired to get a report from the Secretary without previous communication with the President. Both Madison and Monroe during their terms as Presidents experienced

9 Elliot, *Debates*, V, 542.
10 *Writings of Thomas Jefferson*, I, 190.

special difficulties because of the calls of Congress on their Secretaries of the Treasury.[11]

President Jackson left his contemporaries under no doubts as to his theory of the relation existing between him and any Secretary of the Treasury whom he might choose to associate with him. The episode which brought his theory into prominence was the so-called removal of the deposits. In connection with the episode, Jackson, in September, 1833, developed his view of the proper functions and status of a cabinet officer such as the Secretary of the Treasury by virtually saying that, although the Secretary might be required by law to report to Congress instead of to the President, the peculiar provision was never meant to exempt a Secretary from his obligation to sustain the President in all matters of public policy.[12] The matter assumed almost at once a partisan aspect. Opponents of Jackson's policy toward the Bank—such men, for examples, as Henry Clay and Horace Binney—denied that the Treasury was an "executive department." Samuel J. Tilden, then a youth just out of his teens, undertook to defend Jackson's view. Basing his argument upon a well-selected number of historic incidents, Tilden made out a plausible case that since Hamilton's day the Treasury had usually been considered an executive department.[13] It was the same conclusion which the Committee of Ways and Means put upon

[11] *Memoirs of J. Q. Adams,* IV, 217, 500-502. Cf. *Works of John Adams,* VIII, 555.

[12] *Messages and Papers,* III, 5 ff.

[13] February 14, 1834. *Writings and Speeches of Samuel J. Tilden,* ed. John Bigelow (1885), I, 27 ff.

record in an elaborate report read to the House on March 4, 1834.[14]

Two years later, in 1836, an effort was begun for the purpose of amending the Constitution in such a way as to allow Congress to choose the Secretary of the Treasury. And during the succeeding six years opponents of Jackson's executive policy appealed now and again to Congress for similar amendments.[15] The effort was only one feature of the reaction against what seemed to be an unwarranted and high-handed policy on the part of the Democratic party. There were no doubt many sympathizers with the sentiment of Clay when, in the Senate, on January 24, 1842, he burst into the declaration that "during the last twelve years, the machine, driven by a reckless charioteer with frightful impetuosity, has been greatly jarred and jolted, and it needs careful examination and a thorough repair."[16] There was reason in this sort of plea. But nothing in the way of legislation ever came from the effort to put the Secretary of the Treasury's appointment into the hands of Congress. Whatever the intent of the makers of the law of 1789, in practice the Secretary of the Treasury has been regarded from Jackson's day as an officer under executive control. Moreover, in the language of the later law, the Department is

[14] Niles's *Register*, XLVI, 38 ff. (March 15, 1834.)

[15] These efforts may be followed in the *Congressional Globe* under the dates: February 13, 1836, January 2, 1838, January 14, 1839, December 29, 1841, and January 24, February 2, 15, 23, 28, March 4, 21, and August 30, 1842. They marked several sessions of the 24th, 25th and 27th Congresses.

[16] *Globe*, 27 Cong., 2 sess. (1841-1842), p. 164.

recognized as an "executive department." But it should also be noted that the old provision of 1789, which authorized the Secretary to "make report, and give information to either branch of the legislature in person or in writing," has not been altered.[17]

III

The Senate of 1789, acting perhaps on the assumption of a place in the new government analogous to that of the colonial council or upper house—a body which exercised some variety of judicial functions—took the lead in the business of organizing a judicial establishment. Its committee of eight, Ellsworth of Connecticut acting as chairman, appointed as early as April 7, brought in a bill which resulted in the Judiciary Act of the following September.[18] The final section (35) contained a brief provision for the office of the Attorney-General. Aside from his function as federal prosecutor, the Attorney-General was to be legal adviser to the President and heads of departments. This arrangement brought him into the range of executive control and made him, like the Secretaries, a ministerial officer. He was head of no department in 1789, nor indeed—as we shall see later on—until 1870. His rank, like his salary, was distinctly below that of the three Secretaries. Yet from

---

[17] *Revised Statutes* (2d ed., 1878), pp. 38-41. For a recent consideration of the place of the Secretary of the Treasury in our system, see Frank J. Goodnow, *The Principles of the Administrative Law of the United States* (1905), pp. 70 ff.

[18] 1 *Statutes at Large*, pp. 92 ff. September 24, 1789.

the outset Washington reckoned the Attorney-General as an intimate adviser.[19]

The Judiciary Act, while nominally the result of the labors of a Senate committee, was probably shaped largely by the hand of Oliver Ellsworth, its chairman. It was Madison's recollection—expressed more than once—that the Senator from Connecticut drafted the bill, "and that it was not materially changed in its passage into a law."[20] But contemporary jottings on the course of the debate, made by Senator Maclay, himself a member of the committee, make the authorship as ascribed to Ellsworth almost a certainty.[21]

The portion of the Act devoted to the Attorney-General's place is curiously brief. This brevity suggests the marked immaturity of the administrative-judicial system of the central government. Indeed, so far as the central government is concerned, the office was an innovation, for no such office had been known to the Confederation. On the other hand, the English Attorney-Generalship, which doubtless furnished the men of 1789 with a model, was old and well established.[22] Moreover, there had been Attorneys-General in many of the colonies. In Virginia, for example, the office had been established some years

[19] The evidence for this I examine later. See pp. 164 ff., 181 ff.

[20] *Letters and other Writings of James Madison*, IV, 428. Cf. *Ibid.*, 220-222.

[21] *Journal of William Maclay*, ed. E. S. Maclay (1890), pp. 91, 97, 101, 103, 105, etc. William Garrott Brown examines the evidence carefully and presents the general conclusions admirably in his *Life of Oliver Ellsworth* (1905), pp. 181 ff.

[22] Sir William R. Anson, *Law and Custom*, Pt. II (2d ed., 1896), pp. 201 ff.

before 1650. Early in the eighteenth century the
Virginia Attorney-General had been expected to reside
at Williamsburg, at the time the seat of the provincial
government.[23] Some of the states in the Revolutionary epoch had Attorneys-General. And both
Pelatiah Webster in 1783 and Gouverneur Morris in
1787, it will be recalled, included a leading representative of the legal profession in their separate plans
for a council.

IV

We have seen how Congress provided in 1789 for
laws which called for the appointments of three Secretaries and an Attorney-General. Four positions were
created, the occupants of which were to be the assistants of the President. Before turning to the next
subject—the factors which brought these officers into
a President's council—let us observe a statement set
down by Gouverneur Morris, and printed in the spring
of 1789.

The statement in view occurs in a pamphlet by
Morris entitled *Observations on the Finances of the
United States, in 1789.* This pamphlet was partly the
result of Morris's "maritime meditations" on his
journey from America in the winter of 1788, but it was
formulated later and was perhaps influenced by certain conversations between Morris and Jefferson in
Paris, the latter our minister to France. Under date

---

[23] O. P. Chitwood, *Justice in Colonial Virginia* (Johns Hopkins University Studies, July-August, 1905). It is worth observing that the state
of Connecticut had no Attorney-General until 1897. *Public Acts* for 1897,
chap. 191. May 25, 1897.

of May 8, 1789, Gouverneur Morris sent a copy of the pamphlet to his friend, Robert Morris, once Superintendent of Finance. In it there occurs this passage:

On no subject perhaps can it be more needful to take precautions . . . . than on that of finance, both for the public security and for the reputation of the Ministers. It might therefore be wise to provide that the terms on which loans are to be made, and the manner of making them, should be discussed and decided on, not only by the officers of the Finance department, but by the President and the other principal officers of State, such as the Secretary at War, and of Foreign Affairs. These taken together might be very safely entrusted with the appropriation of the revenue . . . . their determinations would be secret.[24]

Here is a statement from the pen of the great protagonist of the conciliar idea in the Philadelphia Convention. It is not surprising that it should be in accord with earlier suggestions as to the advantages of a council of principal officers. But it certainly indicates how very natural was the conception of a President's council just at the period of the active beginnings of the new government in 1789.

[24] J. Sparks, *Life of Gouverneur Morris*, III, 3-4, 471, 476.

NOTE

The first Congress, on May 21, 1789, appointed a
committee of eleven members to prepare bills for
organizing the executive departments. The committee
consisted of Messrs. Baldwin (chairman), Vining,
Livermore, Madison, Benson, Burke, Fitzsimons,
Boudinot, Wadsworth, Gerry and Cadwalader
(*Annals of Congress,* I, 412). There is no clue in
contemporary records to any other than the committee authorship of the act for a Treasury Department. Yet Secretary John Quincy Adams, under date
of January 12, 1819, did not hestitate to ascribe the
authorship of the act directly to Alexander Hamilton,
as follows:

The laws constituting the Departments were . . . . founded
upon the same principle, with the exception of the Treasury
Department, the law to establish which was drawn up by
A. Hamilton, who was himself to be the Secretary, and whose
object was to establish a direct intercourse between the members of the legislature and himself for his own purposes. . . . .
Memoirs of John Quincy Adams, IV, 217.

I have not discovered that any one of Hamilton's
chief biographers takes any account of this statement.
Although it is probably not deserving of much credence, yet I think it worth citing, for it is possible that
in the course of time new evidence on the subject may
be brought to light.

CHAPTER V

THE CREATION OF THE CABINET: 1789-1793

THE Convention had hardly finished its work in September, 1787, when Alexander Hamilton conjectured the probability that Washington would be President in case the new form of government were acceptable to the people. "This," he added, "will insure a wise choice of men to administer the government and a good administration. A good administration will conciliate the confidence and affection of the people and perhaps enable the government to acquire more consistency than the proposed constitution seems to promise for so great a Country."[1]

By the summer of 1789, his election and inauguration having taken place, and Congress having by that time made progress in arranging for the great departments and the judicial establishment, Washington was deeply concerned with the problem of surrounding himself with four assistants, men qualified in foreign affairs, in finance, in army organization, and in the law. The nominations for these appointments were of grave consequence to the first chief magistrate as well as to the country. And in the matter of selection the importance of a few guiding principles was perfectly apparent.

Washington sought for capable and efficient men whose usefulness had stood the test of some experience

[1] *Documentary History*, IV, 290. The remarks of Hamilton, from which the extract is quoted, were undated, but were probably jotted down in the early autumn of 1787.

in colonial, state, or continental places. The whole
Revolutionary epoch was one peculiarly likely to make
or mar reputations. And Washington was well fitted
to judge men who had been associated with him in the
armies at that time. He seems to have been especially
desirous of obtaining tried and worthy men in the
various judicial posts under his control. Moreover,
important places within his power of nomination he
meant to distribute with due regard to the claims of
the various states—the geographical factor was not
to be overlooked. And finally what has been termed
political orthodoxy—intent to support the new system of government—was taken into the account.[2]

While such guiding principles were influential and
to some extent considered in the President's choice of
his principal officers, there can be no doubt that the
claims of friendship played an important part in
directing Washington's search for men to assist him.
Intimately and confidentially associated with him as
these men must be, it was very natural that Washington decided finally to make three of the four
appointments under consideration from among his
personal friends.

I

In the autumn of 1788, several months before the
first Congress assembled, men were gossiping about

---

[2] Miss Salmon discusses these principles carefully in her study of the
appointing power. *Papers of the Amer. Hist. Assoc.*, I, 314-319. Cf.
C. R. Fish, *The Civil Service and the Patronage* (Harvard Hist. Studies,
vol. XI, 1905), pp. 6-10.

the possible incumbents of the principal offices. It was already assumed that newly organized departments of foreign affairs and war, when they should be arranged, would probably be placed under the supervision of the old Secretaries, John Jay and General Henry Knox. Madison, it was remarked, might well be "employed as minister for the home department."[3] But Madison's election to the first national House of Representatives soon placed him outside the range of popular consideration for office. Moreover, as it proved, there was to be no separate home department arranged by Congress. Before Robert Morris was chosen Senator from Pennsylvania, it was natural to regard him as perhaps the most available head of the Treasury Department, should the old Treasury Board be superseded by a single Secretary. Even while the problem of arranging a Treasury Department was being discussed by the House, men referred easily to Morris as an example of what a single man of capacity in the position ought to be. "The gentleman," said Boudinot, "had asked where a proper character for a financier was to be found? America has seen one man equal to the task."[4] "We had once a gentleman," remarked Gerry, "who filled such a department, and I believe the only one in the United States who had knowledge and abilities by any means competent to the business."[5] There was no doubt about Morris as being popularly considered the

---

[3] November 29, 1788. D. Humphreys to Jefferson. Bancroft, *History of the Formation of the Constitution*, II, 485 (Appendix).

[4] May 20, 1789. *Annals of Congress*, I, 410.

[5] *Ibid.*, I, 401. See Note 1 at the end of this chapter.

most marked man for the headship of the country's finances. But as time advanced, at latest by the month of July, 1789, attention had more and more turned toward Alexander Hamilton. It is known that Chancellor Livingston had aspirations for the place. And John Jay may possibly for a time have considered it as within his range of ability.[6]

The appointments of Hamilton and Knox were determined upon by President Washington easily and probably in the early part of the summer of 1789. Hamilton, conscious of having assisted in the movement toward a new constitution, felt an obligation to lend his aid in getting the machine into operation and regular motion. We know from his own statement that he did not hesitate to accept the proffer of the Treasury headship.[7] Both men were on terms of very close intimacy with the President. Associated with him in the Revolution, they had kept up a correspondence with him at intervals ever since. When Knox's income was at a low ebb, he had solicited Washington's recommendation to assist him in getting a place in the employ of the government of the Confederation. And partly through Washington's friendship he had been appointed Secretary at War by Congress in 1785.[8] Knox had certainly approved himself to the public by

[6] *Writings of James Madison* (ed. Hunt), V, 303, 309, 313, 319, 324, 370-371. *Letters and other Writings* (ed. Rives), I, 421, 476-477, 484. III, 67. *Works of Alexander Hamilton* (ed. Lodge), VIII, 204, 254, 259-260. J. C. Hamilton, *Republic*, IV, 504.

[7] May 2, 1797. Dr. A. M. Hamilton, *Intimate Life of Alexander Hamilton* (1910), pp. 14-15.

[8] F. S. Drake, *Memorials of the Society of the Cincinnati of Massachusetts* (1873), pp. 169-173.

his conduct of the old department.[9] In fact, in respect to fitness, the appointments of both Knox and Hamilton were in accord with the most intelligent contemporary opinion.

In July, 1789, Washington was considering Edmund Randolph of Virginia for some place in the federal judicial establishment. Early in the following month, aided by the confidential advice of Madison, he had "almost determined" on the nomination of Randolph to the Attorney-Generalship.[10] When the proffer of the position was made to Randolph late in September, the President then deemed Randolph's acceptance of it as "problematical." The truth is that Randolph accepted Washington's offer with hesitation, partly owing to the disordered condition of his private affairs—a condition which could be altered materially only by more of an income than he could expect as a low-salaried office-holder—and partly because he desired to complete a revision of the laws of Virginia, a task on which at the moment he was engaged. As first Attorney-General of the State of Virginia under its new constitution of 1776, and later as governor of that state who had naturally acted as spokesman of the Virginia delegation in the Philadelphia Convention of 1787, Randolph certainly had a conspicuous claim to some sort of recognition under the new administration, even though his political orthodoxy had not been of the most robust kind. Like Hamilton and

[9] For example, see oration of Judge J. M. Varnum, delivered at Marietta, Ohio, on July 4, 1788. In *American Museum* for May, 1789, V, 454-455.

[10] J. Sparks, *Writings of George Washington*, X, 26.

Knox, he had for years been on terms of intimate friendship with Washington. Indeed, there can be no doubt that the President felt a real affection for him.[11]

If the naming of Randolph as Attorney-General suggests Madison's influence, the naming of Thomas Jefferson as Secretary of State shows it in the clearest possible light.

The appointment of Jefferson is distinctly the most interesting of the four appointments under consideration. John Jay was what might be called the logical candidate for the headship of the country's foreign affairs in 1789. A man of relatively large experience abroad as well as one already known for his dominating influence on administration at home during the later years of the Confederation, and on friendly (though hardly intimate) terms with Washington,[12] Jay seemed to the discerning mind of Madison to be assured of the position in the early summer of 1789.[13] According, however, to the best available authority on Jay's life—that of his son—Washington gave to Jay the choice of "any office he might prefer." And so, at his own request, Jay was named as Chief Justice of the Supreme Court.[14] This decision of Jay probably led Washington directly to the consideration of Thomas Jefferson.

[11] *Writings of George Washington* (ed. W. C. Ford), XI, 432-434, 450-470. M. D. Conway, *Omitted Chapters in the Life and Papers of Edmund Randolph* (1888), pp. 129 ff. J. C. Hamilton, *Republic*, IV, 31.

[12] W. C. Ford, *George Washington*, Memorial ed. (1900), II, 163.

[13] *Letters and other Writings of James Madison* (ed. Rives), I, 476, 477, 483.

[14] W. Jay, *Life of John Jay* (1833), I, 274.

Perhaps Jay helped to turn the President's attention to Jefferson. It seems most probable, however, that Madison was the directive factor in the situation. He certainly did all that he could to bring Jefferson into a mood to accept the place after it had been offered to him. Madison had been for years on terms of the closest friendship with Jefferson. He had kept Jefferson in France intimately informed of the progress of events in the United States ever since Jefferson's departure in 1784. And in respect to the work of the Philadelphia Convention and the years just following, Madison was Jefferson's chief source of information. In May, 1789, Madison had sounded Jefferson for the apparent purpose of testing Jefferson's willingness to accept a possible home appointment under the new government. While both Jay and Madison were relied on by Washington for counsel during the momentous summer of 1789, it seems very probable that Madison's high regard for Jefferson and his well-known intimacy with him made Madison the real source of any special information, apart from Jefferson's reputation, which the President could have desired. Washington and Jefferson, it should be observed, had never been on terms of intimacy. It is true that letters had passed between them occasionally. Long since Washington had expressed his regard for Jefferson, referring to him as ''a man of discernment and liberality.'' Moreover, Washington had eagerly forwarded to Jefferson the Convention's adopted plan of a constitution on the day after the Convention adjourned, September 18, 1787, hoping that he might be first to communicate the document to his fellow-Virginian acquaintance. As for Jefferson's reputation, it was conspicuously well established. He had been very useful at various times in the Continental Congress. Like his friend, Edmund Randolph, he had been governor of Virginia. And in 1789, with Franklin restored to his native land, Thomas Jefferson was unquestionably the best-known American then resident in Europe. He was not only a man of intellectual accomplishments, but he had proved himself as a practical statesman to be at least a man of great promise.[15]

Landing at Norfolk, Virginia, in November, 1789, Jefferson for the first time heard of his appointment. For over two months following he hesitated about accepting it. He was very much disinclined to have other than foreign affairs to attend to in connection with the Department of State. While he was in a doubtful mood, Madison visited him in Virginia for the purpose, it would seem, of trying to obtain his consent to the appointment. Only after this visit and at the renewed and urgent request of Washington, assured that the public was eager for his acceptance of the position, did Jefferson give a half-hearted consent, reluctantly turn his face from France, and take up his new task in New York City on March 22, 1790.[16]

The four nominations were made to the Senate in September, 1789. They were confirmed without delay,

[15] Bancroft, *History of the Formation of the Constitution*, I, 151. *Documentary History of the Constitution*, IV, 427. Jefferson's *Writings* (ed. P. L. Ford), VIII, 368, ft. note.

[16] See Note 2 at the end of this chapter.

and commissions were accordingly issued. Hamilton was first to enter upon his duties on September 11, succeeding the Treasury Board of three commissioners, Messrs. Walter Livingston, Samuel Osgood, and Arthur Lee. The next day General Knox, who had had charge of the old department of war since 1785, formally began his work under new direction. Jay conducted the business of the new Department of State at the request of the President until he was succeeded by Jefferson late in March, 1790. Randolph began his service on February 2, 1790,[17] the day on which the judiciary establishment went into full operation. Soon after that, however, he was obliged to return to Virginia on his wife's account. He was thus so much delayed that he actually handed his resignation of the Attorney-Generalship to Washington. The resignation was not accepted, and Randolph was able to undertake the active duties of his post in the month of May. Only in May, 1790, with Jefferson, Hamilton, Knox, and Randolph in New York City, could the first administration be looked upon as really assembled.[18]

Here, then, were the simple facts previous to that variety of circumstances which were to induce Washington to combine his principal assistants into a coun-

[17] W. G. Brown, *Oliver Ellsworth*, p. 197.

[18] *Executive Journal of the Senate*, I, 25, 26, 32-33. M. D. Conway, *Omitted Chapters*, etc., pp. 133-135. In view of the difficulty of access to the *Senate Executive Journal*, I have found it most convenient, as a rule, on dates of nominations, etc., to cite Robert Brent Mosher's *Executive Register* (1903), an admirably and carefully arranged compilation. Mosher's book contains accurate lists of all the Cabinets down to its date of issuance, including records of all commissions, and dates when active duties were undertaken.

cil. First, the Constitution implied that there were to be principal officers and executive departments. Second, Congress decreed that there should be three departments, and arranged statutes providing for the creation of four principal officers. Third, Washington nominated these officers; and their appointments were made final by the favoring attitude of the Senate and the issuance of commissions.

Neither the Constitution nor the law brought the principal officers into a council. When Senator Henry Cabot Lodge characterized the Cabinet as "statutory," and declared that "the law alone creates the Cabinet," he was either mistaken in his view or careless in his use of language.[19] The law created the principal officers or members of the Cabinet. The Cabinet itself was the creation of President Washington. He began the practice of assembling his principal officers in council. And this practice became in the course of time a settled custom. The simple truth is that the Cabinet is a customary, not a statutory body.

The financial requirements especially conspicuous during Washington's first term, the problems of our commercial and foreign relations, the frontier questions involving the need of an army as well as the determination of our attitude toward the Indians and to British and Spanish neighbors—all these and other matters called not only for the direction of a sagacious President, but also for the assistance of well-qualified experts. With these things in view, we may turn to

[19] "The Senate of the United States," reprinted in *A Frontier Town and Other Essays* (1906), pp. 73-74.

certain features of the historic process making for
executive unity and force.

II

From the outset Washington regarded the principal
officers as his assistants.[20] This view did not prevent
the President from consulting others. But the exercise of his functions was almost certain to bring the
assistant officers into a council. The process of unification, depending to a large extent on personal relations that very naturally often escaped record, was
somewhat unconscious. A few well-authenticated facts
will serve to make the process clear.

Soon after the new government started, Washington
asked for the opinions of his Secretaries on matters
of importance separately, in conversations for the
most part unrecorded, or in writing, in accordance
with the letter of the Constitution. From Jefferson
alone there were at least a dozen written opinions
furnished before the close of the year, 1790.[21] On the
first question of diplomacy which confronted the
administration, in respect to a possible war between
Spain and Great Britain—a matter that involved the
point as to whether a British force should be permitted
to pass through our limits of territory on its way from
Canada for the purpose of attacking the Spanish pos-
sessions in the southwest—Washington asked for
written opinions from Vice-President John Adams and

20 *Writings* (ed. W. C. Ford), XI, 397-398. May 25, 1789.
21 Jefferson, *Writings*, V, 150 ff.

Chief-Justice Jay as well as from the three Secretaries.[22] Jay's opinion, although perhaps defensible, was in reality an encroachment on the advisory function of the Attorney-General.[23] Custom had not yet made the advice of the Vice-President appear irregular. In fact, during the first five years of his Presidency, Washington occasionally appealed to Adams for written advice;[24] and at least once, as we shall see, had Adams summoned to a meeting of the Secretaries.

On August 22 and again on August 24, 1789, Washington, accompanied by the Secretary of War, General Knox, actually appeared in the chamber of the Senate to advise with the Senators in the matter of a proposed treaty with the Southern Indians. According to Maclay's well-known record, the President seemed ready "to tread on the necks of the Senate" and to "bear down" the Senators' deliberations "with his personal authority and presence. Form alone," declared Maclay, "will be left us. This will not do with Americans. But let the matter work; it will soon cure itself."[25] And it did so, for there is no record of any similar meeting in later history.

However prejudiced Maclay may have been in his account of the incident, there is no reason to doubt

---

[22] *The United States and Spain* (ed. W. C. Ford, Brooklyn: 1890), pp. 7, 16, 17, 18, 43, 106.

[23] Mosher, *Executive Register*, pp. 93-94. Here is revealed a similar encroachment, when Chief-Justice Marshall, on February 20, 1821, enlightened President Monroe as to the time when Monroe should take the oath of office, the 4th of March, 1821, falling on a Sunday.

[24] J. Adams's *Works*, VIII, 489, 496, 515. May 17, 1789; August 27, 1790; January 8, 1794.

[25] *Journal* (ed. E. S. Maclay), p. 131.

that the ineffectiveness of any such meeting became once and for all evident to President, Secretary, and Senators. The very ineffectiveness of the method must have tended to make the President more dependent upon his personal assistants, the heads of departments and the Attorney-General, when the business of the government became in time very complicated. As for the incident itself, it was not without points of resemblance to experiences between the colonial governors and their councils.[26] But we may be quite sure that neither Washington nor Knox was aware of any precedents for their conduct in entering the upper house. The President acted upon the assumption of a clear constitutional privilege—a privilege, moreover, which is recognized to-day among the standing rules of the Senate, where provision is made for occasions when the President "shall meet the Senate . . . . for Executive business."[27]

Twice—in January, 1790, and again in November, 1792—the problem arose as to whether the Secretaries were to obtain hearings before the House of Representatives. In the first instance Hamilton was ready and even desirous to present his "Report on Public Credit" in person, in accordance with the statute creating his position. The House refused to permit him to appear before it.[28] In the second instance there was some effort on the part of certain members of the House to get both Knox and Hamilton before that

[26] See Note 3 at the end of this chapter.
[27] *Senate Manual* (edition of February 5, 1905). Standing Rule xxxvi.
[28] *Annals of Congress*, I, 1079, 1081. II, 1446, 1516, 1639, etc.

body in connection with a discussion of the failure of St. Clair's expedition against the Indians. Inasmuch as feeling ran high on this subject, it was perhaps fortunate that the House again refused to permit the Secretaries to appear. It was, at any rate, strongly urged by Madison in this latter case that a precedent might be established which would involve perplexing consequences in the future.[29]

Thus circumstances tended, in the first place, to keep President and Senate apart in matters calling for advice. In the second place, they circumscribed the positions of the Secretaries in such a way that inevitably the Secretaries regarded themselves as essentially and in most respects belonging to the Executive. Accordingly these very circumstances, it may be assumed, helped to unify the President and his personal advisers.

In 1791 we find the earliest evidence on what came to be called cabinet meetings. Congress having adjourned in March, Washington left Philadelphia for a tour in the South. Spending several days at Mount Vernon on the way, he addressed a letter to the three Secretaries under date of April 4. He wrote: "I have to express my wish, if any serious and important cases (of which the probability is but too strong) should arise during my absence, that the Secretaries for the Departments of State, Treasury, and War, may hold

[29] *Ibid.*, 2 Cong., 2 sess. (1792-1793), pp. 679-722. November 13-21, 1792. For a careful study of these matters, see a paper by Miss Mary L. Hinsdale entitled ''The Cabinet and Congress: An Historical Inquiry,'' in *Proceedings of the American Political Science Assoc.* (1905), II, 127-135.

consultations thereon, to determine whether they are
of such a nature as to demand my personal attendance
at the seat of government. . . . . Presuming that the
Vice-President will have left the seat of government
for Boston, I have not requested his opinion to be taken
on the supposed emergency; should it be otherwise,
I wish *him* also to be consulted.''[30] In accordance with
the suggestion, there was a meeting on April 11. The
Vice-President and three Secretaries were present.
Jefferson made a careful report of it in a letter to
Washington. Loans, commerce, foreign relations,
appointments, frontier troubles with the Indians, and
other subjects all came into the discussions. At intervals of about a fortnight during his absence that
spring, the Secretary of State kept the President
informed of the course of events, both domestic and
foreign. But Jefferson made no statement as to holding another meeting of the Secretaries.[31]

If the evidence of the ''Anas'' may be trusted in
this connection, this was the single occasion on which
Vice-President Adams was ever asked to attend a
cabinet meeting.[32] It is true that, at the opening of
John Adams's administration, friends of Jefferson,
then Vice-President, were anxious that he should be
admitted to the meetings of Adams's advisers. But
Jefferson's theory of the office would not have allowed
the practice. ''I consider my office as constitutionally
confined to legislative functions,'' he wrote to Elbridge

[30] Washington's *Diary from 1789 to 1791* (ed. B. J. Lossing), p. 162.
Writings, XII, 34, foot note, 35.
   [31] *Writings*, V, 320 ff.
   [32] Jefferson, *Writings*, I, 165.

Gerry on May 13, 1797, "and .... I could not take any part whatever in executive consultations, even were it proposed."[33]

Although President Washington had taken time to arrange the business of the departments before leaving Philadelphia, apparently it had not occurred to him to suggest meetings of his assistants until he was well on his way southwards. Was his failure to speak of the Attorney-General a mere oversight? It is impossible to say. It may have been simply that the President was aware that no legal problem was likely to arise which would require Randolph's judgment. At any rate the first recorded "cabinet" meeting seems to have been suggested in a singularly casual manner.

In 1792 there are several clear records of "cabinet" meetings. Thomas Jefferson has left some account of two of these, giving a few details. The first meeting was described as follows:

Mar. 31. A meeting at the P's, present Th: J., A. H., H. K. & R[andolph] The subject was the resoln of the H. of Repr. of Mar. 27. to appt a commee to inquire into the causes of the failure of the late expdn under Maj. Genl. St. Clair with power to call for such persons, papers & records as may be necessary to assist their inquiries. The commee had written to Knox for the original letters, instns, &c. The President he had called us to consult, merely because it was the first example, & he wished that so far as it shd become a precedent, it should be rightly conducted. He neither acknowledged nor denied, nor even doubted the propriety of what the house

[33] *Ibid.*, VII, 120. *Life and Correspondence of Rufus King* (ed. Charles R. King), II, 167.

were doing, for he had not thought upon it. . . . . We were
not prepared & wished time to think & enquire.[34]

Taking time to consider the problems, the Secretaries
and the Attorney-General came together once more.
Jefferson outlined the second meeting in this wise:

Apr. 2. Met again at P's on same subject. We had all considered and were of one mind 1. that the house was an
inquest, & therefore might institute inquiries. 2. that they
might call for papers generally. 3. that the Executive ought
to communicate such papers as the public good would permit,
& ought to refuse those the disclosure of which would injure
the public. Consequently were to exercise a discretion.
4. that neither the commee nor House had a right to call on
the head of a deptmt, who & whose papers were under the
Presidt. alone, but that the commee shd instruct their chairman to move the house to address the President. . . . .
Hamilt. agrd with us in all these points except as to the
power of the house to call on heads of departmts. He
observed that as to his departmt the act constituting it had
made it subject to Congress in some points, but he thot himself not so far subject as to be obliged to produce all papers
they might call for . . . . in short he endeavd. to place himself subject to the house when the Executive should propose
what he did not like, & subject to the Executive, when the
house shd propose anything disagreeable. . . . .[35]

The passages are interesting and important. Not
only do they reveal the President and his principal
assistants in council, but furthermore they indicate
clearly the effort on the part of Washington to establish sound precedents, and on the part of the Secretaries and the Attorney-General to protect the execu-

[34] *Writings*, I, 189.
[35] *Ibid.*, I, 189-190. For evidence of other meetings, *Ibid.*, I, 179, 205,
210, etc.

tive from any unfair invasion by the legislative power. In brief, the President's assistants meant to keep the executive department, as far as it was possible, in an independent position in the government.

In 1793 the meetings of the President's advisers were frequent, especially so after Washington's arrival in Philadelphia on April 17. The most notable of these was the meeting of April 19, at which the issuance of the so-called Neutrality Proclamation was unanimously agreed upon.[36] Within a month from that time Jefferson referred to the meetings of the advisers as occurring "almost every day."[37] There is abundant evidence to show that the assistants of the President held many consultations through the summer until early in the month of September. About the first of November meetings were again renewed.[38] The year was a very critical one, filled with problems of policy, about the right solution of which there was often much perplexity and grave doubt.

The crisis of 1793 enforced the necessity of frequent meetings on the part of the President's best-qualified advisers. And in all likelihood it brought the Cabinet for the first time forcibly into popular view as a working body. At any rate during the year the terms "council," "conclave," and "cabinet" were occasionally applied to the four assistants of Washington. The application of these terms rested on the obvious fact that the President was summoning to his aid a

[36] J. Sparks, *Writings of George Washington*, X, 337, Appendix, 533-536.

[37] Jefferson, *Writings*, VI, 250.

[38] *Ibid.*, I, 218 ff. VI, 191 ff.

committee of officials somewhat similar to the English Cabinet Committee. There was nothing essentially new in such a committee, closely related on the one hand to administrative departments, and on the other as advisers to the chief magistrate. There is no evidence but the term "cabinet" to show that in characterizing the President's advisers men took into account anything but the superficial resemblance to the English institution. What probably we did, was to adopt a well-recognized English political term, the significance of which had been pretty well settled in the seventeenth century.

There is an occurrence in the summer of 1793 that should not escape attention, for while the result served to place a restriction on the President and his advisers, it likewise, by reason of that very fact, tended to mark more clearly the important sphere of effort to which the functions of the Cabinet must often be confined. We have already noted the circumstances under which the Senate was found to be ineffective as a possible council of advice. We have also seen the House of Representatives on two separate occasions refuse to admit the Secretaries within their precincts. We may now observe the decision of the judges of the Supreme Court of the United States, when Washington ventured to ask them for an opinion.

· The President and his advisers, perplexed over the many legal problems arising under the treaties with France, concluded on July 12, 1793, to appeal directly for legal advice to the federal judges. The judges declined to respond. "It was, perhaps, fortunate for

the judges and their successors," remarks Professor
Thayer in commenting on the occurrence, "that the
questions then proposed came in so formidable a shape
as they did. There were twenty-nine of them, and they
fill three large octavo pages.[39] . . . . Had they been
brief and easily answered the Court might, not
improbably, have slipped into the adoption of a precedent that would have engrafted the English usage
upon our national system. As it is . . . . while the
President may require the written opinion of his
Cabinet, 'he does not possess a like authority in regard
to the judicial department.' "[40]

This request, it may be added, accorded with a colonial practice of asking the judges for opinions. The
usage went back into fourteenth-century England. It
is, moreover, still maintained to-day in a few of the
states of the Union. Charles Pinckney had submitted
a proposition to the Philadelphia Convention to allow
the supreme executive to "have authority to require
the opinions of the Supreme Judicial Court upon
important questions of law, and upon solemn occasions." But that body had not favored it.[41]

The bitter animosity which had arisen between

[39] Sparks, *Writings of G. Washington*, X, 542-545 (Appendix).

[40] James Bradley Thayer, *Legal Essays* (1908), pp. 53-54, foot note.
Cf. J. P. Bishop, *New Commentaries on the Criminal Law* (8th ed.
Chicago: 1892), I, 30 (§62).

[41] Elliot, *Debates*, V, 445. August 20. J. B. Thayer, *John Marshall*
(Riverside Biographical Series, No. 9, 1901), pp. 70 ff. There are at
least seven states that have provided for obtaining opinions from the
judges of the highest court upon application by the executive or the legislature: Massachusetts, New Hampshire, Maine, Rhode Island, Florida,
Colorado, and South Dakota. Thayer, *Cases on Constitutional Law*
(1895), I, 156, 175-176, 177-178, 181, 183, note, etc.

Hamilton and Jefferson by the summer of 1792, partly the result of natural differences of temperament and opinion, and partly, perhaps, the result of competing ambition, was aroused by the intimate relations that the circumstances of their respective positions enforced. It is certainly remarkable that the association of the first three Secretaries and the Attorney-General could have been maintained as long as it was. It is entirely unlikely that it could have lasted for any such period under any other President but Washington. Jefferson was first in the group to surrender his post, retiring on the last day of December, 1793. Within a period of less than two years his three colleagues had left the administration, Randolph having been virtually dismissed. Others succeeded these four men, but they had little to do with the creation of the Cabinet.

In the next chapter I propose to give some attention to the significance of the term "cabinet," tracing it from its appearance in 1793 to the time when it made its way into a federal statute in 1907.

NOTES

1. ROBERT MORRIS AND THE TREASURY PORTFOLIO:

In the *National Intelligencer* of February 24, 1845, there appeared what purported to be a recollection of George W. P. Custis, grandson of Mrs. Washington, regarding Washington's offer of the Treasury headship in 1789 to Robert Morris. The passage was reprinted and is accessible in the volume entitled *Recollections and Private Memoirs of Washington. By G. W. P. Custis* (1860), p. 349—a posthumous publication which contains notes by Benson J. Lossing and a memoir by Custis's daughter. It reads:

In 1789, when the first president was on his way to the seat of the new government, he stopped in Philadelphia at the house of Robert Morris, and while consulting with that eminent patriot and benefactor of America, as to the members of the first cabinet, Washington observed, "The treasury, Morris, will of course be your berth. After your invaluable services as financier of the Revolution, no one can pretend to contest the office of secretary of the treasury with you." Robert Morris respectfully but firmly declined the appointment, on the ground of his private affairs, and then said, "But my dear general, you will be no loser by my declining the secretaryship of the treasury, for I can recommend to you a far cleverer fellow than I am for your minister of finance, in the person of your former aid-de-camp, Colonel Hamilton." The president was amazed, and continued, "I always knew Colonel Hamilton to be a man of superior talents, but never supposed that he had any knowledge of finance." To which Morris replied, "He knows everything, sir; to a mind like his nothing comes amiss . . . ."

This account is rather too circumstantial to appear trustworthy. The incident is said to have occurred in April, 1789, before Congress had set to work on the task of organizing departments. Washington was quite as well fitted as Morris to know Hamilton's real interests, for he had been on terms of the greatest intimacy with him. There is perhaps a modicum of truth in it. But it is impossible, in view of Custis's general unreliability, and the absence of contemporary evidence, to give it full credence.

2. JEFFERSON'S APPOINTMENT AS SECRETARY OF STATE:

The material for the study of this subject is very abundant. It seems worth while to collect together such sources as have been consulted in formulating the narrative:

W. C. Rives, Jr., *History of the Life and Times of James Madison*, III, 63-64. *Letters and Other Writings of James Madison* (ed. Rives), I, 459, 471-472. *Writings of James Madison* (ed. G. Hunt), V, 435-436. *Writings of Thomas Jefferson* (ed. P. L. Ford), V, 54, 95, 114-115, 134, 139-150. *Writings of George Washington* (ed. W. C. Ford), XI, 438-439, 467-469. J. C. Hamilton, *Republic*, IV, 31, 113, 115-117, 474. *Annals of Congress*, Senate Proceedings, June 16, 18, 1789. John Jay, *Correspondence and Public Papers* (ed. H. P. Johnston), III, 365, 366, 380-381. H. S. Randall, *The Life of Thomas Jefferson*, I, 554-555, 557, foot note. *Memoir, Correspondence, and Miscellanies from the Papers of Thomas Jefferson* (ed. T. J. Randolph, Charlottesville: 1829), I, 87-89, 144-146. George Tucker, *The Life of Thomas Jefferson* (1837), I, 300. *Autobiography, Reminiscences and Letters of John Trumbull from 1756 to 1841* (1841), p. 154. *Diary and Letters of Gouverneur Morris* (ed. Anne C. Morris), I, 230. *Works of Alexander Hamilton* (ed. Lodge), VIII, 260.

There are other references to the friendship existing between Madison and Jefferson, but the student
of the subject will discover them easily in following
up the correspondence between the two men which
extended over a great many years.

3. COLONIAL PRACTICES:

There is an interesting and apposite paragraph on
the colonial practice of the governor meeting with the
legislative council or upper house in South Carolina,
to be found in Dr. W. Roy Smith's *South Carolina as
a Royal Province,* pp. 92-94:

During the proprietary and the early years of the royal
period, His Excellency had a seat in the council in its legislative as well as in its executive and judicial capacities. . . . .
On April 11, 1739, the upper house resolved that the presence of the governor or commander-in-chief during the sitting of the house was of an unparliamentary nature and that
they would enter into no debates during his presence. They
had good precedents for this. Richard West, special counsel
to the Board of Trade, had given an opinion in 1725 that the
governor could not legally vote when the council was sitting
in a legislative capacity. In January, 1736, as the result of
a contest in New York, the Board of Trade decided that
Governor Cosby was neither to sit nor to vote in the council
while it was acting as a branch of the legislature. When
Governor Glen arrived in the province in December, 1743,
he became angry at the attempt to exclude him from the
legislative council, and made a speech endeavoring to show
from the practice of the other provinces and the home government that he had a right to be present. His exclusion, he
declared, was contrary to the British constitution, "for that
the King's Throne in the House of Peers was not placed
there as an ornament to the Room, but because he had a right

to be there, and the Lord Coke says that the Parliament is composed of two houses. The King and House of Lords make one House, and the House of Commons is the other.'' He went on to say that he had the same right to be present that the King had in the House of Lords. Whether or not the council were as ignorant of the British constitution as Governor Glen and were convinced by his arguments is not known. At any rate, they agreed that he might be present, provided he would never take any part in the debates or receive any messages coming to their house or give answer thereto. Glen did not like this purely ornamental position and made the serious mistake of joining hands with the lower house in an attack on the legislative powers of the council. He seems to have attended the meetings occasionally until 1749, and then to have ceased altogether. Finally, he came into their chamber on April 29, 1756, as they were reading a message previously sent by him. The reading was at once postponed and the house adjourned to the afternoon. . . . . A committee report of the upper house, adopted May 7, 1745, during the controversy with Glen, calls attention to the confusion caused by the governor's presence in their chamber. . . . . The governors had not been content to call meetings before or after the assembly business was done, but would have council meetings at intervals between and would continue to sit in the great chair of the council chamber when the upper house met. The result was that members of the assembly coming up with messages were at a loss to know who was the president, as at one time the body would be a council, then again an upper house.

CHAPTER VI

THE TERM "CABINET" IN THE UNITED STATES

T HE practice of consulting his principal officers together in a council was begun by President Washington in the early part of his first term. It was indirectly justified by Alexander Hamilton when, in 1792, he remarked that the "success of every government . . . . must always naturally depend on the energy of the executive department. This energy again must materially depend on the union and mutual deference which subsists between the members of that department, and the conformity of their conduct with the views of the chief executive."[1] This was merely a mode of stating the theory that must have been behind the practice. In the course of years the practice, followed out by the first President's successors, became a settled custom. The custom conformed to the need of any vigorous, well-organized, and carefully directed central administration. In this way an administration could be closely associated and its work unified under the lead of the executive magistrate.

I

To characterize Washington's principal officers as a body of advisers, the English term "cabinet" came into use in 1793. It was well enough known at the time

[1] Hamilton, *Works*, VI, 367.

as applicable to the important source of directive power in the English government, the Cabinet Committee. It had been used by Charles Pinckney as early as 1787 to characterize what he, almost alone among his contemporaries, seems to have foreseen as a probable development—an advisory committee to the American chief magistrate.[2] In 1792 the phrase "cabinet council" was applied locally to a group of New York state officials.[3] But, after much scrutiny of newspapers and printed correspondence, I have never been able to discover the term "cabinet" or "cabinet council" as applied to a combination of the nation's principal officers as a working body before the year 1793.

At the risk of being wearisome, I venture to assemble such characteristic evidence as can be easily found on the usage of the term. In a letter of Jefferson to Madison of May 12, 1793, we find this sentiment: "The Anglophobia has seized violently on three members of our council."[4] On May 19 Jefferson referred to the group as "our conclave."[5] On June 13 Madison was apparently first to apply the well-known English term, writing of the "discussions of the cabinet."[6] Again, on July 22, he spoke of Hamilton's "cabinet efforts."[7] On August 2 Jefferson confided to his "Anas" a reflection on the differences of

[2] *Supra,* chapter III, p. 91.
[3] *Life and Correspondence of Rufus King,* I, 410.
[4] *Writings,* VI, 250.
[5] *Ibid.,* VI, 261.
[6] *Writings* (ed. Hunt), VI, 132.
[7] *Ibid.,* VI, 136.

opinion existing "in our Cabinet."[8] On August 18 Jefferson remarked on a paper "read in cabinet for the 1st time."[9] Senator Rufus King of New York, under date of April 12, 1794, referred in his "Diary" to the "cabinet."[10] Early in the following year Madison, in writing to Jefferson, said: "I fancy the Cabinet are embarrassed."[11] Quoting a letter written in Philadelphia on October 14, 1795, the *American Mercury*, a newspaper published at Hartford, Connecticut, printed the phrase "ministerial cabinet."[12] And on the last day of that year, Jefferson, writing to his friend, William B. Giles, a member of the House of Representatives, said of a certain man that he "never gave an opinion in the cabinet against the rights of the people."[13] Writing of Pickering and Oliver Wolcott to the Secretary of War, James McHenry, a correspondent of McHenry in 1796 declared them to be "without doubt your inferiors as Cabinet ministers."[14] Soon after he reached Philadelphia in the spring of 1797, Jefferson recorded this fact about President Adams: "Monday, the 6th of March . . . . he had met his cabinet" for the first time.[15] Representative William Smith of South Carolina, in a letter to Rufus King, then minister to England, after describing the

[8] *Writings*, I, 253.
[9] *Ibid.*, VI, 394.
[10] *Life and Correspondence*, I, 519.
[11] *Writings*, VI, 232. January 26, 1795.
[12] November 23, 1795.
[13] The reference is probably to Edmund Randolph.
[14] B. C. Steiner, *Life and Correspondence of James McHenry* (1907). p. 166.
[15] Jefferson, *Writings*, I, 273.

inauguration of Adams as President, said, under date of April 3, 1797, that the "Jacobins are flattering him and trying to cajole him to admit the V. P. into the Council."[16]

The instances might be multiplied. But such as I have here collected, chosen somewhat at random over a period of about four years, will indicate clearly enough that the Cabinet was first characterized definitely in the writings of a few leading statesmen who were in close touch as a rule with the affairs of the national government. The institution was soon referred to in the newspapers of the time. I have not discovered any reference to the body in the debates of Congress before the year 1798. On April 25 of that year, while the bill providing for the organization of a navy department was being discussed in the House of Representatives, Edward Livingston, at that time a resident of New York, referred unmistakably to the Cabinet as "the great council of the nation."[17] Not before Jefferson's administration were there any notable references to the Cabinet in Congress. The term "cabinet" may be found used in debate on February 27, 1802, in the House. It appeared again rather less than a year later in a discussion on January 11, 1803. It was freely bandied about and criticised in a sensational argument directed against the administration by John Randolph in March, 1806—an occasion which revealed Randolph in one of his most querulous moods full of sound and fury against his

16 *Life and Correspondence of Rufus King*, II, 167.
17 *Annals of Congress*, 5 Cong., 2 sess. (1797-1798), II, 1552.

opponents. It was one of these opponents, a member
of the House from Pennsylvania, who was moved to
make this reflection as part of his reply. "I wish,"
he declared, "the gentleman had deigned to inform us
what he meant by a Cabinet. I perceive no such thing
in the Constitution or laws. I believe the phrase is
peculiar to the Court of St. James, where the Ministers
of the King are called the Cabinet." Truth, however,
forced the speaker to add at once this statement of
fact: "I have heard the Heads of Departments and
the Attorney-General assembled by the President on
great occasions, called the Cabinet."[18]

There were few variations in the use of the term as
time advanced. Probably by the close of Jefferson's
administration, when the national government had
been in operation for a period of twenty years, the
functions of the Cabinet Committee of experts in aid
of the chief magistrate were popularly understood.
As an institution it had taken a distinct place. Certainly Jefferson could say with good reason that the
"third administration . . . . presented an example of
harmony in a cabinet of six persons, to which perhaps
history has furnished no parallel."[19]

II

The circumstances which brought about the creation
of the Cabinet by Washington have been traced and
set forth.[20] Time and the inevitable demand for a firm

[18] *Ibid.*, 9 Cong., 1 sess. (1805-1806), pp. 561, 564-565, 590, 606, 744.
[19] *Writings*, IX, 307.
[20] *Supra*, chapter V.

executive policy gradually made the conception of the significance of the Cabinet clear and molded the institution into permanence. Here and there, notably in the writings of Hamilton and Jefferson, the reader will come upon evidence to show that the conception of the Cabinet was taking definite form.

Attention has already been called to Hamilton's remarks in 1792 on the subject of the need of energy and unity in the executive.[21] In 1800 Hamilton expressed in a forcible way the theory on which every Cabinet in the American scheme of government must rest. This was his thought: "A President is not bound," he declared, "to conform to the advice of his ministers. He is even under no positive injunction to ask or require it. But the Constitution presumes that he will consult them; and the genius of our government and the public good recommend the practice. As the President nominates his ministers, and may displace them when he pleases, it must be his own fault if he be not surrounded by men who, for ability and integrity, deserve his confidence. And if his ministers are of this character, the consulting of them will always be likely to be useful to himself and to the state. . . . . When, unhappily, an ordinary man . . . . refrains from counselling with his constitutional advisers, he is very apt to fall into the hands of miserable intriguers."[22]

This passage, taken from one of the most bitter

---

[21] *Supra,* p. 135.

[22] "Public Conduct of John Adams" (1800), in Hamilton, *Works,* VI, 419.

political invectives that can be found, reflects the fact that the Cabinet Committee had reached a position at which its general functions could be easily defined by a man of insight. There is a sharp thrust at President Adams's unfortunate experiences with his cabinet advisers, vigorous enough to make any prospective successor of Adams think carefully about the qualities of the men whom he might wish to place in the Secretaryships and the post of Attorney-General. The very contrast that Jefferson's advisers—a most harmonious combination—revealed, is an indication that Jefferson was probably alive to the importance and utility of the institution. At any rate, in 1807, Jefferson expressed himself as follows: "For our government," he wrote, "although in theory subject to be directed by the unadvised will of the President, is, and from its origin has been a very different thing in practice . . . . all matters of importance or difficulty are submitted to all the heads of departments composing the cabinet. . . . . So that in all important cases the Executive is in fact a directory."[23]

It can be shown that the method of cabinet meetings which Washington had first suggested as far back as 1791, Jefferson for the most part followed. Of it he said: "I practiced this method, because the harmony was so cordial among us all, that we never failed by a contribution of mutual views on the subject, to form an opinion acceptable to the whole . . . ."[24] It was not a method sanctioned by a strict interpretation of

[23] Jefferson, *Writings*, IX, 69, 70.
[24] *Ibid.*, IX, 273-274.

the Constitution, as Jefferson was well enough aware. However, it accomplished things quickly and, in view of the many difficult problems before a President, it was inevitably the most satisfactory and natural method.

Even from John Randolph we get a glimpse of the theory of the place of the advisers in the government when, in November, 1803, he declared it to be "the essence of Government that one man cannot execute it alone; and that he is obliged to share it with heads of Departments, or with agents by some other name. The imbecility of human nature is such that he must participate power with others. . . . ."[25]

On the day that President Jefferson retired into private life, March 4, 1809, a close observer of executive practices who had some doubts as to the ultimate stability of the existing form of executive, had copyrighted (and soon after published) a pamphlet entitled *Considerations on the Executive Government of the United States of America.*[26] The author was Augustus B. Woodward. Although he dated his essay at New York, he held at the time the position of Chief-Justice of the Territory of Michigan. The ideas in this pamphlet were to some extent fantastic and impractical. But several of them indicate a man of unusual political sagacity and are worth attention.[27]

The keynote of Judge Woodward's essay was sounded near the beginning where he declared his con-

25 *Annals of Congress*, 8 Cong., 1 sess. (1803-1804), p. 573.

26 Flatbush, N. Y.: 1809, pp. 87.

27 For other reflections on Woodward, see chapter X, pp. 266 ff., and Note 1 on p. 288.

viction that the "first shock which our government must sustain, endangering its existence, or menacing its stability, must be derived from the executive department. It is here the storm will arise," he continued, "and in this quarter may we expect the first blow to our union."[28] With this as a postulate, the author proceeded to set forth sundry matters, three of which have rather special significance in connection with the subject of this chapter. For Judge Woodward was the first writer, I believe, who deliberately presented an intelligent account of the development of the Cabinet. He had a true appreciation of the position of the Vice-President in the national organization. Moreover, he commented with quite exceptional insight on the rank of the Secretaries; he disapproved of the Secretaryship of State as a stepping stone to the office of President; and he doubted whether sufficient care had been shown hitherto in the appointment of Secretaries of War and Navy.

1. "It is understood," wrote Judge Woodward, "to have grown into a practice, under the American administrations, to assemble the respective heads of departments in consultation, on particular, important and leading measures. When thus assembled, popular parlance has appropriated to them the epithet of the cabinet. But is it," he asked, "a constitutional council for the President? He is authorized to require the opinion of any one of them in writing, on a matter falling within his proper department. To embody them, and to render them a council, is not contem-

[28] A. B. Woodward, *Considerations,* p. 12.

plated by the Constitution. Is it expedient that it should be? They are exclusively the selection of the President. Their qualifications for their high appointments are•regulated rather by a particular, and perhaps professional skill, than by the possession of general talent or general confidence. The temptation to display singular abilities, or to increase relative consequence, may prompt their advice. At all times, too, they are dependent on the President for their continuance in office.'' On the whole, he concluded, this method of giving advice makes too great a demand on the official. ''It is too severe a trial for humanity, nor does counsel given in the situation possess a title, as strong as might be desired, to the public respect.''[29]

2. ''From the cabinet,'' he reminded his readers, ''practice has excluded the Vice-President. There is therefore no situation in our government more trying to a man of real worth and sensibility. He may be called upon to mature measures, with the origin and progress of which he is unacquainted; measures to which he may be opposed, and which his intelligence might have corrected in their incipient stages.''[30]

3. ''In our executive departments,'' continued Judge Woodward, ''two have been considered as requiring talent and genius. Of these, practice has given the precedence to the department of state. Twice has it determined the succession. Should it grow into a habit, and there is, perhaps, no reason

[29] *Considerations*, pp. 26-27. I have taken a few liberties with Woodward's old-fashioned punctuation.

[30] *Ibid.*, pp. 27-28.

that it should not, since the public mind must necessarily have a channel for its approbation, and the situation of the Vice-President calls for no particular display of talent,[31] the President becomes virtually invested with the choice of his successor. Although our policy is pacific, yet the impression that the military departments do not require talent or genius, but professional skill and mechanical assiduity alone, ought not to be extensively received. If ever our nation, listening to the dictates of folly or yielding indulgence to her passions, should embark in the mad contests of the world, she may pay, by her existence, the forfeit of her mistake. . . . . ."[32]

We need not concern ourselves with Judge Woodward's complicated plan which—calling of course for an amendment to the Constitution—provided for an executive directory of five persons, a President and four Councillors elected for five years, with machinery so arranged as to allow after the first year for the annual election of one new director, as often as there was a vacancy by regular retirement.[33] The plan must have been summarily relegated at the time to the limbo of quickly-forgotten political fantasies. At all events, that is where it belonged. What is worth emphasis, however, is this: the author's clear statement of the method by which the Cabinet had come into being, and his sagacious reflections on the Vice-Presidency and

---

[31] Cf. Jefferson to E. Gerry, writing on May 13, 1797: "The second office of this government is honorable and easy, the first is but a splendid misery."

[32] *Considerations*, p. 29.

[33] *Ibid.*, Appendix, pp. 45 ff.

the secretariat. He presented his views on these subjects from the standpoint of one familiar with past administrative practices, convinced that, unless steps were taken to reform our political machinery and customs, the Presidency was certain to be involved in future difficulties.

It should perhaps be added that Judge Woodward was reflecting and writing on his original theme as late as 1824. It may well have given him some satisfaction then to note that the "administrations of the fourth and fifth Presidents have not been attended with the same felicitous circumstances, which characterized that of the third—an entire exemption from cabinet explosion and dissatisfaction."[34] His conviction remained strong that the "difficulties of the government of the human species still lie where they have always lain—in the construction and in the action of the executive power."[35] From the Cabinet it was still "the uniform course," as he wrote, "to exclude the Vice-President. Perhaps," he commented, "his constitutional function of being prolocutor of the Senate was deemed incompatible with his being a member of the Cabinet. His attendance would frequently be inconvenient, and his possessing a voice in the deliberations of the Senate might render it indelicate. That any dissatisfaction arose from this course being pursued, either at the time of its adoption, or subsequently, has never been manifested."[36] He continued

[34] *The Presidency of the United States* (New York: 1825. Pp. 88), p. 42.

[35] *Ibid.*, pp. 37-38.

[36] *Ibid.*, p. 9.

to desire some form of council for the President that should be sanctioned by the Constitution or at least by law, although he could not tell exactly how to provide for such a body under the existing scheme of government.[37] But his special contribution in the way of novelty at that time was—as we shall see later on[38]—a project for a department of domestic affairs, concerning the importance and vital necessity of which he felt assured.

Turning once more to Congress, we come upon Josiah Quincy's savage arraignment of the government in power in January, 1813, for the project to invade Canada. In his speech, Quincy seldom made any reference to the chief magistrate, James Madison. His invective was directed almost wholly against what he clearly regarded as the source of administrative policy and national disturbance—the Cabinet. His thought suggests to-day, as it may have suggested at the time it was voiced, the weakness of the chief magistrate. However that may be, the entire speech is peculiarly significant of the place the Cabinet could take by that time in the organization of the national government according to the opinion of a shrewd observer of government practices. At least three passages in the speech deserve attention.

"I have some claim to speak," asserted Quincy near the opening of his remarks, "concerning the policy of the men who constitute the American cabinet. For eight years I have studied their history,

---

[37] *Ibid.*, pp. 66-67.
[38] Chapter X, 266 ff.

characters, and interests. . . . . I say, then, sir, without hesitation, that, in my judgment the embarrassment of our relations with Great Britain . . . . has been, is, and will continue to be, a main principle of the policy of this American cabinet."[39] As he advanced in his argument, he declared: "It is a curious fact, but no less true than curious, that for these twelve years past the whole affairs of this country have been managed and its fortunes reversed under the influence of a cabinet little less than despotic, composed, to all efficient purposes, of two Virginians and a foreigner. . . . . During this whole period the measures distinctly recommended have been adopted by the two Houses of Congress with as much uniformity and with as little modification, too, as the measures of the British ministry have been adopted during the same period by the British Parliament. The connection between cabinet councils and parliamentary acts is just as intimate in the one country as in the other."[40]

It was near the conclusion of his speech that Quincy dwelt at some length on the "Virginia influence" as it had manifested itself in the Presidency. He considered the Cabinet, he declared, as doing everything in its power to keep the succession in the Virginia line, in particular to make Monroe the successor of Madison. This was his grandiloquent and sensational outburst: "This is the point on which the projects of the

[39] Josiah Quincy, *Speeches delivered in the Congress of the United States . . . . 1805-1813* (edited by his son, Edmund Quincy), pp. 379-380.

[40] *Ibid.*, pp. 397-398.

cabinet for the three years past have been brought to bear, that James the First should be made to continue four years longer. And this is the point on which the projects of the cabinet will be brought to bear for the three years to come, that James the Second shall be made to succeed, according to the fundamental rescripts of the Monticellian dynasty."[41]

It is no part of this inquiry to consider the exasperation aroused by this venomous assault of the Massachusetts Federalist upon his Republican opponents. Clay met the attack on the administration a few days later in an eloquent and effective reply. Meantime an insignificant member, Representative Rhea, twitted Quincy because, as he said, "he talks profusely about something he calls a Cabinet, which, according to his talk, must know everything. A cabinet! And pray, sir, what is a cabinet? . . . . in America, under the Constitution of the United States, the word has no meaning applicable to any department of the Government. Ah! but it is delicious to follow anything carrying the fume of Old England."[42] This was thoroughly ineffective—mere balderdash, of course. The element of truth in Quincy's speech that could hardly be overlooked by any intelligent and calm judge was in substance this: that the American government had never been directed from the start "by the unadvised will of the President." That was Jefferson's conviction. No less explicit and truthful was the statement of John McLean some years later when, as

[41] *Ibid.*, p. 402.
[42] *Annals of Congress*, 12 Cong., 2 sess. (1812-1813), p. 577.

Postmaster-General under President John Quincy Adams, he declared to his friend, Edward Everett, that the "policy of those who are most intimately associated with the President, contributes as much, and sometimes more, to form the character of the Administration, than the acts of its head. . . . . ' "43

Men might persist—as they did—in objecting to the word *cabinet* even long after the days of Jefferson and Josiah Quincy. It is nevertheless true that, by that time, term and institution had come into their American place. Henceforth the old English term characterized not so much a committee different in composition from the English Cabinet Committee as one differently related to the government of which it was a part.

III

From most of the foreign visitors to the United States during the first few decades after 1789, there came almost nothing in the way of comment on our political institutions and practices which was either penetrating or informing. These visitors perceived some of the most obvious features of our national government. They frequently sought out and occasionally described cleverly our Presidents or other leading statesmen. But trailing, one after the other, over pretty much the same routes of slow and inconvenient travel, encountering similar types, and undergoing similar experiences, in the course of years they often dropped into rather stereotyped language, borrowed

43 *Massachusetts Historical Society Proceedings*, 3d series, I, 378. Letter of August 27, 1828.

incidents, or otherwise padded their volumes when their own industry and inspiration had given out. But a few of them will repay consideration, for they reflected at least surface appearances and popular impressions.

In the spring of 1795, the Duc de La Rochefoucauld-Liancourt met General Knox in Philadelphia soon after Knox had resigned the Secretaryship of War. Later he visited Knox on at least two separate occasions at his home in the province of Maine. From this acquaintance it is probable that the French nobleman gained intimate knowledge of President Washington's administration. At any rate, in his *Travels,* he commented on the office of President, remarking that it was "not so well provided with the means of execution as not to require some accession of strength from the popularity of the man who holds it, and from the confidence reposed in him by his fellow-citizens."[44] He referred to Jefferson's view of politics as one "adopted in the President's council."[45] But he was careful to point out that the American executive had "no constitutional council."[46]

Henceforth, for many years, the foreign observers said little or nothing about the Presidency. Frances Wright, sometimes known by her married name of Darusmont, came to our shores in 1818 and spent several years. Her book, *Views of Society and Manners in America,* revealed an observer of unusual

[44] *Travels through the United States of North America in the Years 1795, 1796, and 1797* (2 vols., London: 1799), II, 184.
[45] *Ibid.,* II, 515.
[46] *Ibid.,* II, 650-651.

discrimination with prepossessions decidedly in favor
of American institutions. Among other things she
wrote of the President and his Secretaries, contrasting
them intelligently with the English Cabinet.[47]   It was
a point of view seldom easily grasped by English
travellers. After two years in America during the
term of President John Quincy Adams, Captain Basil
Hall remarked casually on the extreme importance of
the executive; but he considered it as not well established even by that time.[48] The violence of the election
contests which preceded Jackson's terms was certain
to arouse comment and some reflections on the presidential office. Many a foreign critic remarked on the
contests, but the attempts to account for them led
foreign writers into many vagaries and indicated much
misconception as to the office of President.

Achille Murat, nephew of the first Napoleon, a resident in America since 1821 and to some extent
identified with Florida politics, recognized that the
Attorney-General had a place as "part of the president's cabinet council." But he was unaware in 1832
that Jackson had for three years been reckoning the
Postmaster-General as one of his regular council
associates.[49]

Two Scotch visitors, James Stuart and Thomas Hamilton—the latter a younger brother of Sir William

[47] London: 1822, 2d ed., pp. 333 ff. Madame Darusmont died at
Cincinnati, Ohio, in 1852.

[48] *Travels in North America, in the Years 1827 and 1828* (2 vols.,
Philadelphia: 1829), II, 36-37.

[49] *A Moral and Political Sketch of the United States of North
America* (London: 1833), pp. 189, 307.

Hamilton—referred with some interest to the Cabinet as they observed it in Jackson's first term. "Instances occurred," remarked Stuart, "even during the short period of my stay at Washington, which led me to think that, instead of the house sending to the ministers for information, it would be attended with advantage that the secretaries of state, even if they had no vote, should be allowed to sit and speak in the house."[50] Hamilton, although meeting President Jackson and his Secretary of State in an intimate way, was unable to straighten out the simple facts about the Cabinet. Like Stuart, he looked upon it as curious that the ministers should be excluded "from even a deliberative voice in either branch of the legislature." Ever ready with explanations, he thus continued:

It proceeds, no doubt, from that extreme jealousy of the executive. . . . . and is necessarily productive of much delay and inconvenience. . . . . It is somewhat strange that the American constitution, which evidently presumes that every man in office is a scoundrel, should have removed, in this instance, one of the strongest and most efficient securities for public virtue. . . . . A British minister cannot skulk in Downing Street, when the Commons of England are discussing the wisdom of his measures, or the purity of his motives. . . . . The oracles of an American minister are issued only from the shrine of his bureau. . . . . The Americans . . . . in excluding their executive officers from all place in their representative bodies, have gratuitously discarded a powerful and efficient security for the honest and upright administration of their affairs.[51]

[50] *Three Years in North America* (2 vols., Edinburgh: 1833), II, 12.
[51] *Men and Manners in America.* By the author of Cyril Thornton. (2 vols., 2d Amer. ed., Philadelphia: 1833), II, 34-36.

There were far more accurate statements of the facts that lay behind the well-known schism in Jackson's first Cabinet, but no careful student or reader should overlook the impressions of it which Mrs. Trollope recorded in her inimitable way.[52]

Before concluding this aspect of the subject, let me cite from a work that appeared in the summer of 1828 under the title, *Notions of the Americans.* Published anonymously, but written by James Fenimore Cooper —then at the height of his renown—it was an attempt to make clear the falsity of European impressions about America. The author adopted as a means toward his object the artificial method of putting his observations and statements of fact into the mouth of a European travelling bachelor, member of a club of cosmopolites, who was persuaded to come to America on a visit and thence to send letters filled with his impressions to his friends. There was in the letters a great deal of current gossip, but some excellent statements of fact, among them this:

You probably know already that the president of the United States is assisted by a cabinet. It is composed of four secretaries (state, treasury, war, and navy), and of the attorney-general. As the president alone is answerable for his proper acts, these ministers have no further responsibility than as their own individual agency is concerned. They have no seats in congress. . . . . It is an unsettled point whether congress has a right to admit the ministers to possess consultative voice in the two houses. I think the better opinion is, that they have; but the practice has never yet been

[52] *Domestic Manners of the Americans* (2 vols. in one. London: 1832), II, 181-182.

adopted. Indeed, there is a sort of fastidious delicacy observed on this subject, which, in effect, prevents the secretaries from attending the debates even as auditors. I have never seen any member of the cabinet in the chamber of either body. . . . . The exclusion of the ministers from the debates is thought, by many people, to be a defect, since, instead of the verbal explanations which they might give, if present, it is now necessary to make formal demands on the different departments for information. On the other hand, it is contended that the existing practice compels members to make themselves familiar with details, and that they are none the worse legislators for their labour. In no case could the ministers be allowed to vote, or even to propose a law, directly. . . . .[53]

IV

It is not necessary to follow the term farther in much detail. As early as 1803 it was used by Chief-Justice Marshall in the Supreme Court decision of *Marbury vs. Madison.*[54] Jackson was the first President, as one might expect, to use the term in an annual message. It appeared in his first message of December 8, 1829, and may be discovered in a few other state papers issued or signed by him.[55] Tyler again employed the term to characterize his advisers in his fourth and last annual message of December 3, 1844. Since Tyler's administration the word has appeared occasionally in the

[53] *Notions of the Americans:* Picked up by a Travelling Bachelor. (2 vols., London: 1828), II, 47-51, *passim.* For an estimate of this work see Professor T. R. Lounsbury's *James Fenimore Cooper* (American Men of Letters Series), pp. 100 ff.

[54] 1 Cranch, *Reports*, p. 170.

[55] *Messages and Papers of the Presidents* (ed. Richardson), II, 448. III, 5, 19, 36, 198, 199, 210, 211, 212, 433, 597.

formal and public papers of some of the succeeding Presidents. But its use has been rare.[56]

There can be no doubt that careful scrutiny of the congressional debates would reveal occasional comments on the Cabinet and on the usage now and again of the term. As a more recent instance than any which has been cited thus far, I may refer to a passage in connection with the debates in 1870, just previous to the act for the re-organization of the judicial establishment. Hon. William Lawrence, Representative from Ohio, had this to say:

We also understand that by usage there are certain officers of the Government, heads of Departments, who are members of what is called by common usage ''the Cabinet.'' I am well aware that there is no law which organizes the Cabinet; but almost from the foundation of the Government the President has been in the habit of calling a council of the heads of Departments and taking their advice upon all important public matters; and these officers acting in that capacity are in common parlance called ''the Cabinet.'' Now, the Attorney General is one of the officers who, in accordance with this usage, has been consulted by the President.[57]

There was some further discussion of the term at that time. But it amounted to nothing but the distinct recognition of the fact of the well-known existence of the institution. The law had as yet taken no notice of it.

That the term *cabinet* has at last gained a place in the language of the federal statute law is remarkable enough to call for a brief explanation. In an act

[56] *Messages*, IV, 350, 659. V, 163, etc.
[57] *Globe*, 41 Cong., 2 sess., Pt. IV, pp. 3065 ff. (April 28, 1870.)

approved and signed by President Roosevelt on February 26, 1907, provision was made for increasing the salaries of the Secretaries, Attorney-General, and Postmaster-General from $8,000—the sum at which they were fixed by law in 1874[58]—to $12,000. The part of the act with which we are concerned read as follows:

Sec. 4. That on and after March fourth, nineteen hundred and seven, the compensation of the Speaker of the House of Representatives, the Vice-President of the United States and the heads of Executive Departments who are members of the President's Cabinet shall be at the rate of twelve thousand dollars per annum each. . . . .[59]

Behind this mature formulation was the customary story of a struggle in Congress over the bill for appropriations for the year, 1907-1908. Introduced into the House on the previous December 7, the bill was debated first, after its second reading, on the 10th. Four days later—Friday, the 14th—Representative Lucius N. Littauer of New York proposed that the compensation of the heads of the executive departments "who are members of the President's Cabinet" should be at the rate of $12,000 per annum. This proposition brought to his feet Representative James R. Mann of Illinois. Mr. Mann recognized at once the appearance in this suggestion of a term hitherto unknown to the statute law, and criticised the language accordingly. "I suppose the gentleman is aware," he began, "that there

[58] Act of 1874, dated January 20. See Appendix A for all changes in the salaries of the President, Vice-President, and principal officers, 1789-1909, p. 396.

[59] 34 *Statutes at Large*, ch. 1635, p. 993. For salary of the Secretary of Agriculture, *Ibid.*, ch. 2907, p. 1256.

is no place in the statutes where there is any recognition of the President's Cabinet. The gentleman in his amendment," continued the speaker, "provides for an increase of salary for the heads of Departments who constitute the President's Cabinet. Would it not be wiser," he asked, "to designate the nine secretaries—the heads of the various Departments—who, in fact, constitute the Cabinet?" There was a brief succeeding colloquy over the matter between Messrs. Littauer and Mann. It had, however, only an ephemeral interest. The significant result was this—that the term *cabinet* went consciously into the statute law of the United States. The course of the bill was not altogether smooth. But neither Senate nor House made any essential alteration in the language first proposed. It was language, as Representative Littauer remarked, which could not be misunderstood, for it designated a perfectly well-known and real institution.[60]

[60] *Congressional Record* (1906-1907), Pt. I, p. 381. The course of the bill may easily be followed from December 7 to February 26, 1907. It passed the Senate on January 14, but there were adjustments to be settled with the House before it reached President Roosevelt.

Mr. Sidney Low called attention to the appearance of the term Prime Minister in the opening clause of the Treaty of Berlin, where Beaconsfield was characterized as "First Lord of Her Majesty's Treasury, Prime Minister of England." This, he thinks, is the first formal appearance of the term in an English public document. *Governance of England* (1904), p. 154. "Until 1906," says Mr. Lowell, "the Prime Minister, like the cabinet itself, was unknown to the law." In that year the position seems to have been recognized by being accorded a place in the order of precedence. *Government of England* (1908), I, 68. See Hansard, *Debates,* 4 Ser., CLVI, 742 (May 3, 1906).

CHAPTER VII

THE ATTORNEY-GENERALSHIP

OF all the great offices established in 1789, that of the Attorney-General was in some respects the least satisfactory in its organization. Attention has already been called to the brevity of that portion of the Judiciary Act devoted to the Attorney-General's place. This brevity suggests the immaturity of the administrative-judicial system of the central government. The office was an innovation in connection with that government. But the incumbent, recognized as legal adviser to the President and the heads of departments, was inevitably brought within the range of executive control, and became, like the Secretaries, a ministerial officer.[1]

When, in 1790, Edmund Randolph, first of the Attorneys-General, wrote of himself as "a sort of mongrel between the State and U. S.; called an officer of some rank under the latter, and yet thrust out to get a livelihood in the former,"[2] he cast no doubtful reflection on the status and relation of his position. He knew that he was head of no department. Moreover, his salary of fifteen hundred dollars was so small that probably he could not have been expected to support himself by it. He was obliged to trust to legal practice to eke out a living. There is no evidence

[1] 1 *Statutes at Large*, p. 92.
[2] M. D. Conway, *Omitted Chapters*, p. 135.

to indicate that he was even expected to remain at the
seat of government, although he was obliged to keep
in touch with the President, at least by occasional
correspondence.   And, should the federal business
warrant it, the President might summon him to a conference with the Secretaries.   He was certainly reckoned an adviser in legal matters by Washington from
the start.

The place and functions of the Attorney-General
remained for many years after 1789 subjects of reflection on the part of thoughtful men.   Several Presidents, beginning with James Madison, urged reform in
the office, although apparently having no clear notions
at first as to what measures of reform were needed.
The Attorneys-General themselves were helpful in the
solution of the problem, none more so than William
Wirt and Caleb Cushing.   The problem became clearer
under the stress of numerous circumstances in the
growth and requirements of federal administration.
By the close of the Civil War it was forced into the
foreground; and Congress, acting in 1870 after long
deliberation, established the office on a new footing,
giving the Attorney-General a place as head of the
department of justice.   The act of 1870, it should be
added, made no change in law as to the duty of the
Attorney-General in giving official opinions and advice.

I

Before the outbreak of the war in 1812, Madison
called attention to the large accumulation of business
in the various departments of the government, in par-

ticular in the war department, which was disproportionately burdened. This accumulation was due largely to the peculiar state of our foreign relations that for years had involved all the Secretaries in exhausting labors. These relations had affected the entire administrative machinery of the federal government.[3] As a farewell word in his last annual message of December, 1816, Madison urged upon Congress the propriety of establishing an additional executive department "to be charged with duties now overburdening other departments and with such as have not been annexed to any department."[4] To another kindred matter he drew attention in these words: "The course of experience," he declared, "recommends . . . . that the provision for the station of Attorney-General, whose residence at the seat of Government, official connections with it, and the management of the public business before the judiciary preclude an extensive participation in professional emoluments, be made more adequate to his services and his relinquishments, and that, with a view to his reasonable accommodation and to a proper depository of his official opinions and proceedings, there be included in the provision the usual appurtenances to a public office."[5]

Such reflections coming from one of the leaders in the Philadelphia Convention, who had since had much experience in administrative work, were not easily

[3] April 20. Special message in *Messages and Papers,* I, 499.
[4] December 3. *Ibid.,* I, 577.
[5] *Ibid.,* I, 577-578.

overlooked by several of Madison's successors in the Presidency. John Quincy Adams, Jackson, and Polk all harked back to his remarks about the position of the Attorney-General. But the reflections, it may be observed, hinted at incidents in the past which have hitherto escaped any careful attention from historians.

In 1814 an attempt had been made to enact a residence requirement. In January of that year a resolution was introduced into the House for the express purpose of inquiring into the expediency of "making it the duty of the Attorney-General of the United States to keep his office at the seat of Government during the session of Congress." Evidently the House regarded the Attorney-General as the proper officer to aid it at times in respect to doubtful points of law. The resolution prepared the way for a bill in conformity with it which, after sundry alterations, was passed by the House in April, but got no farther than a second reading in the Senate.[6]

The bill met Madison's wishes, so far at least as the residence requirement was concerned. "I readily acknowledge," wrote the President, "that, in a general view, the object of the bill is not ineligible to the Executive."[7] But Madison was disturbed when he learned that his able Attorney-General, William Pinkney of Maryland, was ready to resign because of

[6] *Annals of Congress,* 13 Cong., 2 sess. (1813-1814), pp. 766, 852-853, 1114-1115, 2023-2024. Cf. Henry Adams, *History of the United States,* VII, 398.

[7] *Writings* (ed. Rives), II, 581. The same odd use of "ineligible" may be seen in No. 50 of *The Federalist,* one more slight piece of evidence favoring Madison's authorship of that disputed number.

the residence requirement likely to be enacted into law. Pinkney in fact did resign[8] some months before the fate of the resolution was known, for he was probably chiefly dependent on private practice in Baltimore, the city in which he resided. In accepting his resignation Madison wrote: "There may be instances where talents and services of peculiar value outweigh the consideration of constant residence; and I have felt all the force of this truth since I have had the pleasure of numbering you among the partners of my public trust."[9] Madison exacted the stipulation from Richard Rush, Pinkney's successor in the office, that during sessions of Congress he must reside at the seat of government.[10]

The salary of the Attorney-General was at this time three thousand dollars. It had started in 1789 at half that amount, but was gradually increased and at length doubled in 1800. But Congress was thereafter slow in increasing it. And it was not until 1853 that the salary of the office was placed on a par with that of the Secretaries and of the Postmaster-General. By the appropriation act of that year[11]—so far, at any rate, as salaries could mark unity and equality—the five Secretaries, along with the Postmaster-General and the Attorney-General, stood upon an equal footing.

It will be observed that Madison implied that the

[8] January 25, 1814.

[9] *Writings*, II, 581.

[10] *Annals of Congress*, 14 Cong., 2 sess. (1816-1817), p. 699.

[11] March 3, 1853. For salaries, see Appendix A to this volume, p. 396.

Attorney-General might have a certain amount of private practice apart from his duties as a federal official. The truth is that such practice was undertaken often by the early Attorneys-General. And I can find no very pronounced opinion regarding it until the days of Caleb Cushing when Cushing recorded himself against it in a very vigorous way, as we shall see later in this chapter.

Madison had said quite enough on the subject of the Attorney-Generalship to attract the attention of Congress. And in the session opening in December of 1816, there was some effort made to work out various alterations. But nothing was immediately accomplished. Economy was the watchword of the epoch. Nevertheless the reader of the congressional debates may gain some important truths about the position and office of the Attorney-General from a stray letter of Monroe, at the moment Secretary of State, but about to take office as President—a letter which Monroe addressed to Lowndes, chairman of the House Committee of Ways and Means. This letter was produced in the House on January 21, 1817.[12]

"The Attorney General," said Monroe, "has been always, since the adoption of our Government, a member of the executive council, or cabinet. For that reason as well as for the better discharge of his other official duties, it is proper that he should reside at the seat of Government. . . . . His duties in attending the cabinet deliberations are equal to those of any other member. . . . . Being at the Seat of Govern-

[12] *Annals of Congress*, 14 Cong., 2 sess. (1816-1817), pp. 699-700.

ment throughout the year," Monroe continued, "his labors are increased by giving opinions to the different Departments and public officers. . . . . Being on the spot, it may be supposed that he will often be resorted to verbally in the progress of current business. Such is the fact." Then turning to another aspect of the theme, Monroe declared: "The present Attorney-General [Richard Rush] has not embarked in the practice of the local courts of the city of Washington. The practice is, in itself, of little moment; and to engage in it upon a scale to make it, in any degree, worth his attention, would be incompatible with the calls to which he is liable from the Executive, and the investigations due to other official engagements." Monroe knew that the office had been shabbily treated at the hands of Congress, for after calling attention to the facts that it had no apartment for business, no clerk, and not even a messenger, he added that it had had neither stationery nor fuel. "These have been supplied," he concluded, "by the officer himself, at his own expense."

Monroe's letter is an extraordinarily interesting and authoritative commentary on the primitive conditions that surrounded an officer of some rank in the national government of 1817. It came from the most experienced and tried administrative official serving Madison, for Monroe had held both the office of Secretary of State and that of Secretary of War, sometimes sustaining them together for brief periods during the six years preceding. It revealed a man thoroughly prepared to appreciate the need of a capable occupant

of the office. Although it took Monroe some time to
select his Attorney-General, he had good reason, as
we shall presently see, to feel by the close of his
administration as President great satisfaction over
his choice.

II

William Wirt of Virginia accepted the post of
Attorney-General offered him by President Monroe
late in October, 1817, with a clear understanding that
there was nothing in the duties of his office to prevent
him from carrying on general practice in Washington,
where he took up his residence, or from attending
occasional calls to Baltimore, Philadelphia or elsewhere, if time allowed.[13] He knew, however, that his
first obligation was to Monroe and to the regular
duties of his new position.

On the very day of his commission, November 13,
he sketched on the fly-leaf of a record-book a simple
plan which revealed his purpose of keeping careful
records and of obtaining from the various heads of
departments who might consult him copies of all documents concerning which he might be asked for opinions.[14] Some months later, under date of March 27,
1818, Wirt addressed a letter to Judge Hugh Nelson,
chairman of the Judiciary Committee of the House of
Representatives. In this letter he set forth what he

[13] J. P. Kennedy, *Memoirs of the Life of William Wirt* (1st ed.,
1849), II, 32.

[14] Original record quoted in J. S. Easby-Smith, *The Department of
Justice: Its History and Functions* (1904), p. 10.

conceived to be certain defects of the law of 1789, that portion of the Judiciary Act which established the office, and drew attention to such improvements as he hoped that Congress might be induced to make. It was an informing if not a constructive statement. It probably accomplished little, if any, change, for it never reached the House directly, so far as I can discover, but was filed away with other committee material, and gained publicity only in 1849, fifteen years after Wirt's death, when it was printed at length in the *Memoirs of the Life of William Wirt,* written by Wirt's friend, John Pendleton Kennedy. At that time it attracted attention, especially among the members of the legal profession. Its substance merits consideration.[15]

Wirt began with an examination of the Judiciary Act of September 24, 1789. There the duties of the Attorney-General were briefly set forth. They had not been more clearly elaborated in any later enactment. Wirt next sought for the records of opinions as given by his predecessors in the office—for letter-books, official correspondence and documentary evidence, but could not find a trace of these. Accordingly he concluded that there could have been neither consistency in the opinions nor uniformity in the practices of the Attorneys-General. He indicated that in various ways he had discovered that his forerunners had been called on for opinions from many sources—committees of

[15] Kennedy, *Memoirs,* II, 61-65. The *Monthly Law Reporter* for December, 1850, reprints from Kennedy the Wirt letter of 1818, comments on Kennedy's book, but makes several misstatements about the Attorney-General.

Congress, district attorneys, collectors of customs and of public taxes, marshals, and even courts-martial. Clearly these practices went far beyond the provisions of law. Resting on courtesy merely, they impressed Wirt as dangerous. It was his opinion that "from the connection of the Attorney-General with the executive branch of the government . . . . his advice and opinions, *given as Attorney-General,* will have an *official influence,* beyond, and independent of, whatever intrinsic merit they may possess; and whether it be sound policy to permit this officer or any other under the government, even on the application of others, to extend the influence of his office beyond the pale of law, and to cause it to be felt, where the laws have not contemplated that it should be felt is the point which I beg leave to submit."[16]

The conclusions which Wirt drew may be summarized. First, and above all things, provision should be made in law for keeping the records and preserving the documents of the office. This would make for consistency of opinions and uniformity of practices. Second, there should be a depository in the office of the Attorney-General for the statutes of the various States, statutes which might be needed at short notice for aid in solving legal problems. In this matter Wirt was asking simply for a special library to facilitate his work. Finally, he suggested that legal restrictions be placed on the duties of the officer for the obvious reason that one man could not find time to perform the work if he were obliged to attend to such miscella-

16 Kennedy, II, 64.

neous calls as had been made upon the time and energy of his predecessors. The experience of several months had already shown to him that "very little time is left to the Attorney-General to aid the salary of his office by individual engagements," a fact, he thought, which might account in part for the number of resignations which had occurred among his predecessors.

This letter marks what may be regarded as the beginning of a new epoch in the history of the Attorney-General's office. So far as the position of Attorney-General could be shaped and its functions vitalized, Wirt meant that these things should be done. It cannot be said that Wirt's suggestions influenced directly congressional action, for there is no direct proof of such influence. But there was at last a man in the Attorney-Generalship who had a few definite ideas on the subject of organization which he was ready to make effective. This, at any rate, Congress must have understood. After his long occupancy— from 1817 to 1829—the office had certainly risen in importance and was probably considered as more closely allied to the whole executive administration than ever before.

The details of administrative organization it is not the province of this chapter to examine. It is enough to say that Wirt was provided by Congress with a clerk in 1818 and a small sum of money ($500) for office-room and stationery. In response to criticism over inequalities in the salaries of the Secretaries, these salaries were raised and equalized in 1819; and the salary of the Attorney-General was increased at the

same time to thirty-five hundred dollars. Some
other improvements of a minor character were
accomplished.[17]

Early in his term Wirt had intimated to the House
that by the law creating his position he could not be
reckoned legal counsellor to that body. When, in
January, 1820, the House sent an order for his official
opinion on a certain subject then before them, he
deliberately declined to give the opinion. "It is true,"
he reasoned, "that, in this case, I should have the sanction of the House . . . . and it is not less true that
my respect for the House impels me strongly to obey
the order. The precedent, however, would not be less
dangerous on account of the purity of the motives in
which it originated. . . . . I may be wrong in my view
of the subject; the order may be sanctioned by former
precedents; but my predecessors in office have left
nothing for my guidance."[18] He was no less explicit
about his duty when, sought by the Secretary of the
Navy a few months later for aid, he declared: "As my
official duty is confined to the giving my opinion on
questions of *law,* I consider myself as having nothing
to do with the settlement of controverted questions of
fact.'"[19]

A month after Wirt's death, his friend, Samuel L.

---

[17] *Annals of Congress,* 15 Cong., 1 sess. (1817-1818), II, 1779, 2566
(Act of April 20, 1818, sec. 6). *Ibid.,* 2 sess. (1818-1819), I, 21 ff.,
II, 2486 (Act of February 20, 1819). Easby-Smith, *Department of
Justice,* p. 10, for sundry details.

[18] *House Documents,* No. 68, p. 2 (16 Cong., 1 sess., vol. V). Wirt's
letter to the House was dated February 3, 1820.

[19] *Opinions,* p. 254. April 3, 1820. (*House Executive Documents,* 26
Cong., 2 sess., No. 123.)

Southard—for some years his colleague in the Cabinet—gave a public address on Wirt's career, speaking on March 18, 1834, in the hall of the House of Representatives at Washington. In discussing Wirt's opinions as Attorney-General, Southard said: "They all relate to matters of importance in the construction of the laws. . . . . They will prevent much uncertainty in that office hereafter; afford one of the best collections of materials for writing the legal and constitutional history of our country; and remain a proud monument to his industry, learning and talents.'"[20]

In 1841, seven years after Wirt's death, the first volume of the series known as the *Official Opinions of the Attorneys-General* was authorized by Congress and issued.[21] Similar volumes have been compiled and printed at intervals ever since; and they constitute to-day a well-known and useful set. They amount to official justifications of the conduct of our Presidents. Unlike our custom, it is the practice in England to regard the opinions of the law officers of the Crown as confidential—a practice which is considered by some writers as a very serious loss to the body of English jurisprudence.[22]

In the first volume, Wirt's opinions filled over five hundred pages in a total of 1471. Not one of his eight predecessors was represented by much over thirty pages. The five men who came after him, serving in the office for almost exactly eleven years—from 1829

[20] S. L. Southard, *A Discourse on the Professional Character and Virtues of the late William Wirt* (1834), p. 36.
[21] *House Ex. Doc'ts*, No. 123 (26 Cong., 2 sess.).
[22] 38 *American Law Review* (November-December, 1904), pp. 924-925.

to 1841—equivalent in time to Wirt's single term, left on record 704 pages. No doubt the legal business of the federal government increased considerably under Jackson and his immediate successors. But perhaps Wirt's admirable example of industry may have had something to do with the activity of the Attorneys-General following him.[23]

In refusing to be led beyond the limits prescribed by law, Wirt doubtless contracted the action of his office. The restrictions thus placed upon it, however, must have made its relations to Congress on the one hand and to the executive department on the other clearer and altogether better defined. They certainly tended to increase the usefulness of the Attorney-General as a member of the Cabinet.

III

The administrative work of the government had by 1830 increased enormously. This was due to some variety of causes: expansion of territory, growth of population, and development of commerce and wealth. The executive departments and the judiciary—confined, as they were for the most part, to their primitive and original organizations—were inadequately performing their functions. John Quincy Adams had appreciated this fact, and called attention to it in his

---

[23] The figures in this paragraph are the result of a detailed calculation of the pages in the volume of *Opinions* already cited. To make the matter quite clear, it should be said that included in the total of 1471 pages there was an appendix of odd opinions, which extends from page 1383 to page 1471.

first annual message.[24] Apparently, however, he failed to accomplish anything toward remedying it.

When Jackson became President and referred to the particular need of attending to the business of reorganizing the Attorney-General's office, and of placing that officer "on the same footing in all respects as the heads of the other departments," he found a Congress ready to heed his suggestion. Originally, as I have shown, the office had left its incumbent time for private practice. By Jackson's day it was reckoned "one of daily duty." Jackson believed it important that the Attorney-General should not be summoned away from the seat of government on anything but federal business. With a reasonable increase in salary and a residence requirement, the officer, he thought, could be charged with the general superintendence of the government's legal concerns.[25]

In the spring of 1830 a bill bearing on the suggested reform was introduced into the Senate. These were its chief objects: to reorganize the office of the Attorney-General in such a way as to erect it into an executive department; to transfer to it from the Department of State the work of the Patent Office; to give to the Attorney-General the superintendence of the collection of debts due the government; and to raise the salary of the Attorney-General to six thousand dollars—exactly the salary that was by that time provided for every one of the four Secretaries. Such arrangements, it was argued, would do away with the

[24] *Messages and Papers*, II, 314-315.
[25] *Ibid.*, II, 453 ff., 527 ff.

necessity, at any rate for some time to come, of organizing a Home Department—a subject which had been vigorously discussed for a good many years. The plan of the bill would, it was assumed, debar the Attorney-General from practice other than what he would be called on to conduct on behalf of the government in the Supreme Court. But the anomalous position of an Attorney-General so burdened must have been soon apparent. In particular the plan evidently ignored the essential fact that the Attorney-General was primarily a law officer. Accordingly it was easily defeated.[26]

Senator Daniel Webster opposed this bill. He had no faith in the attempt thus to forestall a Home Department. Moreover, he wished the Attorney-General still to enjoy the privilege of accepting private practice without too much restriction. The old salary ($3,500) was relatively low for the position, but not too low, it was urged, because the Attorney-General could more than make up to himself the amount of compensation received by the Secretaries who were confined strictly to the work in their offices.[27] According to the views of another Senator, to permit the Attorney-General to engage in private practice was not only a legitimate but even a desirable way of aiding him in his equipment for performing well his official duties.[28]

Although the bill failed, a plan was finally matured largely through Webster's efforts, formulated, and

---

[26] *Register of Debates* (1829-1830), VI, Pt. I, pp. 276, 322 ff., 404.

[27] *Ibid.*, VI, Pt. I, p. 324.

[28] *Ibid.*, VI, Pt. I, p. 323.

enacted into law, by which a new official known as
Solicitor of the Treasury was provided, for the special
purpose of aiding the Attorney-General in all suits
pertaining to treasury claims. And for the additional
responsibility involved in the new relationship, the
salary of the Attorney-General was raised to four
thousand dollars—an amount at which it remained
until 1853.[29]

It is clear, from certain reflections in his second
message of December 6, 1830, that President Jackson
was dissatisfied with any such compromise measure.
However useful in itself the provision for a Solicitor
of the Treasury might be, it was not, according to the
President, ''calculated to supersede the necessity of
extending the duties and powers of the Attorney-
General's Office. On the contrary,'' Jackson asserted,
''I am convinced that the public interest would be
greatly promoted by giving to that officer the general
superintendence of the various law agents of the
Government, and of all law proceedings, whether civil
or criminal, in which the United States may be interested, allowing him at the same time such a compensation as would enable him to devote his undivided attention to the public business.''[30]

I cannot discover that Jackson ever again expressed

[29] 4 *Statutes at Large,* chap. cliii, sec. 10. ''*And be it further enacted,*
That it shall be the duty of the attorney general . . . . at the request
of said solicitor, to advise with and direct the said solicitor as to the
manner of conducting the suits, proceedings, and prosecutions aforesaid; and the attorney general shall receive in addition to his present
salary, the sum of five hundred dollars per annum.'' May 29, 1830.

[30] *Messages and Papers,* II, 527.

himself in print, after these utterances of 1830, on the subject of reforming the office of the Attorney-General. Something had been accomplished to remedy defects. After Jackson, no President before Polk had anything to say on the subject.

Polk argued in a vein similar to that which Jackson had made familiar. He, too, wished to increase the duties and responsibilities of the officer; and he recommended that he be placed on the same footing as the heads of departments, for, as Polk said, "his residence and constant attention at the seat of Government are required."[31] Even then Congress paid no heed to the matter for several years. There can be no doubt that any projects of administrative reform were seriously interfered with by the war with Mexico.

In this connection account should perhaps be taken of a curiously interesting paragraph that may be found in a circular letter addressed by Polk, under date of February 17, 1845, to all the men to whom he extended invitations to become his cabinet associates. "I disapprove the practice which has sometimes prevailed," he wrote, "of Cabinet officers absenting themselves for long intervals of time from the seat of government, and leaving the management of their departments to chief clerks, or other less responsible persons than themselves. I expect myself to remain constantly at Washington, unless it may be that no public duty requires my presence, when I may be occasionally absent, but then only for a short time. It is,"

[31] *Messages*, IV, 415.

he continued, ''by conforming to this rule that the President and his Cabinet can have any assurance that abuses will be prevented, and that the subordinate executive officers connected with them respectively will faithfully perform their duty.''[32]

Polk of course exacted this significant condition from his first Attorney-General, John Y. Mason of Virginia. But the Attorney-Generalship had two other occupants, Nathan Clifford of Maine and Isaac Toucey of Connecticut—as it happened, the only two appointments (outside the circle of original holders) to cabinet positions during the whole course of the administration from 1845 to 1849. From a very brief statement in the recently published *Diary* of President Polk, it appears that Polk exacted this original condition from Clifford.[33] There is no evidence about it in the case of Toucey. What we may be sure of is that Polk intended, so far as it was within his power, to establish the custom of keeping his cabinet associates in Washington during their terms of service, except for the briefest possible absences.

IV

There is good reason to believe that Caleb Cushing was the first Attorney-General of the United States who held himself strictly to the residence obligation—

[32] *Works of James Buchanan* (ed. John Bassett Moore, 1909), VI, 110-111.

[33] *The Diary of James K. Polk* during his Presidency, 1845 to 1849 (ed. Milo Milton Quaife, Chicago: 1910), II, 193. Polk's memory would seem here to be at fault in referring to the letter addressed to each member of his Cabinet as ''in March, 1845.''

an ideal, as we have seen, that had been gaining ground since 1814—and refrained from the general practice of the law during his term as a federal officer.

Coming into office in March, 1853, just after the salary of the Attorney-General had been raised to eight thousand dollars, Cushing at the start was placed, in respect to salary, on a footing of equality with his cabinet associates. He had accordingly no very valid reason for entering into private practice in or outside of Washington. Like the other cabinet associates of Pierce, Cushing kept his place throughout the four years' term. He left behind him a collection of official opinions that for extent alone has never been equalled either before or since his day. They fill three in the series of volumes known as *Official Opinions*, twenty-seven of which have thus far (1911) been issued.[34]

It may be doubted whether Pierce had an abler associate among his advisers than Cushing, although Jefferson Davis was Secretary of War and William L. Marcy was at the head of the Department of State. Certainly there was no man in the Cabinet more trusted by the President. Pierce held him in the highest regard. That he was of great assistance in keeping the Cabinet together is a matter of authentic history.[35]

Cushing left to posterity quite the most careful considerations on the historic development of the

[34] Cushing's opinions fill volumes V, VI, and VII, extending over upwards of 2000 pages.

[35] *Memorial of Caleb Cushing* (Newburyport: 1879), pp. 169 ff. 7 *Opinions of the Attorneys-General*, pp. 453-482.

Attorney-Generalship up to his time. These have been occasionally quoted since they were written and are well known. Like Wirt, Cushing determined to understand the structure and functions of his office so far as the laws and the practices of his predecessors could reveal them. Instead of presenting his conclusions— as Wirt had done—to the chairman of a committee of the House, he offered them directly to the President, in itself an acknowledgment of the relationship of his position. They were written under date of March 8, 1854, at the end of his first year's experience. With the technical portions of the "Opinion" relating to the Attorney-General and the courts, this inquiry is not concerned. But it is important to notice occasional reflections which were obviously intended to throw light on the relation of the office to the executive.[36]

According to the original theory of the office, the Attorney-General was prompted, if not authorized by the President, to engage in private practice of the law. This custom in the case of the English Attorney-General[37]—from whose office, it seemed probable to Cushing that we had borrowed certain features—was perfectly well understood in 1789.

Cushing doubted the expediency of allowing the head of a department to continue in the practice of the law "under any circumstances." He was willing to admit that such a custom might once have been

[36] 6 *Opinions of the Attorneys-General*, pp. 326-355. I have found it convenient to use the opinion as it appeared in the *American Law Register* (December, 1856), V, 65 ff.

[37] Anson, *Law and Custom of the Constitution*, Pt. II, pp. 201-202.

justifiable. "Formerly, in an age of simple manners, when the public expenditures were less, the number of places less, the population of the country less, the frequentation of the capital less, the ingenuity of self-interest less . . . . a secretary, eminent in the legal profession might, without the possibility of reproach or suspicion of evil, take charge of private suits or interests at the seat of government. He may do so now, perhaps; but that is not so clear as it formerly was; and it is not easy to perceive any distinction in this between what befits one and another head of department." As for himself, he remarked that, however "all these things may be, the actual incumbent of this office . . . . experiences that its necessary duties are quite sufficient to task to the utmost all the faculties of one man; and he willingly regards those recent acts, which have at length placed the salary of his office on equal footing with other public offices of the same class, as intimation at least that the Government has the same precise claim on his services, in time and degree, as on those of the Secretary of State or the Secretary of the Treasury."[38]

It must be clear from the passage that Cushing regarded himself not only as the peer of his cabinet associates, but as in some sense head of a department, although he occupied what the law termed an "Office." This was the conception of the position to which General Benjamin F. Butler alluded when, in 1879, in paying a tribute to Cushing, he declared that he had "raised the office of Attorney-General, and organized

[38] *American Law Register*, V, 93.

it to be in truth and in fact a department of the Government.''[39] At any rate, many of Cushing's suggestions for a better organization of the work of the Attorney-General were enacted into the laws between March, 1854—the date of his ''Opinion''—and June, 1870, when the Attorney-General was named in the law as head of the Department of Justice.[40]

The English Attorney-General has never been recognized as a member of the English Cabinet.[41] When Richard Rush was in England in 1818, after an experience of several years as Attorney-General under President Madison, he could not help considering the absence of the English Attorney-General from the Cabinet as strange and worthy of comment, and later he said that ''in the complicated and daily workings of the machine of free government throughout a vast empire, I could still see room for the constant presence of the attorney-general in the cabinet.''[42] The comment came naturally out of his own experience, and probably reflected Rush's familiarity with the American tradition, for since the beginning of our government the Attorney-General had been reckoned an intimate adviser of the President. We have an indirect statement from Washington on the point.[43] Monroe expressed himself clearly in the matter, as we

[39] *Memorial,* op. cit., p. 169.

[40] Easby-Smith, *The Department of Justice,* pp. 15 ff.

[41] Anson, *Law and Custom,* Pt. II, p. 202.

[42] *Memoranda of a Residence at the Court of London* (2d ed., Philadelphia: 1833), p. 63.

[43] C. W. Upham, *Life of Timothy Pickering* (1867 ff.), III, 226. I have cited definite instances, in chapter V of this volume, of records of cabinet meetings under Washington which Randolph attended.

have seen. And such intimate sources as the *Memoirs* of John Quincy Adams, the *Diary* of President Polk, and—more recently still—the *Diary* of the Secretary of the Navy, Gideon Welles, have furnished ample proof of the American practice.

Cushing's reflections on the Cabinet were particularly illuminating. It was, he perceived, an important means of attaining unity in executive decision and action. This unity, he declared, "cannot be obtained by means of a plurality of persons wholly independent of one another, without corporate conjunction, and released from subjection to one determining will."[44] It was in substance the very point of view that Alexander Hamilton had taken of the matter as far back as 1792.[45]

With reference to the principal officers Cushing remarked that "the established sense of the subordination of all of them to the President has . . . . come to exist, partly by construction of the constitutional duty of the President to take care that the laws be faithfully executed, and his consequent necessary relation to the heads of departments, and partly by deduction from the analogies of statutes."[46] About a year and a half after he had written these reflections he devoted an entire "Opinion" to a consideration of the relation of the President to the executive departments.[47]

[44] *American Law Register*, V, 81.
[45] *Supra*, chapter VI, p. 135.
[46] *American Law Register*, V, 71.
[47] August 31, 1855. 7 *Opinions of the Attorneys-General*, pp. 453-482.

Cushing's usefulness to Pierce as a cabinet counsellor, his talents, his learning, and his persistent industry on behalf of the administration—all these matters should not make us overlook certain weaknesses of which his contemporaries were aware. In 1847 James Russell Lowell—at the time rather less than thirty years of age—satirized Cushing in the *Biglow Papers*:

> Gineral C. is a dreffle smart man;
> He's ben on all sides thet give places or pelf;
> But consistency still wuz a part of his plan,—
> He's ben true to *one* party—an' thet is himself. . . . .[48]

Senator Benton of Missouri, in a speech delivered in July, 1856, acknowledged that Cushing was the "master-spirit" of Pierce's Cabinet, but—cleverly adapting a well-known passage from *Hamlet*—he burst into the assertion that he was "unscrupulous, double-sexed, double-gendered, and hermaphroditic in politics, with a hinge in his knee, which he often crooks, that thrift may follow fawning." In a word, Cushing governed by subserviency.[49]

Cushing was never able to win completely the trust of his fellows. Yet he proved to be a useful statesman. Both Buchanan and Grant at different times sought his aid. He was among the legal experts chosen as counsel to assist the Geneva Tribunal. President Grant actually named him as Chief-Justice of the

[48] Quoted by J. F. Rhodes, *History of the United States since the Compromise of 1850* (1892 ff.), I, 392.

[49] The whole passage was used by Von Holst, *History of the United States*, IV, 263, foot note.

Supreme Court, but was virtually forced at the last moment to withdraw his name from the Senate. Looking back over a long life, which extended from 1800 to January, 1879, it still seems fair to conclude that in no task did Caleb Cushing prove himself more useful than in that of the Attorney-Generalship. He was the ablest organizer that the office had had since its establishment in 1789.[50]

V

The innumerable legal problems created by the Civil War or following closely in its train brought great pressure of work on the office of the Attorney-General. By that period an administrative-judicial organization had been developed that proved under the new circumstances distinctly out of joint. Various legal officers in the separate departments gave opinions to the Secretaries which were at times inconsistent with, if not actually opposed to, those of the Attorney-General. Tasks were duplicated. In brief, there was no definite provision in law which tended to unify or bring to one master-mind the direction of the legal work of the government. As a consequence that work lacked symmetry and consistency.

The four chief law-officers in 1861—with the dates of their separate establishments—were the Attorney-General (1789), the Assistant Attorney-General (1859), the Solicitor of the Court of Claims

[50] I have depended, for this sketch, upon Rhodes, Von Holst, and the material in the *Memorial* of 1879. The generalization is based upon these and the parts of Cushing's ''Opinions'' that I have used.

(1855), and the Solicitor of the Treasury (1830). The latter officer was, as we have seen, a rather anomalous factor in the Treasury Department who, for certain purposes, was under the direction of the Attorney-General. Subordinate to these and controlled by the Attorney-General from 1861 there was a large corps of scattered district attorneys.[51] The whole organization was very loosely knit and disjointed. It was truly said that the law business of the government during the period of the Civil War "greatly outgrew the capacity of the persons authorized to transact it, and the number of outside counsel . . . . appointed subsequently to 1861 was greater than all the commissioned law officers of the Government in every part of the country.'"[52]

The cost of this extra counsel was large—how large, it would be quite impossible to say with any assurance of accuracy. Figures were brought forward in the House of Representatives to show that nearly half a million dollars ($475,190.42) could be thus accounted for during a portion of the years from 1861 to 1867. More than half that amount ($258,018.44) went, it was said, to pay for extra legal counsel employed during the years 1868-1869. To William M. Evarts alone, fees for occasional legal aid to the government amounted, by 1867, to approximately fifty thousand dollars ($47,545.86). It is certainly well within the range of truth to say that the government was obliged

[51] Easby-Smith, *Department of Justice*, pp. 16, 28-30.

[52] *Congressional Globe*, 41 Cong., 2 sess., Pt. IV, p. 3035 (April 27, 1870).

to pay a hundred thousand dollars annually during the decade 1860-1870.[53]

These were significant facts. They were used, moreover, in Congress to direct attention to many administrative weaknesses in the federal organization. Whatever changes of organization might be accomplished, it was felt that a department of justice must be provided. As late as the spring of 1870, when the bill for such a department was almost matured, Thomas A. Jenckes of Rhode Island declared that the special reason why the committee had reported it "earlier than any other relating to the organization of the Departments is the great expense the Government have been put to in the conduct of the numerous litigations involving titles to property worth millions of dollars, rights to personal liberty, and all the numerous litigations which can arise under the law of war."[54]

The heritage of war expenditures had assumed such ominous proportions that in 1867 Congress appointed a so-called Joint Committee on Retrenchments. This committee, impelled perhaps by certain recommendations concerning the reorganization of the office set forth by Attorney-General Henry Stanbery, in December of that year, was attracted to an investigation of the legal work of the government. On December 12, 1867, Representative Lawrence of Ohio offered a resolution looking toward a consolidation of all the law

[53] The figures are gathered from the debates in the House of April 27, 1870.

[54] *Globe*, April 27, 1870.

officers of the government at Washington into one department. That resolution seems to mark the beginning of legislative effort. For more than two years following, the subject remained in the background of public discussion. It was lost to sight largely because of subjects of a more pressing and sensational nature. But it may be traced during the sessions of the Thirty-ninth, Fortieth, and Forty-first Congresses. Finally, after a vigorous effort early in 1870—admirably directed in the House by Jenckes—a measure was enacted and approved by President Grant on June 22, 1870. This act erected the old Office of the Attorney-General into the Department of Justice.[55]

The chief purpose of this chapter is to reveal the historic features of the Attorney-Generalship which throw light on the relations of the Attorney-General as a more or less efficient adviser and assistant to the President and his cabinet associates. Hence the act of 1870, apart from its more technical details, has a peculiar interest, for it represented a mature and honest effort to make effective an ideal with respect to the Attorney-General that had been occasionally formulated since Andrew Jackson's day. The act really created no new department. Legal business in the various departments, hitherto scattered and at loose ends, was transferred to the Attorney-General. By placing the Attorney-General at last upon "precisely . . . . the same footing as the other heads of Departments," the act made him in fact the chief law

[55] *Globe*, op. cit., p. 3039. Easby-Smith, *Department of Justice*, p. 17. 16 *Statutes at Large*, pp. 162-165.

officer of the government. In brief, it transformed the old office into a symmetrical organization.[56]

There was an occasional remark during the debates that revealed perfect familiarity with old traditions, as when Representative Lawrence declared that the Cabinet "is the creature of usage only. But since the establishment of the office of Attorney-General," he commented, "the Attorney-General has been a member of the Cabinet by usage just as much as any head of a Department. He ought to be in the Cabinet. There ought not to be a Cabinet without a law officer."[57] We may be certain that Richard Rush, had he been alive, would have taken the same view of the matter.[58]

A chief object of the act of 1870 was to make it possible to create a staff sufficiently large to transact the law business of the government in all parts of the country. If assistant counsel were employed, these extra men were to be designated either as assistant district attorneys or as assistants to the Attorney-General; and so, holding commissions as such, they could be made—in fact they became—strictly responsible to the Attorney-General for the performance of duties that might be assigned to them.[59]

During the development of administrative-legal work, law officers had been provided in the various executive departments from time to time as they were needed. "Following the precedent set in the creation

[56] *Globe*, op. cit., p. 3067. April 28.
[57] *Ibid.*
[58] *Supra*, p. 181.
[59] *Globe*, op. cit., p. 3035.

of the Solicitor of the Treasury by the act of 1830,''
remarked one speaker, ''we have authorized the
appointment of an assistant Solicitor of the Treasury,
and also a Solicitor of the Internal Revenue; and
during the war we had a Solicitor of the War Department and an assistant Solicitor of the War Department. . . . . We also created a law officer for the Navy
Department, and in the course of time a law officer has
been created for the Post-Office Department.''[60] Such
facts revealed at once the possibilities of contradictory
opinions coming from the various legal officers, and
the consequent confusion.

In what way this confusion might affect the
Attorney-General under the old régime, and so the
President, may be readily seen from another passage
in the debates of 1870. The President takes the opinions of the heads of departments, it was declared;
''yet, as the law now stands, it is perfectly apparent
that the law officers of the several Departments may
advise the heads of Departments in one way upon
subjects of public importance affecting their Departments, and the Attorney-General may advise the
President and the Cabinet, when they are assembled,
in a totally different way upon the same subject. Now
. . . . it is utterly impossible that the President can
intelligently advise Congress or act without embarrassment on affairs relating to our international
rights, obligations and duties when there is a law
officer in the State Department, as now, advising the
head of that Department in one way while the

[60] *Ibid.*, p. 3036.

Attorney-General may be advising the President in a different way. . . . . We have an officer called an examiner of claims, the law officer of the State Department, advising the Secretary of State in matters affecting our foreign relations, our duties and obligations, while the President and Cabinet are receiving advice from the Attorney-General.''[61]

The act of 1870 brought the solicitors in the various departments under the ultimate control of the Attorney-General. Whatever official opinions these solicitors might be called upon to give, must henceforth be recorded in the office of the Attorney-General. There, before they could become the executive law for the guidance of inferior officials, these opinions were stamped with the Attorney-General's final approval. ''It is,'' asserted Representative Jenckes, ''for the purpose of having a unity of decision, a unity of jurisprudence, if I may use that expression, in the executive law of the United States, that this bill proposes that all the law officers therein provided for shall be subordinate to one head.''[62]

The act made provision for the creation of one new law officer of large importance—the Solicitor-General of the United States. It was proposed to have in this new position ''a man of sufficient learning, ability and experience that he can be sent to New Orleans or to New York, or into any court wherever the Government has any interest in litigation, and there present the case of the United States as it should be pre-

---

61 *Globe,* op. cit., p. 3065.
62 *Ibid.,* p. 3036.

sented.''[63] The express language of the law required him to be ''learned in the law''—a requirement that had originally, in the law of 1789, been exacted of the Attorney-General, but for some unknown reason was omitted in the law of 1870, so far as the latter officer was concerned.

According to the characterization of Representative James A. Garfield, the act of June, 1870, was ''substantive legislation.'' There was comparatively little opposition to it in Congress, for it was easily seen that it placed the government's law work on an orderly and well-arranged basis.

VI

By an act approved on January 19, 1886,[64] the Attorney-General was definitely reckoned as fourth in the line of possible succession to the Presidency in case of the removal, death, resignation or inability of President and Vice-President. This act was due largely to the persistent efforts of Senator George F. Hoar of Massachusetts. The occasion of these efforts was the conviction in the public mind—aroused by the attempt in July, 1881, to kill President Garfield—of the grave and serious necessity of placing new safeguards about the life of the chief magistrate.

The original law of March, 1792, which provided for the succession to the Presidency, had declared that, in case of vacancy, ''the President of the Senate *pro tempore,* and in case there shall be no President of the

[63] *Ibid.*, p. 3035.
[64] 24 *Statutes at Large*, p. 1.

Senate, then the Speaker of the House of Representatives, for the time being, shall act as President of the United States, until the disability be removed, or a President shall be elected."[65]   Even at the epoch of its formulation the principle underlying this language was not considered sound by such men as Madison, Gouverneur Morris, Livermore and Fitzsimons. There were suggestions at the time that it might be wiser to call on the Chief Justice of the Supreme Court or the Secretary of State.   And in the Philadelphia Convention, on August 27, 1787, Madison—with what seems in the light of the law of 1886 almost prophetic insight—had "suggested that the executive powers during a vacancy be administered by the persons composing the council to the President."[66]   But the Senate, having originated the form of statement of the law of 1792, were unwilling to alter it.   Accordingly the above language was at length adopted and went into the statute-book.[67]

The subject of the succession was next brought conspicuously into public notice in June, 1856, by Senator John J. Crittenden of Kentucky.   Crittenden had become impressed by the fact that from the fourth of March to the first week of December in every second year there was no Speaker of the House of Representatives.   He was accordingly moved to present a resolution to the Senate which called on the Judiciary Committee of that body to examine the subject and

[65] 1 *Statutes at Large*, p. 240.

[66] Elliot, *Debates*, V, 480.

[67] *Annals of Congress* under dates of December 20, 1790, January 10, 13, October 24, November 15, 23, 30, December 1, 21, 1791, etc.

make a report. On the following August 5 a report—
familiarly known as the "Butler Report" from
Senator Pierce Butler of South Carolina, chairman—
was read to the Senate. The Report was concluded
with a carefully formulated bill. The bill was never
acted upon. The Report, buried in a volume of Senate
documents, was lost sight of and apparently forgotten
for many years.[68]

The Butler Report attempted to supplement the
original law of 1792. On the assumption that there
was no President of the Senate *pro tempore* or
Speaker of the House, it declared "that the duties
prescribed by act of Congress shall devolve on the following officers: first, on the chief justice, when he has
not participated in the trial of the President; and next,
on the justices of the Supreme Court, according to the
date of their commissions."[69] This was the single constructive recommendation. It is, however, worthy of
note that the authors first of all stated their belief that
the members of the Cabinet "in some prescribed
order" were "the proper functionaries to fill the
vacancy. In cases of death," continued the record,
"they would be the persons most fit for the occasion.
There are other circumstances, however, which would
make the cabinet officers unfit to occupy the place of
the President. In case of his impeachment for high
political offences, the cabinet might be implicated, as
participes criminis, and ought not to be in position of

[68] *Senate Documents* (1855-1856), II, No. 260, pp. 7. The debate may
be followed in the *Congressional Globe,* 34 Cong., 1 sess. (1855-1856),
Pt. II, pp. 1476, 1930-1931, 2020.

[69] *Butler Report,* p. 5.

allies.'' The question, moreover, as to whether the
Cabinet could be considered an official body after the
functions of the President—its head—had terminated
or were suspended, was puzzling to the committee,
and was left unanswered.[70]

Within a week of the shooting of Garfield, the Butler
Report was referred to in the public discussions over
the possible consequences of the tragedy. In particular Senator James B. Beck of Kentucky called attention to it in a letter to the Louisville *Courier-Journal*.[71] In the following autumn—Garfield having died
on September 19—it happened that the country was
without either a President of the Senate or a Speaker
of the House of Representatives, for Congress had not
yet assembled. Should the immediate successor of
Garfield, President Arthur, die, there existed no provision in law for a new President. Statesmen were
alarmed over a possible predicament. Efforts to
remedy the defect of the law were begun almost as
soon as Congress assembled in December, 1881. And
these efforts were continued at intervals during three
successive Congresses—the Forty-seventh, the Forty-
eighth, and the Forty-ninth. Senator Hoar's persist-
ency was finally rewarded early in 1886.

Hoar was the author of the bill that became the law.
''I drew and introduced the existing law,'' he remarked
many years later in his well-known *Autobiography of
Seventy Years,* where he saw fit to quote the statute
in its entirety.[72] The substance of his bill seems to

[70] *Butler Report,* pp. 4-5.
[71] *Congressional Record,* December 16, 1885.
[72] II, 170-171.

have been suggested to him by certain remarks of his brother, Hon. Ebenezer R. Hoar, in a speech made by the latter in the House of Representatives sometime between 1873 and 1875.[73] Introducing the subject of succession in the last stage of his effort, Senator Hoar remarked that one of the important alterations to be made in the existing law—that of 1792—was the substitution of "members of the Cabinet in the order of their official seniority—the order in which the various Departments were created, except that the head of the Department of Justice, which is the last Department created by law, is continued in his old place as Attorney-General, ranking the heads of the Departments created since the original establishment of the Cabinet.'"[74]

The passage furnishes an admirable statement of the principle that the statute of 1886 carried into effect. In accordance with the passage the Attorney-General, who had been regarded as a cabinet-associate of the President from Washington's administration, was definitely acknowledged as a peer among his colleagues—a position that he had actually held since 1853.

[73] I have not been able to discover this speech after scanning the *Congressional Record* over the years, 1873-1875. Hoar acknowledged his indebtedness to his brother on December 16, 1885.

[74] *Congressional Record,* December 16, 1885.

NOTE

THE ATTORNEY-GENERAL AND PRIVATE PRACTICE SINCE
    1854:

There is no conclusive evidence that I can discover
which would indicate that Caleb Cushing (Attorney-
General from 1853 to 1857), or any of his successors
in the Attorney-Generalship, have ever taken private
law cases while they were acting as federal office-
holders. This opinion is based upon a careful effort
to exhume evidence that would justify a contrary point
of view.

The problem may be formulated in this way:

In case the Attorney-General found his salary inadequate,
and determined for this or any other reason to take a small
amount of private practice, would he be violating any custom or rule of honor in undertaking it? In other words:
Are there any instances between 1854—the date of Cushing's well-known argument against the custom—and 1909,
to indicate that the Attorney-General has at times, either
with or without the knowledge of the President, accepted
private cases which have not involved the interests of the
federal government?

At various times I have taken opportunity to pro-
pound this problem to men living in Washington, D. C.,
who seemed likely to be able to throw light upon it. I
have examined many law cases, in hopes of finding
some clue here or there in the State Reports. In a
vain effort to secure printed evidence, I was obliged to
fall back on two different opinions, both of them
common enough in Washington.

A. An official associated for a great many years with the Attorney-General's office, both before and since 1870, is positive that the Attorneys-General continued, with perhaps an occasional exception, to accept private practice down to President Cleveland's first administration (1885). This official, indeed, specified a few instances since that time among the Attorneys-General who, he was sure, accepted private cases. He assumed that in these various instances no rule of honor and no custom were considered to be violated.

B. The other opinion is a direct denial of this view. "No Attorney-General," runs the statement, "would think for a moment of accepting a private case while occupying the federal office." A well-known ex-Secretary of State, who has been deeply interested in the history of American diplomacy and political practices, holds to this view. Yet this particular gentleman was obliged, after careful inquiry, to admit that he discovered that opinion A was firmly believed by several officials with whom he had spoken.

Of course men summoned from the active practice of the law to the Attorney-Generalship must frequently take the office while law cases in which they are interested are still pending. It seems entirely probable that in such instances there may have to be a confidential understanding with the President in order that a man's regular practice may not suffer because of his new occupation. At any rate, lawyers owe certain obligations to their clients which cannot be surrendered at once. Often, especially where an Attorney-General is a member of a firm, the legal work may be assumed and carried on by the firm. Such leading firms in the past as Black & Phelan (J. S. Black, Attorney-General, 1857-1860), Speed & Smith (Joshua Speed, Attorney-General, 1864-1866), Thayer & Williams (G. H. Williams, Attorney-General, 1872-1875), and Harmon, Colston, Goldsmith & Hoadley (Judson Harmon, Attorney-General, 1895-1897), were not dissolved because their leading member went to Washington in an official capacity.

I submit the problem to the reader. I should be glad to know where to find evidence that would afford a solution of it.

CHAPTER VIII

ESTABLISHMENT OF THE SECRETARYSHIP OF THE NAVY

ON April 30, 1798, on the eve of probable war with France, President John Adams approved and signed a bill formulated for the purpose of establishing an executive department to be called the Department of the Navy. The bill, enacted into law,[1] was the outcome of various ideas and circumstances which had tended toward its formulation since the early days of the American Revolution.

I

The first impulse toward a naval administrative organization came largely from New England, the commercial center of the colonies. It may be detected in 1775, soon after the outbreak of the Revolutionary War. The agricultural South showed, from the first discussions of the subject in the Continental Congress, some opposition to a navy.

Neither the navy nor a naval administration, it should be remembered, came suddenly into existence. They were both the results of necessity. The very circumstances of war forced men to consider and to plan measures of protection on the sea, and some sort of central directive organization. Rhode Island was the first colony to commission vessels for a local or State navy. It should also be credited with bringing to the

[1] 1 *Statutes at Large*, pp. 553 ff.

attention of Congress a set of resolutions which served, after a hearing, as the starting point in the autumn of 1775 for a central administration of naval affairs.[2]

The naval administration of the Revolutionary epoch proved in fact to be a series of rather crude experiments. Above the details of administration, standing out as the more or less responsible centers of control, there were four executive organs. With reference to chronology they may be arranged as follows:

1. The Naval Committee: October, 1775, to January, 1776.
2. The Marine Committee: February, 1776, to December, 1779.
3. The Board of Admiralty: December, 1779, to July, 1781.
4. The Agent of Marine: September, 1781, to November, 1784.

The changes were neither quite so sudden nor so definite as the foregoing divisions and dates might lead the reader to believe. By a process of merging and absorption the so-called Naval Committee lost its identity in the succeeding Marine Committee. As time elapsed—during the years, 1778-1779—Congress hit upon the idea of executive boards, relatively small groups containing men outside Congress as well as members of that body. Such boards were utilized in other parts of the continental or central administration, notably in connection with the finances and the

[2] *Journals of Congress,* October 3-December 22, 1775 (*passim*). John Adams's *Works,* I, 155, 187-188. II, 462-463, 479-481, 485. III, 6-12. IX, 464. Cf. C. O. Paullin, *The Navy of the American Revolution:* its Administration, its Policy, and its Achievements (1906), pp. 31 ff.

practical business of the direction of the war. But nowhere did they work smoothly or effectively. In 1780 an effort to place the various administrative organizations under separate heads or Secretaries was, as elsewhere we have seen, matured and approved in Congress, favored by such leading men as Hamilton, Jay, Washington, and the two Morrises. The effort was vigorously opposed by Samuel Adams and a respectable following. But the "constructive" or "concentrative" school, as it has been variously termed, finally gained the day in the spring of 1781.[3]

On February 7, 1781, Congress adopted a plan which provided for the establishment of a Secretary of Marine, and prescribed that officer's duties. Two days later, February 9, the salary of the Secretary was fixed at five thousand dollars. Near the end of the month, on February 27, Congress elected Major-General Alexander McDougall of New York to the new position. Months before, McDougall had been thought of as a fit incumbent for the place by Alexander Hamilton. In various ways well qualified, McDougall made such conditions as to accepting the appointment that Congress felt forced finally to veto it. And there is no evidence that any other choice for the Secretaryship was ever again seriously considered. Thus the attempt to establish and fill the new office failed. But it could hardly have been forgotten.[4]

---

[3] Paullin, *op. cit.*, pp. 31 ff., 48, 82, 86-87, 90, 181 ff., 193, 208, 210 ff., 226. Guggenheimer in Jameson's *Essays*, pp. 138 ff., 160 ff. The term "concentrative" is Paullin's; Francis Wharton uses "constructive." *Revolutionary Diplomatic Correspondence*, I, Introd., p. 252.

[4] *Journals of Congress* under dates indicated, and March 30, 1781.

In the summer of 1781 the subject of naval administration was on several occasions before Congress. Three committees tried at different times to solve the administrative problems involved in the naval situation. Late in August the third committee adopted a makeshift policy, agreeing "that for the present an agent of marine be appointed, with authority to direct, fit out, equip, and employ the ships and vessels of war belonging to the United States, according to such instructions as he shall, from time to time, receive from Congress."[5] A few days later, on September 7, Robert Morris, Superintendent of Finance, was asked by Congress to assume all the powers and duties of the office "until an agent of marine be appointed by Congress."

Morris accepted the office on the following day, holding it until he resigned his Superintendency on November 1, 1784. By that time the need of a continental navy for protection had passed. Such naval business as remained related chiefly to the settlement of naval accounts; and it was placed in the hands of a few subordinates, men who had served under Morris, until the Board of Treasury, organized in 1785, wound it up.[6]

That for more than three years Robert Morris not only managed the finances of the Revolution, but also

[5] August 29.

[6] The bare details are easily followed in the *Journals of Congress*, VII-X. Paullin has thrown new light from an examination of the "Records and Papers of the Continental Congress" in Washington. See his chapter, "The Secretary of Marine and the Agent of Marine," in his *Navy of the American Revolution*, pp. 210-251.

shouldered the burdens of naval administration, are facts that help to reveal his extraordinary capacity. He had been for a time vice-president of the old Marine Committee. And during the trying winter of 1776-1777, while Congress was at Baltimore, he remained in Philadelphia; and there, with very little assistance, he administered naval affairs.[7] After Congress in 1781 had failed in their efforts to appoint McDougall as Secretary of Marine, it is curious to observe the way that naval affairs gravitated to Morris. No better characterization of this phase of his career has ever been written than this of Dr. Paullin. "He was invited," says Paullin, "to take upon himself more or less of the naval business by the urgent need of sending the cruisers on important errands, the helplessness of the Board of Admiralty, the inertia of Congress." "The figure," he continues, "that Morris presents at this time is that of the strong and confident man of affairs, sagacious, expeditious, and painstaking, who is surrounded by weaker men, hesitating, vacillating, and procrastinating in their administrative attempts."[8] In brief, Morris stands as the first important figure in the national administration of naval affairs, just as he holds a similar place in the history of American financial administration.

II

In any satisfactory scheme of government—such, for example, as men were groping for during the years of the Confederation (1781-1788)—a Secretary of

[7] Paullin, *op. cit.*, p. 90.
[8] *Ibid.*, pp. 219, 225-226.

Marine was not usually overlooked. It was assumed that any robust and vigorous government must sustain a navy and provide for its effective administration. Yet to most men of that time it is probable that the conclusion of the Revolutionary War signified the disappearance of the need for a navy. Other matters seemed to be of relatively greater moment. The common view was sufficiently well expressed by John Adams. In a letter written to Thomas Jefferson at Paris, Adams remarked that a "disposition seems rather to prevail among our citizens to give up all ideas of navigation and naval power, and lay themselves consequently at the mercy of foreigners."[9] The sentiment should not, however, disguise the fact that commerce at this time was already reviving and reaching out to some extent in the direction of Oriental ports. This commercial interest, characteristic of peaceful conditions, was bound to foster any incipient movement, such as can be found, toward a naval establishment.

For years a navy had been one of John Adams's cherished projects. In the opening years of the Revolution he had labored for some efficient form of naval administration; and he was the chief author of the rules for the government of the American navy, and articles to be signed by the officers and men employed in that service, a code re-adopted much later, as we shall see, under the Constitution.[10] While residing in

9 Adams's *Works*, VIII, 412. Letter dated at London, July 31, 1786.
10 *Journals of Congress*, November 23, 25, 28, 1775, etc. Paullin, *op. cit.*, pp. 43 ff. *Proceedings of the U. S. Naval Institute*, XXXII, 1009.

London, in letters written during 1785-1786, Adams occasionally touched upon the subject of an American navy. He wrote to Jefferson, saying: "I wish I could know the number of foreign ships which have entered the ports of the United States since the peace. . . . . If all these ships and seamen were American, what materials would they furnish for a navy in a very few years, not more than eight or ten."[11] About a year later, on July 3, 1786, he expressed to Jefferson his conviction that a war with the Barbary States, which then seemed not impossible, might prove to be "a good occasion to begin a navy."[12] He was willing to go almost any length, as he admitted, in urging on the government of the United States a naval establishment. Moreover, Jefferson himself was at the time distinctly in favor of war and against further payment of tribute to the Barbary powers, and hence quite as strong a believer as Adams in an American navy. He too considered a marine force a necessity, and remarked that it could "never endanger our liberties."[13] It seems highly probable that, had either Adams or Jefferson been members of the first Congress in 1789, when that body was debating the whole problem of the organization of departments, they would both have urged the creation of a separate department of the navy.

[11] August 8, 1785. *Works,* VIII, 296.

[12] *Ibid.,* p. 407.

[13] August 11, 1786. Letter to Monroe. Jefferson's *Writings* (ed. Washington), I, 606. Dr. G. W. Allen has discussed carefully the two views of Adams and Jefferson in *Our Navy and the Barbary Corsairs* (1905), pp. 35 ff.

In 1786 the Congress of the Confederation, stirred by the news of the depredations of the Mediterranean corsairs on American shipping, went on record to the effect that "it is proper and expedient for the federal government to turn their earliest attention to the Marine Department, and that a committee be appointed to frame and report an ordinance for organizing the same."[14]   The next year, late in the session of the Philadelphia Convention, Gouverneur Morris declared that a "navy was essential to security, particularly of the Southern States."[15]   But, notwithstanding such suggestions, there was to be no separate naval establishment for the present, for Congress determined in 1789 to place such naval business as there might be directly in charge of the Secretary of War.

The first section of the statute creating the Department of War referred to naval matters as clearly of minor importance.[16]   But naval business could not long remain so.   For, in the first place, the Constitution had given Congress certain powers with reference to maintaining a navy.   The President, moreover, was commander-in-chief of the navy.   And since no State could

[14] Quoted by Paullin from "Records and Papers of the Continental Congress," No. 25, vol. II, 459, in *Proceedings of the U. S. Naval Institute*, XXXII, 1002.

[15] Elliot, *Debates*, V, 490.   August 29.

[16] 1 *Statutes at Large*, p. 50.   ". . . . the Secretary for the Department of War, who shall perform and execute such duties as shall from time to time be enjoined on or entrusted to him by the President . . . . agreeably to the Constitution, relative to military commissions, or to land or naval forces, ships, or warlike stores . . . . or to such other matters respecting military or naval affairs."   Not another reference to a navy occurs in the law.

own ships of war in times of peace, circumstances were sure in future to force some of these constitutional powers into active employment.

In 1790 the Secretary of War, General Knox, was considering the possibility of getting together some armed vessels of war for the uses of the government. Early in January, 1791, the Senate, enlightened by Jefferson, Secretary of State, as to the conditions of Mediterranean trade, resolved ''that the trade of the United States to the Mediterranean cannot be protected but by a naval force; and that it will be proper to resort to the same as soon as the state of the public finances will admit.''[17] Nothing came of this suggestion. But it reveals clearly enough that circumstances beyond American control were already arousing and helping to shape public interest in a navy. These circumstances were to enforce vigorous action on the part of the national government, as we shall presently see, in 1794.

III

From the year 1794 we may reckon what Knox termed the ''second commencement of a navy for the United States.''[18] By a law of March 27, 1794, Congress provided for the building of six government vessels, a fleet sufficiently large, it was thought, for ''the protection of the commerce of the United States against the Algerine corsairs.'' By a special provision

[17] *American State Papers, Foreign Relations,* I, 108.
[18] December 27, 1794.   Report to the House of Representatives in *American State Papers, Naval Affairs,* I, 6.

it was determined that "in case of peace with Algiers all work on the frigates should stop." Peace with Algiers came the next year (1795), but was not formally ratified by the Senate until March 2, 1796. The work of building the frigates had by that date reached such a stage of advancement that President Washington soon requested Congress to consider the problem of loss to the government in case work were summarily suspended. In response to this suggestion Congress decided, by an act of April 20, that the President should "cause to be completed, with all convenient expedition," three frigates. These ships, "launched the following year, were the United States, Constitution, and Constellation. They were the first of a long and honorable list."[19] The United States, built at Philadelphia, was launched on May 10, 1797; the Constitution, built at Boston, was launched October 21 following; and the Constellation, built at Baltimore, was launched on September 7. Pickering and Washington together helped to name the frigates.[20]

There was opposition to the enactment of March, 1794. As the opposition to a navy in the Revolution came at the outset chiefly from the South, so now, long after the navy of the Revolution had disappeared, there came similar opposition from the same region. Although the enactment was directed to a specific object, it was generally regarded as likely to lead to

[19] G. W. Allen, *Our Navy and the Barbary Corsairs*, p. 58. The whole subject is admirably treated in this author's fourth chapter, "Peace with Algiers," pp. 43-58.
[20] C. O. Paullin, in *Proceedings of the U. S. Naval Institute*, XXXII, 1008-1009.

a permanent naval establishment. Madison saw in a navy grave danger of international complications. Others opposed a navy on financial grounds: the country was poor; let the public debt be first of all discharged. It would be better, it was suggested, to buy peace of the Algerines, as European states had done for many years. A few considered the navy as a real menace to liberty. But the more liberal majority— among whom should be reckoned William Smith of South Carolina—passed the law. Relying on the probable improvement of the nation's credit, sure of the need of organized protection to American commerce on the high seas, inasmuch as trade was rapidly increasing, this majority forced through Congress a measure that was to prove on the whole beneficent and necessary.[21]

In Washington's last annual message there was a memorable passage in this connection, in which the President dwelt on the desirability of building up a navy. "To an active external commerce," he wrote, "the protection of a naval force is indispensable . . . . it is in our own experience that the most sincere neutrality is not a sufficient guard against the depredations of nations at war. To secure respect to a neutral flag requires a naval force organized and ready to vindicate it from insult or aggression. This may even prevent the necessity of going to war by discouraging belligerent powers from committing such violations of the rights of the neutral flag as may . . . . leave no other option. . . . . These considerations," he concluded,

[21] Based upon Paullin and Allen.

"invite the United States to look to the means, and to set about the gradual creation of a navy . . . . so that a future war of Europe may not find our commerce in the same unprotected state in which it was found by the present."[22]

With numerous circumstances all tending to emphasize the great utility of a national navy, with the counsel of eminent statesmen advocating conservative but definite action looking toward the creation of a navy, together with the fact that there was already a small nucleus of national ships about ready to be launched, John Adams's administration opened in March, 1797.

IV

From 1794, when navy business first assumed vital importance, to May, 1798, three Secretaries of War endeavored successively to manage that business in consultation with Presidents Washington and Adams. The truth has been very succinctly expressed in this way: "Knox superintended the navy for a little less than a year; Pickering for a little more than a year; and McHenry for a little more than two years."[23] Let us observe a few of the facts in the situation.

The initial difficulties of the tasks of naval organization were shouldered by Knox. It was Knox who planned the work of constructing six ships, of procuring materials and of selecting officers, naval agents, and skilled constructors. As early as June, 1794,

---

[22] *Messages and Papers*, I, 201.
[23] Paullin in *Proceedings of the U. S. Naval Institute*, XXXII, 1005.

Washington appointed six captains in the navy, among these being John Barry, Samuel Nicholson, Richard Dale and Thomas Truxton. These six officers were each to superintend the construction of a vessel, although Joshua Humphreys, a shipbuilder of Philadelphia, was the designer of all the frigates.[24] For the sake of distributing benefits among different localities, the six vessels were to be built at as many different ports. In each shipyard such officials as were needed were provided. Thus a business organization was developed quickly near the start.

Pickering for a brief period carried on the work that his predecessor had laid out. The keels of six vessels were completed and laid upon the blocks. Five of the six vessels were named. The work went on under McHenry. But the strained relations between the United States and France—the actual imminency of war early in 1798—forced upon McHenry a grave responsibility such as neither Knox nor Pickering had known.[25]

In his first message addressed to the special session of Congress—a message dated May 16, 1797—President Adams, calling attention to the growing interest in commerce, spoke urgently of the need of establishing a permanent system of naval defence.[26] The sentiments of Adams were in accord with Washington's well-known views, and likewise with those of many less

[24] A good sketch of Humphreys is given by G. W. Allen, *Our Naval War with France* (1909), pp. 42 ff.

[25] For this and the preceding paragraph I have depended much on Paullin's article already cited, pp. 1005-1010.

[26] *Messages and Papers*, I, 236-237.

distinguished members of the Federalist party. They were expressed only six days after the frigate United States was launched at Philadelphia, but before any one of the three vessels was equipped for service. On July 1 following, Congress was moved to authorize the President to man and employ these vessels, and thus—as Dr. Paullin observes—really committed the country to a naval establishment. In accordance with this July law, the navy was to be governed by the rules and regulations of the old Revolutionary navy, the code which John Adams had conceived nearly twenty-two years before.[27]

On November 22 Adams once more urged on Congress the need of protecting American commerce and of looking after the interests of seafaring citizens as well as those of others. In the following March, moved by the increasing danger of war with France as well as perhaps by the President's words, Congress prepared to act. On March 8, 1798, a committee of the House of Representatives reported in favor of a commissioner of marine in the War Department "who should be employed in the immediate superintendence of the naval concerns of the United States." A fortnight later, on March 22, McHenry proposed separating the naval business from that of the War Department.[28]

Results were sure to follow. On Monday, April 2, Senator William Bingham of Pennsylvania made a

[27] Paullin's article, p. 1009.
[28] *Messages and Papers*, I, 251, 256. *Annals of Congress* under March 8. B. C. Steiner, *Life and Correspondence of James McHenry*, p. 302. *American State Papers, Naval Affairs*, I, 33-34, 39.

motion favoring the appointment of a committee "to take into consideration the propriety of instituting a separate executive department, for the purpose of superintending and regulating the various objects connected with the Naval Establishment of the United States."[29] In accordance with this motion a committee of three was appointed the next day. This committee reported a bill to the Senate on April 11. The bill passed that body, apparently without much opposition, on April 16. The report of the Senate debate is very meagre. But we know that two Senators, Marshall of Kentucky and Paine of Vermont, each from an inland state, tried to limit the proposed measure in time, so that a navy department should serve only as a temporary expedient.[30]

The real ordeal came on April 25, in the debate in the House of Representatives on the question of allowing the bill to pass to its third reading. By a close vote—forty-seven to forty-one[31]—the bill went to its final reading, then was passed by the House—forty-two to twenty-seven—and was approved and signed by President Adams on April 30.

The opposition in the House was vigorous. It lay to some extent along party lines, for the measure was regarded as distinctly Federalist. But it was governed also by economic considerations. In general the agricultural states opposed it, and the commercial states—chiefly north of the Potomac River—favored

[29] *Annals of Congress,* 5 Cong., 2 sess. (1797-1799), I, 534.
[30] *Ibid.,* I, 539-542.
[31] See Table at the end of this chapter.

it. It may be noted, however, that a majority of the
Representatives from both New York and Pennsylvania were recorded against it, while the six Representatives from South Carolina were equally divided.
Some of those who opposed the measure argued that
a separate navy department was under the circumstances unnecessary. Gallatin took this view. He
believed that it might be wise to increase the personnel
of the War Department if the business of naval administration demanded additional effort. From his
standpoint, to organize a separate department was not
only unnecessary but uneconomical. The new department would, he believed, increase expenses out of all
proportion to its utility. To the suggestion made
several times in the course of the debate that the Secretary of War had already too many burdens, and that
a naval organization really demanded expert knowledge on the part of a Secretary, it was answered that
it might prove expedient to appoint a War Secretary
capable of understanding both army and navy administration. There was doubtless some reflection here
on McHenry, who was not a man of large ability. But
in any event the difficulties of securing such double
qualifications in one man were obvious.

In the course of his remarks in opposition to a technical expert on ships as well fitted for the new place,
Edward Livingston of New York was reported as
saying that "if a shipbuilder was to have the appointment, he could not think such a person fit to be one of
the great council of the nation; and it must be recol-
lected," he added significantly, "that the person who

holds this office will become one of the counsellors of the President on all great concerns.''[32] Quite unwittingly Livingston here made the first clear reference to the President's Cabinet—reckoning from 1789—that I have found in the records of the debates of either the Senate or the House of Representatives.

The circumstances of the political situation favored the quick passage of the bill. There was already a nucleus, sure to grow, of a national navy. Moreover, the practices of the Revolution, with which men were in 1798 perfectly familiar, had set an earlier standard for a naval administration separate from that of war. President Adams was deeply interested in having a national naval organization. Most European countries had such separate administrative organizations. Harrison Grey Otis, speaking on behalf of a separate naval Secretary, remarked that ''it was necessary, even for the sake of appearances, to establish an office of this kind . . . . we ought to do it in conformity to the opinion of the European world. He thought $5,000 a year would be well expended in purchasing the good opinion of the European nations in this respect, and particularly that of France.'' Such language was likely to arouse hostile comment, as it did. When the same speaker reminded his colleagues from the agricultural states that a thriving, well-protected commerce meant certain gains to agriculture, he adduced a truth that could be neither overlooked nor denied.[33]

[32] *Annals of Congress,* op. cit., II, 1552. April 25, 1798. *Supra,* chapter VI, p. 138.

[33] The account rests on the reports of the debate in the *Annals of Congress,* 5 Cong. (1797-1799), I, 534-541. II, 1426, 1522, 1545-1554,

On the first of May, John Adams sent to the Senate the name of George Cabot of Massachusetts to be Secretary of the Navy. The nomination was ratified on May 3, and a commission was issued on that day. Pickering notified Cabot of his appointment two days later, and at the same time sent him a personal letter to urge his acceptance. "In this new office," wrote Pickering, "the President wishes to find not only a person of practical knowledge in maritime affairs, but a statesman. . . . . The public advantages to be derived from your conducting the department you can fully estimate, and your friends have anticipated. Although the formation of a navy has been contemplated these four years, it is at the present moment only that the establishment may be considered as commencing."[34]

Cabot declined the appointment on May 11, probably from an honest belief in his own unfitness. He was a staunch Federalist—a man of ability according to contemporary judgment, and in touch and sympathy with such men as Pickering and Wolcott, members of the Cabinet. But he was naturally indolent, according to the view of his own great-grandson and biographer, and disliked publicity.[35] The place certainly called for a man of force and thorough industry. Adams was fortunate in finding just such a one in Benjamin Stoddert of Maryland. Nominated to the office on May

supplemented by some suggestions taken from Paullin's article entitled "Early Naval Administration under the Constitution" and hitherto cited.

[34] H. C. Lodge, *Life and Letters of George Cabot* (2d ed., Boston: 1878), pp. 155 ff.

[35] *Ibid.*

18, Stoddert was confirmed by the Senate and commissioned on May 21. But he did not undertake the active duties of the position until the eighteenth of June.[36]

V

The Secretary of the Navy was the first official since 1789 who became a member of the President's Cabinet. In the debates in Congress over the establishment of the new executive department it was assumed, as we have seen, that the official at its head would become a counsellor. And in practice President Adams made him one, setting an example in 1798 which has been followed ever since. Benjamin Stoddert was the first principal officer of Adams's own selection who entered the Cabinet. All the others—excepting John Marshall and Samuel Dexter who were chosen later and served in the Cabinet for comparatively brief periods—were a heritage from Washington's Presidency. Stoddert was not only a capable and far-sighted administrator —the true founder of the office; but in the days following, when Adams was exasperated by intrigues among his confidential assistants, Stoddert seems to have remained faithful to his chief. It was especially important at the time that the President should have an intimate and expert assistant on whom, in naval matters, he might depend, for—as Dr. Gardner W. Allen has recently pointed out—hostilities between the United States and France continued to be acute for almost three years, and amounted to actual war, although war was declared on neither side.[37]

[36] Mosher, *Executive Register*, p. 59.
[37] *Our Naval War with France*, Preface, p. vii.

There is one aspect of the establishment of the Secretaryship that should not be overlooked. The office developed naturally out of the necessity of differentiating the administrative tasks which were burdening the War Department. There was no popular demand for it. It had to be forced into being—extracted from a Congress that contained both hostile and inert elements —by a few leaders who appreciated the more immediate needs of the government, and saw in the future the possibilities of a disastrous war as affecting a steadily increasing commerce. The larger aspects of the problem were set forth—as they should have been —by both Washington and John Adams. These men, with the aid of their administrative assistants and certain enlightened members of Congress, after some years of effort, brought about the act of 1798.

The Cabinet Council thus became a body composed of five regular members. It will be the aim of the next chapter to account for the addition to the Cabinet of a sixth member—the Postmaster-General.

NOTE

Table showing the votes on the question of allowing the bill for the establishment of a separate Navy Department to go to its third reading in the House of Representatives on April 25, 1798:

	VOTES FOR	VOTES AGAINST
Vermont	1	1
New Hampshire	3	0
Massachusetts	10	2
Rhode Island	2	0
Connecticut	6	0
New York	4	5
New Jersey	4	0
Pennsylvania	2	4
Delaware	1	0
Maryland	6	1
Virginia	4	12
North Carolina	1	8
South Carolina	3	3
Georgia	0	2
Tennessee	0	1
Kentucky	0	2
Total votes	47	41

CHAPTER IX

It is a matter of common knowledge that Jackson was the first President to reckon the Postmaster-General a regular member of the Cabinet. In the latter part of the summer of 1828, about six months before Jackson's inauguration, Edward Everett—at the time a Representative in Congress from Massachusetts—in a letter written to Postmaster-General John McLean, remarked that the "Postmaster-Genl. is not, by usage, a member of the Cabinet Council; but, as you justly observe, his functions are as delicate and important as those of any officer." In the opinion of both Everett and McLean, the Postmaster-General was in control of the greatest amount of patronage—greater by far than that of any other officer. Looking back over five years of service to 1823, the year of his appointment, McLean was inclined to believe that at that time the position of Postmaster-General was "the least desirable office in the country."[1] It had certainly increased in importance under McLean's able management. But in order to explain the rise of the office to cabinet rank, it will be necessary briefly to consider some phases of its history.

I

Crude postal arrangements for the benefit of the King and his Court existed in England from the early

[1] Correspondence between Edward Everett and John McLean in *Massachusetts Historical Society Proceedings,* 3d ser., I, 361, 367.

part of the sixteenth century. These were under the direction of an official known as Master of the Posts. In the seventeenth century the postal service was organized for the convenience of the more general public. It was administered by one or more persons —a Postmaster-General and his deputies—who acted under the supervision of one of the Secretaries of State. In 1710 an act of Queen Anne[2] introduced uniformity and consistency into an administration that had been hitherto crude and poorly arranged. The act was clearly designed to bring the distant parts of the realm and the colonies into closer touch with the central governmental organization in London. From 1710 to 1823 there were as a rule two English Postmasters-General.[3]

In colonial America there is very slight evidence of post roads and offices until the second half of the seventeenth century. It is true that Massachusetts as early as 1639 and New Netherlands in 1657 made certain regulations for the purpose of securing the proper and safe transmission and delivery of letters "coming from beyond the Seas, or . . . . sent thither." Moreover, we are safe in surmising that such offshoots from the parent colony as the settlements on the Connecticut River, and Rhode Island and Providence Plantations were a probable means of enforcing the need of occasional communication, and so tended to encourage the establishment of at least a rough system of roads. About 1672 efforts were made to arrange

[2] 9 Anne, c. 10 in *Statutes at Large* (London: 1763), IV, 434-445.
[3] Anson, *Law and Custom of the Constitution,* Pt. II, pp. 182-183.

postal communication between Boston and New York. Although not at first successful, these efforts probably mark the time for the real beginnings of domestic postal service in the colonies. Other colonies followed the examples of New York and Massachusetts, or were induced by their own particular needs to organize some sort of system for transmitting letters from place to place, so that by 1689 at latest the subject of postal service had been widely discussed. Here and there actual plans were being carried out with some degree of success. Attempts on the part of the home government after 1660 to consolidate the colonies certainly had a tendency to foster a general plan for post roads and offices which should include most of the colonies within its range. Moreover, such men as Governor Dongan of New York, Sir Edmund Andros, Lord Cornbury, and William Penn all showed an active interest in making the movement effective.[4]

Early in the last decade of the century a certain Thomas Neale, Master of the English Mint from 1679 to 1699, obtained a patent from William and Mary which granted to him or to his executors and assignees for a period of twenty-one years the right to establish a post—

for the conveying of Letters within or between Virginia Maryland Delaware New Yorke New England East and West Jersey Pensilvania and Northward as far as our Dominions reach in America. . . . .

[4] Mary E. Woolley, ''Early History of the Colonial Post-Office,'' pp. 33 (Providence, R. I.: 1894), in No. II of *Papers from the Historical Seminary of Brown University* (ed. J. F. Jameson).

Neale and his successors were likewise privileged to nominate fit officers in the colonies to carry out the details of organization—the arrangement of offices, roads, postal rates, and other matters essential to the efficacy of the plan. The patent was dated at Westminster February 17, 169½. We are fortunate in having an exact copy of it easily accessible and in print.[5] It was the means of instituting the first royal intercolonial post in the American colonies. In April, 1692, Neale nominated, and the English Postmasters-General appointed, Andrew Hamilton as manager of the general Post-Office in America, thus arranging for an officer who served as deputy Postmaster-General. Many of the colonies—notably New York and New Jersey (of which latter colony Hamilton became governor)—did their best to aid the measure. And although the organization limped along for some years, involving Neale in debt, it seems probable that it was useful to the colonies, and that it had attained some degree of success by the time that the act of Anne, already referred to, went into effect.

Thomas Neale was a character of no great prominence in England. He seems for many years to have been a favorite at Court. As early as June 20, 1664, he was noticed in Pepys's *Diary*. Thirty years later he fell under the observant eye of John Evelyn who had something to say about his business ventures and money-making schemes. He probably belonged to the class of confirmed officer-holders, and was a "deter-

---

[5] *Ibid.*, pp. 27-33. Here first printed by Professor Jameson who obtained an exact copy from the Public Record Office in London in 1894.

mined and adventurous speculator, quick to seize any opportunity for personal profit.'"[6] He died about the close of the century, perhaps in 1699. There is not as yet the slightest evidence to indicate that he ever came to America. But his patent and the resulting postal organization form an interesting commentary on his life, and certainly marked an epoch in the history of an American institution.

Neale's experiment did not prove remunerative to him. In fact, after a few years he found himself without resources, and shortly before his death, deeply in debt, he assigned his interest in the colonial organization to Hamilton and an Englishman by the name of West, to both of whom he was owing money. In the spring of 1703 Andrew Hamilton died, and for three or four years his widow and West together seem to have managed the posts. By 1706 Mrs. Hamilton and West urged that the patent, which still had seven and a half years to run, might be extended for another term of twenty-one years. But the English Postmasters-General, Cotton and Frankland, objected to the proposition, and favored the purchase of the patent by the home government. This accordingly was done in 1707, and the American postal .service became thereby vested in the Crown. John Hamilton, son of Andrew, was appointed to his father's old place of deputy Postmaster-General, and retained it until 1722, when he resigned.[7]

[6] Jameson, *Ibid.*, p. 25. I have relied on Professor Jameson's notes on Neale's career, which are added to Miss Woolley's monograph.

[7] Herbert Joyce, *The History of the Post Office* from its Establishment down to 1836 (London: Bentley, 1893), pp. 114, 116. Mr. Joyce

The act of 1710 which reorganized the English Post-Office, although it was partly arranged in order to provide a war revenue, represented a phase of the general policy of William and Mary, and their immediate successors. Henceforth the Crown meant to exercise its prerogative over various colonial matters. The act involved the control in America of a deputy Postmaster-General. Yet it was not necessary for a while to disturb John Hamilton in his position. He had, from the time of the sale of the old patent in 1707, been under direction of the Crown authorities. It is perhaps worth noting that there was no express statement in the act directly referring to an American official. But frequent allusions to ''her Majesty's Postmaster-General . . . . and his Deputy and Deputies by him thereunto sufficiently authorized'' gave clear legal basis for an American appointment. The ''chief Letter Office'' in the colonies was designated as being at New York.

There was some slight objection to the act of 1710 as a measure of taxation, for there were explicit terms about the rates of postage. According to Lieutenant-Governor Alexander Spotswood, writing to the Board of Trade in 1718, the people of Virginia objected to the rates as a kind of tax which should have had the consent of their own General Assembly.[8] But the act was designed only incidentally to produce revenue. So far as it concerned the American colonies, it was prob-

has written from the sources an excellent chapter on ''American Posts, 1692-1707,'' pp. 110 ff.

[8] G. L. Beer, *British Colonial Policy, 1754-1765* (1907), p. 34, footnote 4.

ably primarily intended to bring them into closer relations with the home government, although it could
hardly help bringing them into closer union among
themselves.

Numerous colonists held the office of deputy Postmaster-General in America. Spotswood of Virginia,
having for years been interested in perfecting
postal arrangements, served in the position from 1730
to 1739. But quite the most capable and distinguished
occupant of the office before the Revolution was
Benjamin Franklin. Franklin made the American
colonial postal organization not only efficient, but also
lucrative. It was said to have yielded to England by
1774 a regular annual income of £3000 sterling.[9] The
period of Franklin's service as deputy Postmaster-
General extended from 1753 to 1774. In the latter year
he was dismissed as one result of the dramatic and
scathing invective directed against him by Solicitor-
General Wedderburn before the Committee of the
Privy Council—an attack upon him for the part he had
taken in procuring and making public the letters of
Hutchinson and Oliver which were supposed to be distinctly slurring on colonial men and measures. This
bitter attack, followed by Franklin's ignominious dismissal from office, aroused the American colonists to
a high pitch of feeling against the English government,
and induced them under what they regarded as the
pressure of necessity to turn to the creation of an independent or so-called constitutional American Post-
Office.

[9] *American Archives*, I, 501.

All through the early part of 1774 William Goddard, an energetic printer and newspaper editor of Philadelphia and Baltimore, worked hard to organize an American postal establishment independent of England. His plan, although clearly against the statute of 1710,[10] met with very general encouragement. Various colonial Assemblies approved it. Moreover, it commended itself to several of the delegates to the First Continental Congress. There can be no doubt that Goddard's efforts were influential in bringing about the first formal action in the matter which Congress took on July 26, 1775. On that day it was determined "That a postmaster General be appointed for the United Colonies, who shall hold his office at Philad*, and shall be allowed a salary of 1000 dollars per an: for himself." To fill the position thus created, Benjamin Franklin was unanimously chosen on the same day. There were numerous details of organization arranged for by Congress at the time. These need not concern us. It is simply important to observe that this action marked the true beginning of an independent postal service under the direct control of the central continental government.[11]

Throughout the period of the Revolution there were obvious difficulties in the way of any successful postal organization. These difficulties of various kinds, but largely of an administrative nature, can be traced by

[10] Section 17.

[11] Goddard's work can only be understood from an examination of the materials collected in *American Archives*, I, 500-504. II, 536-537, 650, 803, 981-983, 1160. IV, 184. VI, 1012-1013.

means of rather scanty entries in the *Journals* of Congress.[12] It is enough to say that the Post-Office, like other administrative work, was managed through committees of Congress, although it was probably true that considerable freedom of direction had to be left to the Postmaster-General himself. Franklin went to France in 1776, the year following his appointment. His place as Postmaster-General was taken by his son-in-law, Richard Bache. Bache in turn was succeeded early in 1782 by Ebenezer Hazard. Hazard retained office until Washington named his successor under the new government in the autumn of 1789. It was certainly natural that the three holders of the office from 1775 to 1789 should have come from Pennsylvania. For most of that period Pennsylvania—occupying a central geographical position well suited for administrative work that involved the interests of the thirteen communities—was the seat of the central governmental organization.[13]

It should perhaps be noted that in October, 1782, a new ordinance—the result of experience and of an effort on the part of Congress to combine various scattered recommendations which had been offered from time to time—was formulated with rather exceptional care. This October ordinance remained the fundamental law of the postal organization until September, 1789.[14]

[12] December 2, 1775; February 1, August 29-30, September 3, 1776, etc.

[13] The dates for the respective appointments of Bache and Hazard were November 7, 1776, and January 28, 1782. See *Journals.*

[14] *Ibid.,* October 18 and December 24, 1782.

II

From the standpoint of 1789 the postal organization had already proved to be an important factor in helping to unite the colonies and the states which were formed during the Revolutionary epoch. The roots of the organization extended farther back into colonial times than those of any central institution for administrative purposes. In fact it must have gradually assumed many of the characteristic features of an executive department from the days when, under Neale's patent early in the last decade of the seventeenth century, it began to be efficient and generally useful.[15] It was not strange that the proper readjustment of the postal organization under the new government took time to work out. On the other hand the Post-Office as a rather distinctively business or administrative organization, as distinguished from those political organizations like the Treasury and the Department of State on which the very life of the nation depended, could be safely conducted, for a time at any rate, on the basis which the Congress of the Confederation had provided.

On September 9, 1789, the House of Representatives proposed to continue postal arrangements on the basis of the old ordinances—''according to the rules and regulations prescribed by the ordinances and resolutions of the late Congress.'' The Senate was disinclined to accept this suggestion, but it went no farther than to draw up a bill which provided for the

[15] Professor Jameson called attention incidentally to this point of view in his notes to Miss Woolley's monograph of 1894, *op. cit.*, p. 25.

temporary establishment of a Post-Office. This was finally passed and became the law, with President Washington's approval, on September 22. Three days later, on September 25, Washington sent the name of Samuel Osgood to the Senate as first Postmaster-General under the Constitution. The nomination was ratified on the following day. Osgood entered upon his duties at once.[16]

Osgood, the first Postmaster-General, was a man of education and experience. He graduated at Harvard College in 1770. Besides serving as an officer during the early days of the Revolutionary War, he had taken an active part in framing the constitution of Massachusetts. He was elected to the Massachusetts Senate, but soon went to the Continental Congress. There, after several years of service, he was chosen in 1785 as one of the three Treasury Commissioners— offices that he and his two colleagues had recently surrendered in order to make way for Hamilton, the new Secretary of the Treasury.[17]

There is abundant evidence clearly to indicate that the temporary arrangement of the postal organization was regarded at the time as far from satisfactory. Energy in its administration was lacking, and revenues were small. In the first four annual messages of Washington the need of adequate legal provision for the postal service was regularly brought to the attention of Congress.[18] But Congress, while by no means

[16] 1 *Statutes at Large*, p. 70. *Annals of Congress*, I, 80-82, 922-923, 927-928. R. B. Mosher, *Executive Register*, p. 10.

[17] Appleton, *Cyclopaedia of American Biography*, IV, 600.

[18] *Messages and Papers of the Presidents*, I, 66, 68, 83, 107, 128, 132.

inclined to disregard the subject, was occupied with matters of more immediate importance. At length, after several temporary measures had been provided, a bill was signed on May 8, 1794, by Washington, which formed the first adequate legal and working basis for a permanent national Post-Office as a settled establishment.[19]

If the statutes which apply to the postal organization over the first forty years of its existence under the Constitution are closely observed, it will be found that the term "Department" was not used to characterize it for many years after 1789. At the outset the Postmaster-General was, in the eyes of the law, an official in charge of the "Post-Office." At least as early as 1810 the postal organization was definitely termed the "Post-Office Establishment."[20] The phrase "Post-Office Department" may be found in the statute law of Monroe's administration.[21] Finally, in the matter of legal phraseology, attention may be called to the fact that the Post-Office department was not termed an "Executive Department" until the revision of the statutes in 1873. This last matter is worth a moment's attention.

Soon after the close of the Civil War, Congress had

[19] 1 *Statutes at Large,* pp. 178, 218, 232, 357. The references are to the acts of August 4, 1790; March 3, 1791; February 20, 1792; May 8, 1794.

[20] 2 *Statutes at Large,* p. 592. April 30, 1810.

[21] 4 *Statutes at Large,* p. 102. March 3, 1825. The appearance of the word "department" in the acts of March 2, 1799, and April 30, 1810, was merely incidental. *United States* vs. *Kendall* (1837) in 5 Cranch, *Reports of Cases . . . . in the United States Circuit Court of the District of Columbia* (1853), p. 275.

forced upon it the task of revising, consolidating, and amending the statutes relating to the Post-Office Department. Over a period of several years the subject was carefully considered until the law of June 8, 1872,—the most elaborate statute in the legal history of the organization—was enacted.[22] Curiously enough there was no reference in the entire act to the Department as being reckoned in terms "executive," although for years the Postmaster-General had been a member of the Cabinet. In the following year the first edition of the Revised Statutes was prepared. The edition was approved by President Grant on June 22, 1874. There the language was for the first time explicit: "There shall be at the seat of Government an Executive Department to be known as the Post-Office Department." It seems probable that the failure to characterize the Department as "Executive" in 1872 was a mere oversight. Certainly the Post-Office Department was an Executive Department by virtue of construction rather than express legislation before the law of 1874 actually termed it "Executive."[23]

Turning back to the early years of the postal organization, it is clear from the debates in 1791 that there was at that time some fear of the executive power acquiring an influence over the Post-Office. There was

---

[22] 17 *Statutes at Large*, p. 283. The debates which led up to the act may be found in the *Congressional Globe*, 42 Cong., 2 sess. (1871-1872), December 5, 1871-June 3, 1872, *passim*.

[23] Mr. Middleton Beaman, librarian of the Law Library of Congress ᴩⁿ   ⁿreme Court, has reassured me as to the soundness of this   ı. Private letter of April 1, 1909. Cf. 5 Cranch, *Reports*, ᴜₚ.   204, 210-211, 232, 233, 272-274, *passim*.

an impression that the organization, penetrating into all parts of the country, might somehow prove to be a dangerous political instrument if it should come under the control of ambitious and unscrupulous Presidents or Postmasters-General. "Through the medium of the post-office," remarked Representative Thomas Hartley of Pennsylvania, "a weighty influence may be obtained by the Executive; this is guarded against in England by prohibiting officers in the Post-Office Department from interfering in elections." On the same occasion Vining of Delaware expressed the hope that the President would be given no power in the business of establishing offices. To a good President, he argued, such power would be a burden. To an unscrupulous President, on the other hand, it would be dangerous "in those places only where his interests would be promoted." By removing offices of long standing, such a man might "harass those he might suppose inimical to his ambitious views."[24]

According to the original act of September 22, 1789, the Postmaster-General was "to be subject to the direction of the President of the United States in performing the duties of his office." This provision placed the officer from the outset within the range of executive control. But it should be observed that it implied that the President might determine various matters, about which the law was silent, in accordance with his own judgment. It was Jefferson's opinion that postal affairs would come under the general supervision of the Secretary of State, inasmuch as the

[24] *Annals of Congress,* 2 Cong., 1 sess. (1791-1793), December 6, 1791.

State Department was intended to include many matters of a domestic nature. President Washington, however, adopted a different view. "The post office (as a branch of the Revenue)," he wrote to Secretary Jefferson on October 20, 1792, "was annexed to the Treasury in the time of Mr. Osgood; & when Col° Pickering was appointed thereto, he was informed, as appears by my letter to him dated the 29 day of August, 1791, that he was to consider it in that light."[25] This explained why the first annual report of Postmaster-General Osgood was addressed in 1790 to Hamilton, Secretary of the Treasury.[26] But it should also be observed that the theory of the Post-Office as part of the revenue system was in accord with that of the English government, and was favored and acted upon by the American Congress.

As early as 1792 the law provided that the Postmaster-General should render a quarterly account to the Secretary of the Treasury.[27] The provision reappeared in the matured statute of 1794.[28] In 1797 the law prescribed an annual report from the Postmaster-General concerning certain post roads, such report to be rendered to Congress.[29] In 1799 that officer was explicitly required to report annually to Congress "every post road which shall not, after the second year from its establishment, have produced one third of the

[25] Gaillard Hunt, quoting from MS. sources in *American Journal of International Law* (January, 1909), III, 145-146.

[26] *Annals of Congress*, II, 2164.

[27] 1 *Statutes at Large*, p. 232.

[28] *Ibid.*, pp. 357 ff.

[29] *Ibid.*, p. 512.

expense of carrying the mail on the same.'"[30] The evidence of the law proved clearly that Congress regarded it as its duty to keep close watch of the postal organization as a factor in the revenue system of the government.

The practice of the Postmaster-General of making an annual report on the condition and needs of his Department to the President—a practice familiar enough to-day—originated in an apparently casual way under President Monroe. John Quincy Adams left this slight piece of evidence as a record of the origin of the practice. Commenting on Postmaster-General John McLean—the official whom he had reappointed at the beginning of his term in March, 1825, but who had served in the place under his predecessor, President Monroe—Adams wrote:

I desired him to make me a report upon the concerns of the Department, which has been usual yearly since he came into the Post Office [in 1823]. It had not heretofore been customary, but the practice was introduced within these few years by Mr. Monroe, and appears to be much approved.[31]

The practice, it would seem reasonable to conclude, indicated at the time of its origin an increasing perception on the part of Monroe of the desirability of a more intimate knowledge of administrative needs, as well perhaps as a purpose to strengthen his power of directing the administration of an official whose work was becoming daily of greater importance to the government. At any rate, from Monroe's day to this

[30] *Ibid.*, p. 741.
[31] *Memoirs of John Quincy Adams*, VII, 54. November 17, 1825.

the practice has been followed, and amounts to an established custom.

III

The four Postmasters-General who succeeded Samuel Osgood—reckoning from Osgood's retirement in August, 1791, to July, 1823,—were men of no very marked distinction, with the single exception of Timothy Pickering. As a rule they had had college educations, were lawyers by training, and had attained to some degree of political prominence in their various local communities or states before they were summoned to take charge of the national postal establishment. Gideon Granger of Connecticut assumed the office at the comparatively youthful age of thirty-four years, and held it continuously for upwards of twelve years, from November, 1801, to February 25, 1814. His son, Francis Granger of New York, served in the same office under President W. H. Harrison and for a few months under Harrison's successor, President Tyler. The choice by Monroe of John McLean in 1823 brought to the head of the establishment as sixth Postmaster-General a young man of large ability and of positive merits as an organizer. In fact, McLean was the first really remarkable figure in the history of the office since 1789.[32]

Although a native of New Jersey, where he was born in March, 1785, John McLean came to Washington from Ohio. There he had won a high reputation as a

[32] Mosher, *Executive Register*, pp. 10, 52, 58, 65, 78, 85, 90, 95, 123-124, 128, 132.

lawyer. In 1812, at the age of twenty-seven, he was
sent to Congress from Cincinnati. Later he was
elected a judge of the Ohio Supreme Court, a position
which he resigned for the sake of becoming Commissioner of the General Land Office in 1822. This latter
place as well as the Postmaster-Generalship he probably owed to his friendship for John C. Calhoun, Secretary of War in Monroe's Cabinet.[33] McLean acted
as Postmaster-General for nearly six years (1823-
1829), having been retained—like Southard and Wirt
—by President John Quincy Adams in 1825. When he
died in April, 1861, he had served for more than thirty
years as an Associate Justice of the United States
Supreme Court, a distinction conferred upon him by
President Jackson in March, 1829. A consistent oppo-
nent to the extension of slavery, he made himself particularly well known to men of anti-slavery views by
the circumstance of his opinion in the Dred Scott case
in 1857, when he dissented along with his colleague,
Justice Benjamin R. Curtis, from the decision rendered at that time by Chief-Justice Taney. On the eve
of President Adams's administration he had been suggested as fitted for a cabinet position.[34] And, though
he was acting on the Supreme Court bench, President
Tyler, in September, 1841, nominated him as Secretary of War. The Senate confirmed the nomination
without delay; and he was actually commissioned to
the office. But he declined the appointment.[35] He was

---

[33] Adams's *Memoirs,* VII, 364. November 30, 1827.
[34] *Ibid.,* VI, 506, 516. February 11, March 2, 1825.
[35] Mosher, p. 131.

not merely among the list of men "mentioned" for the Presidency many times between 1830 and 1860. The Anti-Masonic party in 1830 intended to nominate Judge McLean as their candidate for the office of President, but were obliged finally to agree upon William Wirt. In 1835 the Ohio Legislature named McLean for President. In the Whig convention of 1848 he received two votes for President on the first ballot. Again in 1856 he was considered as an eligible candidate by the American party. Finally, his name appeared on the first three ballots taken at the Chicago convention—the Republican gathering which distinguished itself by nominating on the fourth ballot Abraham Lincoln. By that time he was, of course, too old a man to be considered seriously for the burdensome position of President, for he had passed his seventy-fifth birthday in the previous month of March.[36]

McLean's years spent in Washington at the head of the postal administration were full of activity and accomplishment. He impressed the contemporaries of that epoch in his career—notably John Quincy Adams and Edward Everett—as a man of force and

[36] Besides authorities already cited in this paragraph, I have depended on E. Stanwood, *History of the Presidency* (1898), pp. 156, 183, 230, 236, 264, 270, 289, 294; J. B. Thayer, *Cases on Constitutional Law*, I, 492 ff.; W. B. Sprague, *A Discourse delivered Sunday Morning, April 7, 1861, in the Second Presbyterian Church, Albany, in commemoration of the late Hon. John McLean, LL. D.* (Albany: 1861); D. W. Clark, *The Problem of Life;* a funeral discourse on the occasion of the death of Hon. John McLean, LL. D. . . . . Preached in Wesley Chapel, Cincinnati, at the joint request of the Pastor and the family of the Deceased, April 28, 1861 (Cincinnati: 1861); Appleton, *Cyclopaedia of American Biography,* IV, 144.

ability. From the outset, whatever the rank of his office might be—and he rated it low, as we have seen— he was considered as the social if not the intellectual equal of such men as Calhoun, Wirt, and others high up in administrative circles. Shortly before his inauguration as President, Secretary of State Adams and his wife dined at McLean's house in Georgetown.[37] And later, President Adams was on terms of familiar intimacy with his Postmaster-General, consulting him on many matters which concerned the postal service.

Adams's *Memoirs* are particularly enlightening on the more general features of McLean's work as Post-master-General. "Mr. McLean has greatly improved the condition of the Post-Office Department," commented the President on October 23, 1827, ". . . . and is perhaps the most efficient officer that has ever been in that place. But it is a place of more patronage and personal influence than those of all the other heads of Departments put together."[38] About a month later Adams remarked: "This officer, who came into that place in 1823, has given great satisfaction in the administration of it. For three or four years before, it had been a burden upon the Treasury, requiring annual appropriations of nearly a hundred thousand dollars a year. Its condition since then has been constantly improving, and this year the receipts exceed the expenditures more than a hundred thousand dollars."[39]

[37] *Memoirs*, VI, 373, 451, 479, 488, 495.
[38] *Ibid.*, VII, 343.
[39] *Ibid.*, VII, 363-364. November 30. The figures in McLean's Report of 1827 were $100,312. *Senate Documents*, 20 Cong., 1 sess.

McLean's administration of postal affairs was orderly and economical. His first annual reports which, as we have seen, he was induced to make by President Monroe, were brief. As a rule, however, they revealed improving conditions in the finances of the establishment, notwithstanding conspicuous increases in the number of post-offices and the mileage of post roads, as well as a large and steadily growing corps of employees which numbered in 1829 nearly thirty thousand.[40] By the close of McLean's term the country could reckon nearly eight thousand post-offices, although there had been but seventy-five in 1789. In 1827, as evidence on the part of Congress of appreciation of the increasing burdens of the position, McLean's salary was advanced from four to six thousand dollars.[41] The Postmaster-General was thus placed in this respect on an equality with the four Secretaries in the Cabinet.

The friendly relations existing between President Adams and his able Postmaster-General at the outset of the administration were not destined to last through the four-year term. As time elapsed, Adams became suspicious of McLean. He was clearly disturbed lest McLean, a friend of Calhoun and Andrew Jackson, might be induced to use his position and influence

(1827-1829), I, 259. From 1789 to 1834 there were only eleven years in which the Post-Office Department did not turn in some surplus to the Treasury. W. L. Wilson, ''The American Post-Office,'' p. 259 in *The Ship of State*, by Those at the Helm (Boston: 1903).

[40] McLean's Report of 1828 gives 26,956 persons. *Senate Documents, 20 Cong., 2 sess.*, I, 180.

[41] 4 *Statutes at Large*, p. 239. See Appendix A to this volume, p. 396.

against the real welfare of the administration that he was serving. Clay, Secretary of State and distinctly the leading member of the Cabinet, was also suspicious of McLean, and revealed to the President in the spring of 1825 his bitter feeling against him.[42] It was a time of small factions and disintegration of parties—a transition epoch in politics. But Adams was not the man to act hastily, or to allow mere impressions to get the better of his judgment of McLean. Only toward the close of his Presidency do his *Memoirs* show deep-seated bitterness and contempt for what he was wont to call McLean's "duplicity."

There had been some disagreements between Adams and McLean about certain Post-Office appointments and other business relating to the postal administration when, in the spring of 1828, the President was contemplating McLean's dismissal from office. Even then Adams felt obliged to admit that he could fix upon no positive act on McLean's part that would really justify dismissal. Clay was certainly eager to get rid of McLean, and probably influenced his cabinet associates as well as Adams by his hostile feelings, for the Cabinet was occasionally inclined to minimize McLean's claims to ability and accomplishment. There is not enough evidence on the basis of which to determine the whole ground of President Adams's later impression of McLean. He suspected him of intrigue and partisanship—it was neither necessary to prove it, nor perhaps possible to do so. The suspicion was enough to inter-

[42] Adams's *Memoirs*, VI, 539. April 30, 1825.

fere with friendly relations, even though it did not lead to an actual dismissal.[43]

McLean held decided views as to the general functions of the Cabinet. Moreover, being a man of spirit, he was not likely to keep himself in strict subordination to a Cabinet which contained hostile elements which he could not quite respect. Recently it has become possible to state McLean's views, for they were set forth by the Postmaster-General in a confidential correspondence with Edward Everett on the subject of patronage in elections—a correspondence first communicated to the Massachusetts Historical Society in February, 1908.[44]

In the course of a letter to Everett of August 27, 1828, McLean wrote:

A wide distinction exists between the members of the Cabinet, and other officers of the government. There must be unity in this part of the executive. The members of the Cabinet are the sustainers of the President, and as questions are often, if not generally, decided by concurrence of the majority of them, it becomes the decision of the Cabinet, and each member is bound to support it. This is the condition on which the office is accepted. But, as other officers of the government are not consulted, and can have no influence in the policy of the Cabinet, the same obligation is not imposed on them.

Referring directly to himself, McLean said: ''I would scorn to hold any office, as a creature of any administration. The Cabinet shall never think and decide for me, unless I am a member of it.''[45]

[43] *Memoirs*, VI, 539. VII, 275, 343, 349, 355, 363-364, 544. VIII, 51.
[44] *Proceedings*, 3d series. I, 359-393.
[45] *Ibid.*, I, 387.

McLean sounded an unmistakable note of defiance in these utterances. He was evidently on the defensive. But, viewed from another standpoint, his words lead one straight to the thought that he had at least considered the question of his right, or rather his claims, to a place in the Cabinet. There, at any rate, he could have better defended himself against slurring insinuations, or the direct criticism which his colleagues in the administrative work of the government might make against him. Although many circumstances had helped to develop the office of Postmaster-General from 1789 to 1828, McLean, we may be sure, could claim to have done much to raise the office near to the rank of the Secretaryships. The subject of appointments was necessarily often before the Cabinet. Regarding appointments the Postmaster-General had often to be consulted outside the Cabinet. Why should not that official be given a place in the select group of the President's special advisers?

There is but one clear instance, so far as I have yet been able to discover, of a Postmaster-General being invited into a cabinet council before this time. The instance was recorded by John Quincy Adams as occurring on January 5, 1822, when Postmaster-General R. J. Meigs, Jr., was summoned into a meeting of the Cabinet at President Monroe's, while an appointment—that of General Van Rensselaer to the Albany, N. Y., post-office—was under consideration.[46] While no doubt exceptional, it seems unlikely that this instance can be unique. Moreover, it may well be

[46] *Memoirs,* V, 480 ff.

doubted whether McLean himself would have sub-
scribed his signature to the confidential statement
made to Everett—that "other officers of the government are not consulted, and can have no influence in
the policy of the Cabinet"—had his words been
intended for publication. He probably knew better.

IV

In the latter part of February, 1829, the list of Jackson's proposed cabinet advisers became known. On
February 23 Webster spoke of the "prodigious excite-
ment . . . . produced by the new Cabinet List." He did
not give the list, but he remarked that it "has set all
Washington in a *buz*—friends rage, & *foes laugh.*"[47]
Two days later, without one word of comment, John
Quincy Adams recorded the list in his Diary. McLean
was named third on the list as Postmaster-General,
following Van Buren as Secretary of State, and
Ingham as Secretary of the Treasury.[48] On February
26 the same list appeared in the Washington *Telegraph,* a paper looked upon as the official organ of the
new administration, and was copied widely. The
announcement was of course a very interesting news
item, but it was at once criticised as an act of dis-
courtesy to the Senate, which must ratify the names
before they could become appointments. The real
innovation—and as such, quite worth comment—was
the inclusion of the office of Postmaster-General in the
Cabinet.

[47] *Letters of Daniel Webster* (ed. C. H. Van Tyne), pp. 141-142.
[48] *Memoirs,* VIII, 99.

John McLean was never nominated by Jackson to the Senate as Postmaster-General; but he served in that capacity—probably at Jackson's ·request—from March 4 to March 9, 1829. The duties of that office fell to William T. Barry of Kentucky. Barry as Post-master-General became a cabinet associate just as McLean was first intended to be. Something had occurred between February 26 and March 7 to induce Jackson to alter his original plan, for on the latter day McLean was appointed as an Associate Justice of the Federal Supreme Court.[49]

In the absence of direct evidence from Jackson or McLean on the nature of what occurred, late in February or early in March, to change the original plan, we are obliged to depend upon at least three records left by three men, all of whom were in Washington at the time. The three men were ex-President John Quincy Adams; Amos Kendall, an editor, politician, and friend of Jackson who served as Barry's successor at the head of postal affairs; and Nathan Sargent, also an editor and newspaper correspondent who was employed during the latter part of his life in certain subordinate positions in the government service. As historic evidence these records are by no means of equal value, as the reader can easily determine.

1. Under date of March 6, 1829, Adams stated that he had heard from Southard, former Secretary of the Navy in his Cabinet, that McLean "was nominated a Judge of the Supreme Court . . . . a totally new arrangement, made within the last two days—and

[49] Mosher, *Executive Register,* p. 108.

Mr. Barry of Kentucky, Postmaster-General.'' Four days later, on March 10, Adams wrote that McLean ''declined serving as the broom to sweep the post-offices.''[50]

2. The evidence of Amos Kendall was much more circumstantial, and read as follows:

I was not consulted, and did not seek to know, the reasons which controlled the selection of the new Cabinet Ministers. In only one instance was I in any way made acquainted with those reasons. John McLean . . . . was a political friend of General Jackson who gave him the option of remaining at the head of the Post-Office Department, or accepting a seat on the bench of the Supreme Court then vacant. He decided to remain in the Department, but was soon induced to change his mind by the management of Duff Green. Green was extremely proscriptive and many postmasters were very obnoxious to him, some of them deservedly so. He presented certain cases to Mr. McLean and asked whether he would remove them, and was answered in the negative. He presented the same cases to General Jackson, inquiring whether they ought not to be removed, and was answered in the affirmative. Mr. McLean was an aspirant to the Presidency, and very popular with the postmasters; and when he found that he should probably not be able to protect them from removal without losing the favor of the President and his friends, he changed his mind and signified that upon reflection he preferred the judgeship.[51]

3. Sargent's record was remarkably elaborate. While in essential accord with the evidence of both Adams and Kendall, it introduced several new ideas.

[50] *Memoirs*, VIII, 99, 109-110.

[51] *Autobiography of Amos Kendall*, ed. by his son-in-law, William Stickney (1872), pp. 304-305.

"What I am about to relate," wrote Sargent, "in regard to Judge McLean's appointment was stated by General Cass, at General Porter's in my presence, on the evening after the conversation between General Jackson and Judge McLean . . . . occurred, and which, he said he had just had repeated to him by the latter gentleman, with whom we knew he was on very intimate terms. Mr. McLean had been Postmaster-General about six years . . . . and was understood, as he was 'a Jackson man,' to be an aspirant for the position of Secretary of War. But, as General Jackson had determined to put Major Eaton at the head of that department, Mr. McLean's wishes could not be gratified. But the General proposed that if he should remain where he was, the salary of the office should be raised, and it should be made a cabinet office. With this Mr. McLean was content, and the new arrangement was soon publicly understood. It was known, however, that General Jackson would adopt the policy indicated by the *Telegraph* in the preceding November : viz., that of '*rewarding his friends and punishing his enemies.*' As Mr. McLean had always refused to make appointments and removals upon the ground of party affinities, and had strongly condemned such a practice, the inquiry was naturally made, 'If General Jackson adopts this policy, what will Mr. McLean do? Will he carry it out or refuse?'"

At this point of the narrative Sargent proceeds to tell of the happenings as follows :

The question was so often put, and so emphatically answered by his nearest friends in the negative, that the General deemed it proper to come to an understanding with, and sent for, Mr. McLean, to whom he stated that he should adopt the policy of removing from such offices such persons as had, during the canvass for President, taken an active part in politics, and asked whether he had any objection to this line of action. To this Mr. McLean replied in the negative, "but," said he, "if this rule should be adopted, it will operate as well against your friends as those of Mr. Adams, as it must be impartially executed." To this General Jackson made no reply; but after walking up and down the room several times, as if cogitating with himself, he said, "Mr. McLean, will you accept a seat upon the bench of the Supreme Court?" This was answered in the affirmative; and he was in due time nominated, as we, who had had the story related to us, expected.[52]

Adams's brief statement that McLean declined to serve as "the broom to sweep the post-offices" would seem to contain the important truth. With McLean perfectly clear regarding the need of unity in the Cabinet, it is inconceivable that he should have accepted a place among Jackson's regular advisers under circumstances almost certain to compromise him. His principles would never have permitted him to countenance the dictation of an outsider such as Duff Green, editor of the *Telegraph*. There was no reasonable basis for Sargent's belief that the question of salary had anything to do with McLean's accepting or refusing the Postmaster-Generalship. The office was already paid as well as any of the Secretaryships. On the other hand, Sargent's view that McLean would

[52] *Public Men and Events* from the Commencement of Mr. Monroe's Administration, in 1817, to the Close of Mr. Fillmore's . . . . in 1853 (Philadelphia: 1875), I, 165-166.

be content with a cabinet place is interesting and plausible, for it is in accord with the unmistakable impression which McLean had already conveyed confidentially to Everett in his letter of the previous summer. It is indeed possible that McLean himself may have suggested to Jackson the importance as well as the desirability of giving a place in the Cabinet to the Postmaster-General. There is, however, no evidence on the point. We may be certain of this: that so soon as McLean was convinced that Jackson had determined to use the postal organization for personal and partisan purposes, he knew that he could accept no place within Jackson's formal circle of reputable advisers, for he had indicated to Everett, and presumably to other friends, that he had clear ideals about the uses of political patronage. The Associate Justiceship afforded him an honorable and, doubtless, a desirable way out of the dilemma.

V

In introducing the Postmaster-General into the circle of the Cabinet for the first time, President Jackson inaugurated a practice that has become a settled custom. There were, no doubt, reasons personal to Jackson for acting as he did in the matter. And these personal reasons have been dwelt upon by every writer who has attempted to study the epoch. On the other hand, far too little attention has hitherto been given to certain features in the situation which tended in the long run—if not in Jackson's eyes—to justify the practice. The postal organization in 1829 had reached a stage in its development when it may have seemed to the chief magistrate to demand closer relations between him and its administrative head, the Post-master-General. It looked very much as though President Monroe, late in his second term, had come to some such conclusion when he asked for an annual report from Postmaster-General McLean. Again, the fact that the significance of postal development—itself the result of complex and very far-reaching processes— was brought clearly before his contemporaries by McLean, revealed McLean as a man of marked admin-istrative ability and judgment whom Jackson could hardly afford to overlook. Already the burdens and responsibility of the office had assumed such import-ance in the eyes of Congress that that somewhat inert body had been willing to place it on a footing of equality with the Secretaryships in respect to salary. In future the salary alone would be enough to attract rather a better type of man to it.

There were, of course, dangers in introducing the Postmaster-General into the Cabinet, if it were assumed that the officer could become in that way the mere puppet of an unscrupulous President bent upon manipulating every appointment within his range to his personal ends. No doubt these dangers were to some extent realized under Jackson. And there was occasional criticism directed to exactly this aspect of the matter.[53] But, after all, the presence of the Post-master-General in the Cabinet, or his absence from it,

[53] Pliny Miles, *Postal Reform:* Its urgent Necessity and Practicability (1855), p. 103.

could hardly restrain an unscrupulous President from questionable methods of influence over appointments within the postal organization. In any case, the power of that influence was bound to be to some degree in the President's hands. In introducing the Postmaster-General into the Cabinet, Jackson began a practice that probably tended, in the long run, to invigorate the workings of the postal establishment, notwithstanding the fact that Barry, successor to McLean in the office, made a conspicuously dismal record.[54]

By a curious coincidence in the following year— late in the autumn of 1830—an English Postmaster-General, the fifth Duke of Richmond, was for the first time in the history of the English office given a seat in the Cabinet. The Duke of Richmond thus served in the ministry of Lord Grey until the spring of 1834.[55] Since the opening of Queen Victoria's reign in 1837 the English office has been regarded as political, usually changing its occupant with every change of ministry.[56] The English Postmaster-General has often been reckoned a member of the Cabinet since that time, although it was not until 1866 that he could be a member of the House of Commons. Among the more notable occupants of the office, who have been members of English Cabinets, may be named: the Marquis of Clanricarde (1846-1852); the Duke of Argyll (1856-

[54] *Messages and Papers*, III, 116-117. *Senate Documents*, 23 Cong., 1 sess. (1833-1835), I, 41-47. *Ibid.*, 23 Cong., 2 sess., I, 40-45. Kendall, *Autobiography*, p. 331. Webster, *Works* (ed. 1851), IV, 148 ff.

[55] Based upon an examination of lists of the ministries which appeared year by year in the *Royal Kalendars* from 1808. See Greville, *Memoirs* (ed. Henry Reeve, 1875), II, 66-68. III, 88.

[56] Lowell, *Government of England*, I, 113.

1859); the Earl of Elgin (1860); Lord Stanley of
Alderley (1861-1865); Lord Hartington (1869-1872);
and the Right Honorable Lord John J. R. Manners
(1875-1880). The English Postmaster-General has
held a seat in nearly every Cabinet since 1892.

There can be no doubt that, in both the English and
the American governments, the office of Postmaster-
General has been regarded for the better part of a
century as worthy of high political distinction. Moreover, in each country that distinction would seem to be
largely due to a recognition of the immense importance
to the people of a well-administered postal organization.

CHAPTER X

THE Secretaryship of the Interior established in
1849[1] is the last of the principal administrative
offices which went back for its inception to the notable
decade of 1780-1790, the epoch during which the Constitution was drawn up and ratified. The particular
circumstance which forced the need of its establishment on Congress was the enormous burden of work
that rested on the shoulders of the Secretary of the
Treasury. This burden was partly due to the war with
Mexico which involved such resulting acquisitions of
territory by the United States as New Mexico and
California. It was increased by the addition of the
Oregon country, which came to us in 1846 by treaty.

Although the ideal which the statute of 1849 made
effective was considerably older, the statute itself was
the indirect result of suggestions on the part of Presidents, statesmen, and others familiar with administrative needs, which had been expressed from time to time
since the days of Madison's Presidency.

I

When Pelatiah Webster printed his remarkable
pamphlet in 1783 entitled *A Dissertation on the Political Union and Constitution of the Thirteen United*

[1] 9 *Statutes at Large,* pp. 395 ff. March 3, 1849.

States of North-America, he then proposed in his scheme of government that there should be a "Secretary of State," an official who, as he phrased his thought, "takes knowledge of the general *policy* and *internal* government. . . . . I mention a *Secretary of State,*" he added, "because all other nations have one . . . . the multiplicity of affairs which naturally fall into his office will grow so fast, that I imagine we shall soon be under necessity of appointing one."[2]   Four years later, in his project of a Council of State presented to the Philadelphia Convention, Gouverneur Morris arranged for a Secretary of Domestic Affairs whose business it should be to "attend to matters of general policy, the state of agriculture and manufactures, the opening of roads and navigations and the facilitating communications through the United States."[3]   Likewise, in his plan of government for France drawn up a few years after 1787, Morris made provision for a "Minister of the Interior."[4]

In fact, the conception of some such administrative official, however crudely or variously expressed, was perfectly familiar to the epoch.   Charles Pinckney's *Observations* contained references to a Home Department.   Pinckney expressed himself as convinced of "the necessity which exists at present, and which must every day increase, of appointing a Secretary for the Home Department."   Apparently he meant that such an officer should be made a member of the Cabinet

[2] *Essays,* pp. 213-214.   The pamphlet was first printed at Philadelphia and published on February 16, 1783.

[3] Elliot, *Debates,* V, 446.

[4] Sparks, *Life of Gouverneur Morris,* III, 481 ff.

Council.[5] In the autumn of 1788 Madison was popularly considered as the right sort of man to be placed in charge of a Home Department under the Constitution, should Congress decide to provide for such an organization.[6] In the early summer of 1789, during the course of the debates on the proper number and arrangement of departments, Representative John Vining of Delaware was the leading figure to propose and urge the establishment of a "Domestic" department.[7]

While Congress was not inclined to establish an independent Home Department, it could not escape altogether the force of sentiment and the arguments in favor of the suggested department. Accordingly it provided a combination of the duties of a Home Department with those of Foreign Affairs. In other words it substituted a Department and Secretary of State in place of its first intention, a Department and Secretary of Foreign Affairs.

In the winter of 1789-1790, while Jefferson was hesitating about accepting the appointment as Secretary of State, he gave as one reason for hesitation his objection to having domestic as well as foreign business to attend to. Jefferson confided the first hint of his objection to his friend, William Short, in a letter of December 14, 1789.[8] The next day Jefferson put his thought

[5] Charles Pinckney, *Observations on the Plan of Government submitted to the Federal Convention,* pp. 10-11.

[6] D. Humphreys to Jefferson, writing from Mount Vernon, November 29, 1788, in Bancroft, *History of the Formation of the Constitution,* II, 485.

[7] *Annals of Congress,* I, 385-386, 412, 692-695, *passim.*

[8] Jefferson, *Writings* (ed. Ford), V, 139.

in these words addressed to President Washington: "But when I contemplate the extent of that office, embracing as it does the principal mass of domestic administration, together with the foreign, I cannot be insensible to my inequality to it."[9] On the following January 4, Madison, who had recently seen Jefferson at Monticello, made Jefferson's objection quite clear to Washington. "I was sorry to find him," wrote Madison, "so little biassed in favor of the domestic service allotted to him, but was glad that his difficulties seemed to result chiefly from what I take to be an erroneous view of the kind and quantity of business annexed to . . . . the foreign department. He apprehends," added Madison, "that it will far exceed the latter which has of itself no terrors to him."[10]

The theoretical stage of the problem was concluded when Jefferson took office in March, 1790, and began to administer the business of the Department of State. Within a few months of that time he sent to his colleague, Secretary Hamilton, an estimate of department expenses, reckoning them from April, 1790, for one year. It should be observed that Jefferson divided the expenses on the basis of the "Home Office" ($1836) and the "Foreign Office" ($2625). The figures are enough to indicate that the domestic functions of the Secretary of State were almost certain to be extensive.[11] Moreover the next twenty years were to deter-

[9] *Writings*, V, 140.

[10] H. S. Randall, *Life of Thomas Jefferson* (1858), I, 557, note 1.

[11] Gaillard Hunt in *American Journal of International Law* (January, 1909), III, 148. Washington placed the Mint under Jefferson's charge. *Ibid.*, p. 145.

mine unmistakably that the Secretary of State was to be overburdened with his manifold duties. In fact, by the spring of 1812, all the administrative departments were so pressed with work that President Madison addressed a special message to both House and Senate on the subject.[12]

II

Madison's brief word written in the face of impending war sounded a note of warning that could not easily be overlooked. Some minor changes, it is true, had already been accomplished, revealing the fact that Congress had not been quite heedless of the need of reforms and alterations in the departmental organizations.[13] But these changes were not fundamental enough to afford relief. On June 12, exactly six days before the formal declaration of war with England, we come upon the first clear recommendation of a Home Department arising from a congressional source after 1789.

Near the beginning of a report read to the House of Representatives on that day—a report chiefly concerned with conditions that had prevailed for many years in the Patent Office as a subordinate division in the State Department—there occurred this definite suggestion: "Your committee, without entering into any detailed reasoning on the subject, offer for the con-

[12] *Messages and Papers*, I, 499. April 20.
[13] *Annals of Congress*, 10 Cong., 2 sess. (1808-1809), pp. 347 ff., 352, 387-388, 437, 443, 450-452, 461, 1546, 1549, 1553, 1559-1560, 1575, 1833-1835 (text of act).

sideration of the Legislature the propriety and necessity of authorizing a *Home Department,* distinct from
the departments already established by law.   Such
departments,'' continued the record, ''are known to
other Governments, and their benefits have been recognized in territories far less extensive than those of the
United States.''[14]   This came from a committee of
which Adam Seybert of Pennsylvania was chairman
which had been appointed to examine into the organization and workings of the Patent Establishment.[15]   On
May 25 Seybert had addressed a letter to Monroe, the
Secretary of State, asking for his observations on the
subject, saying at the same time that the occasion
might afford Monroe an opportunity to outline a plan
for separating the Patent Establishment from the
State Department.[16]   Monroe was harassed with work.
However, he gave the matter some attention, and
answered Seybert's letter on June 10.   In general
Monroe was opposed to all inferior independent
departments.   The Patent Office, he thought, might as
well remain in charge of the State Department.   He
admitted, however, that foreign affairs constituted in
themselves a sufficient trust for the person at the head
of the Department of State.   ''They are,'' he reflected,
''very extensive, complicated and important, and are
becoming more so daily.''[17]

There was an ominous tone in Monroe's reply which

[14] *Annals of Congress,* 12 Cong. 1 sess. (1811-1813), Pt. II, p. 2179.
[15] *Ibid.,* p. 1435.
[16] *Ibid.,* pp. 2190 ff.
[17] *Ibid.,* p. 2192.

could not have escaped attentive ears. At any rate Seybert's committee felt free to broach the subject of a new department to the House, declaring that foreign relations were essentially distinct "from many objects in the interior of our country." The report was printed. But no action was taken on its special suggestion of a Home Department, for the country was soon experiencing the stress and strain of war.

By 1815 serious weaknesses extending down from the principal offices through all the national administrative organizations had become more real and were more evident than ever. Arrangements within the War Department were most unsatisfactory. Within this department Indian affairs had proved to be peculiarly troublesome. On March 2, 1815, the Senate passed a resolution requesting President Madison to instruct the Secretary of War to make a report on Indian affairs chiefly for the purpose, it would seem, of obtaining a sound basis of information on which to reorganize that subordinate branch of administration. There was already some disposition to place Indian affairs in a department quite by themselves.[18]

At the moment the headship of the War Department was in a state of transition, consequently more than a year elapsed before the Senate's request was answered. Then came a report on Indian affairs from Secretary William H. Crawford; it was dated March 13, 1816, and was communicated to the Senate on the following day. It was a long and well-considered document. From

[18] *Ibid.*, 13 Cong., 3 sess. (1814-1815), III, 287-288.

certain casual statements one gathers a clear impression that Crawford was aware of the burdens to which most of the Secretaries in the separate departments had long been subjected. He merely hinted at "the creation of a separate and independent department" without giving any details of a plan. But he was sure that if a new department were established "much of the miscellaneous duties now belonging to the Department of State, ought to be transferred to it."[19]

Rather more than a month later—on April 20—Macon of North Carolina presented to the Senate a resolution. This was passed and yielded unforeseen results. The resolution follows:

Resolved, That the Secretaries of the Departments be directed to report jointly to the Senate, in the first week of the next session of Congress, a plan to insure the annual settlement of the public accounts, and a more certain accountability of the public expenditure, in their respective departments.[20]

The peculiar merit of the resolution was that it brought the principal officers together on the subject of the general organization of administrative work. By the following December these officers, in consultation with the President, had formulated a careful report. This report, after reviewing the principles on which the several departments were organized, dwelling with marked stress on the burdens of the Secretary of War, and commenting on the notable incongruity in having Indian affairs managed in connection with the

[19] *American State Papers, Indian Affairs,* II, 26-88.
[20] *Annals of Congress,* 14 Cong., 1 sess. (1815-1816), pp. 331-332.

military establishment, proceeded to outline on the grounds of actual experience the first clear plan for a Home Department in our history. This was the plan which lay behind the recommendation of Madison made in his last annual message of December 3, 1816, where he remarked on "the expediency.... of an additional department in the executive branch of the Government .... to be charged with duties now overburdening other departments and with such as have not been annexed to any department."[21]

Although the inspiration for it may have come in part from the Senate resolution, this first plan for a Home Department signed by all the principal officers except Attorney-General Rush may be truly termed a cabinet measure. It provided for a Secretary whose duty it should be to execute the orders of the President in so far as they concerned the following five administrative divisions: (1) Territorial Governments; (2) National Highways and Canals; (3) General Post-Office; (4) Patent Office; and (5) Indian Department. The plan was communicated to the Senate by Madison on December 9.

Meantime steps had been taken in both the Senate and the House to consider that portion of the message which related to the possible establishment of an additional executive department. William Lowndes of South Carolina, chairman of the committee of seven in

[21] *Messages and Papers,* I, 577; *Annals of Congress,* 14 Cong., 2 sess. (1816-1817), pp. 23-30. The report appeared in the *National Intelligencer* of Saturday, December 21, 1816, and in Niles's *Register* of that date.

the House chosen to consider the subject, addressed a letter to the Secretaries on December 22, asking among other questions whether the accountability of public officers might not be sufficiently served without a new executive department.[22] The Secretaries answered the letter carefully on December 31. Their conclusion in response to Lowndes's particular query was this : "We have no doubt that the just principles of accountability would be better preserved, and economy promoted, by the adoption of that measure. Equally satisfied are we," they added, "that other essential advantages would result from it."[23]

On January 6, 1817, a bill for the purpose of establishing a Home Department was reported to the Senate by Senator Nathan Sanford of New York. The bill was similar in most respects to the "cabinet plan"; but it introduced the "District of Columbia" as a division of administration in the new department and omitted the division of "National Highways and Canals." Among minor readjustments it placed the Mint under the supervision of the Secretary of the Treasury. It ran a brief course in the Senate. On January 29, by a vote of twenty-three to eleven, the Senate refused to listen to a third reading. Two Senators of distinction opposed the measure, Rufus King of New York and Nathaniel Macon of North Carolina, the latter a member of the special Senate committee which had introduced the bill. King recalled the discussions of 1789 on a similar project, dwelling at length upon the oppo-

[22] *Annals*, 14 Cong., 2 sess., pp. 697-698.
[23] *Ibid.*, p. 699.

sition at that time. He admitted that times had
changed, yet he failed, he said, to find much reason
for multiplying departments or for having—as he
expressed it—two Departments of State. A new
department implied that the Secretary "would have a
place in the Cabinet, and be one of the President's
counsellors." The bill reached the House on January
20. The next day Lowndes read his correspondence
with the Secretaries. Although the reply of the Secretaries of December 31 was judicious, it could hardly
have helped the progress of the bill, for it was in no
way compelling or conclusive of the need of a new
department.[24]

The failure to establish a Home Department in 1817
calls for a brief comment. President, Secretaries,
certain Senators and Representatives, and doubtless
many of the more thoughtful citizens at all well
informed about government administration were inclined to favor the measure, yet when the measure
came to the point of actual construction and enactment, it was halted and in the end cast out. To the
reader of congressional and newspaper evidence covering the years 1816-1817, two questions will be frequently suggested. It is impossible, moreover, to
escape the belief that both questions were occasionally
before the minds of men living in those days.
(1) Could a Home Department be organized and
administered with a view to economy? (2) Would its
creation be a constitutional measure?

[24] *Ibid.*, pp. 18-19, 23-30, 33, 47, 52, 59, 60, 70, 74-75, 88, 234-235,
697-699.

It should be remembered that the plan of a Home Department, while enforced by the growing burdens of administration—some of these burdens doubtless the direct result of the war, and others of much longer standing—originated in an effort to bring all the existing departments into clear accountability for their expenditures. Without more definite principles of accountability than had hitherto existed, any additional department would tend not only to increase the financial burdens of the government but to render the solution of the basic problem more difficult. From the standpoint of improved administration a Home Department would seem to have been amply justified by 1817. From the standpoint of national economy—a subject of special moment for the next decade—it was a measure of doubtful consequences and might, in view of other needs, be indefinitely postponed.

There was doubt about the constitutionality of a Home Department. This was plainly revealed by an anonymous writer in the *National Intelligencer* who printed his reflections on the organization of executive departments on February 20 and 22, 1817.[25] Among other things this writer proposed to obtain a ''general enactment for the construction of the departments''

[25] The writer, whoever he was, showed some ingenuity. He favored four principal departments: (1) Revenue; (2) Domestic Affairs; (3) Foreign Affairs; (4) War. ''Domestic Affairs,'' he wrote, ''naturally claim attention anterior to foreign affairs.'' The War Department he divided into two divisions—army and navy. The heads or ''conductors'' of these two divisions were to constitute a ''Board of War.'' Domestic affairs he placed in five divisions, including Indian Affairs, the Post-Office, the Land-Office, the Patent Office, and the Mint. Were these articles written by Judge A. B. Woodward?

in the shape of an amendment to the Constitution. Belief in the absence of constitutional power undoubtedly made certain minds in 1817 peculiarly sensitive to and critical of what Jackson characterized many years later as the "supposed tendency to increase .... the .... bias of the federal system toward the exercise of authority not delegated to it."[26]

In this connection it should be noted that the project of a Home Department was inevitably entangled with that series of speculations which marked the entire movement for internal improvements—a movement which had its sources in the fundamental question of the proper disposition of the nation's money. There was apprehension lest the establishment of a Home Department would be used as an argument for enlarging the sphere of domestic legislation by the general government.

III

In 1824 new light is shed upon the path of the investigator bent upon accounting for the establishment of the Department of the Interior in 1849. Clay could declare in 1824 with conviction that "a new world has come into being since the Constitution was adopted."[27] Already, three years before this utterance in the House of Representatives, John Quincy Adams, forced by what he characterized as "the increase of the inquisitive spirit in Congress" to make investigations into

[26] December 8, 1829. *Messages and Papers*, II, 461-462.
[27] January 30, 1824.

his own department, recorded these comparisons and contrasts:

The foreign correspondence . . . . remained much the same now as it was in 1800. . . . . But the interior correspondence then was with sixteen States; it is now with twenty-four. It was then with a population of less than five, and now of more than nine millions. . . . . At that time there were in Congress about one hundred and thirty members; there are now upwards of two hundred and thirty. Then two or three octavo and one folio volume constituted all the documents printed at a session. Now there are from fifteen to twenty volumes published every year. There are assuredly five calls from Congress for information and documents from the Departments for one that there was then. Every call requires a report.[28]

It was clear from these facts that the Secretary of State, unless he were robust and capable, might find his post burdensome in the extreme.

There appeared in the *National Journal* of 1824—a paper of that day recently established in Washington and edited by Peter Force—various articles written by Judge Augustus B. Woodward. The first of these articles that concerns this inquiry was entitled "On the Necessity and Importance of a Department of Domestic Affairs, in the Government of the United States." Appearing on April 24, it was followed at irregular intervals by others which touched upon the subject of administrative organization or gave detailed consideration to different historical aspects of the Presidency. Judge Woodward had been a student of the American executive for years. Whatever he wrote

[28] *Memoirs of J. Q. Adams,* V, 239-240. January 19, 1821.

on his favorite theme was likely to be read by statesmen and other careful observers of public affairs. On
friendly terms with John Quincy Adams, he is occasionally mentioned in Adams's *Memoirs*. Under date
of July 24, 1824, Adams wrote of Woodward's articles
on the Presidency which were then appearing with
some regularity. ''They are,'' remarked Adams,
''speculative and historical, referring to past events,
but bearing so much upon those of the present time
that I told him he was treading close upon warm
ashes.''[29]

Elaboration was the most notable feature of Judge
Woodward's plan for a Department of Domestic
Affairs. Under the Secretary for such a department
he would have included eight commissioners to be
charged with the oversight of the following bureaux
or administrative divisions: Science and Art, Public
Economy, Posts, Public Lands, Mint, Patents, Indian
Affairs, and Justice. He included in the bureau of
Public Economy the superintendence and execution of
internal improvements such as roads and canals, and
such other matters as the care of unsettled public
lands, the conservation of forests, slavery, mines,
fisheries, and general police. The scheme attracted
widespread notice and gained favorable comment here
and there. But it lacked simplicity and failed to
impress men high in administrative circles with its
feasibility.[30]

[29] *Ibid.*, VI, 401-402. See Note 1 at the end of this chapter.
[30] *National Journal*, April 24, May 29, 1824. The same articles were
reprinted about a year later in the *National Intelligencer* of April 23,

In the autumn of 1824 President Monroe contemplated recommending to Congress a Department of the Interior. His reason for not doing so was recorded by John Quincy Adams under date of April 25, 1825. According to Adams, Monroe, having determined to recommend an increase in the number of the judges of the Supreme Court, was apprehensive lest "it would have too much the appearance of a projecting spirit to recommend also additions to the Executive Department."[31] Nevertheless, just at the close of the second session of the Eighteenth Congress, on March 3, 1825, a member of the House offered a resolution in favor of the establishment of a Home Department for the purpose of promoting agriculture, manufactures, science and the arts, and trade between the states by roads and canals. The resolution was promptly voted down —stamped at once with the disapprobation of the House.[32]

Such Washington papers as the *National Intelligencer* and the *National Journal* persisted in keeping track of the general project. As late as November 10, 1825—not many weeks before the assembling of the Nineteenth Congress—the *National Journal* copied a series of "Remarks" on the subject of a Home Department which had appeared in the *American Athenaeum.* "We shall feel grateful," concluded the writer in the *Athenaeum,* "if any gentlemen will favour us with a paper on this subject, writing in a truly national spirit,

26, and 28, 1825. Woodward communicated some of his ideas to Madison. *Writings of Madison* (ed. Hunt), IX, 206 ff.

[31] *Memoirs*, VI, 532-533.

[32] *Register of Debates*, 18 Cong., 2 sess. (1824-1825), I, 740.

and tending to elucidate the *advantages or disadvantages* that may be expected to result from the establishment of a *Home Department* for the United States.''

John Quincy Adams was the first President after Madison to call public attention to the need of an additional executive department. Under the obligation of an ''indispensable duty,'' he did so in his first annual message of December 6. Remarking that ''the Departments of Foreign Affairs and of the Interior, which early after the formation of the Government had been united in one, continue so united to this time, to the unquestionable detriment of the public service,'' he went on to refer deferentially to Madison's suggestion and said:

The exigencies of the public service and its unavoidable deficiencies . . . . have added yearly cumulative weight to the considerations presented by him as persuasive to the measure, and in recommending it to your deliberations I am happy to have the influence of his high authority in aid of the undoubting convictions of my own experience.[33]

Both Madison and Adams could speak with all the more authority on the subject because they had each had eight years of experience as Secretaries of State before they entered upon the work of the Presidency.

This recommendation of President Adams had been carefully discussed by the Cabinet before it was made public, as we know from the record of the *Memoirs*.[34] Rush of the Treasury Department urged the immediate

[33] *Messages and Papers*, II, 315.
[34] VII, 62-63.

communication of the recommendation in the message. Clay, Secretary of State, while admitting that a new executive department "was of most urgent necessity," was inclined to believe that Congress could not be persuaded to take any action in the matter. Nevertheless, the House promptly sought light on the subject, appointing a special committee, of which Daniel Webster was chairman.[35] Little could Webster have dreamed that his interest in the subject, first aroused in 1825, was to continue over an interval of almost a quarter of a century, and that finally he was to take a leading part in the passing of the bill of 1849 which actually established the Interior Department.

On the evening of December 16, Webster called on the President for the purpose, among other things, of obtaining from Adams his ideas. The President, like Clay, was in doubt about the attitude of Congress toward any such measure. From his record of the interview with Webster the reader may obtain a clear impression of his thought.

I said [wrote Adams], if it was possible in any manner to obtain this from Congress it must be by a very short Act, expressing in very general terms the objects committed to it— the internal correspondence, the roads and canals, the Indians and the Patent Office. I referred him to the papers of Judge Woodward on a Home Department in the *National Journal,* but observed that was a plan upon a scale much too large for the approbation of Congress, to begin with. I have indeed no expectation of success with this Congress for any such establishment even upon the simplest plan.[36]

[35] *Memoirs,* VII, 83; *Register of Debates,* 19 Cong., I sess. (1825-1826), p. 797.
[36] *Memoirs,* VII, 83-84.

The interview was apparently only the starting-point in the search for information. In the following January Webster addressed a letter on the subject to the four heads of departments, Clay, Rush, Barbour, and Southard. For some unknown reason Wirt, the Attorney-General, was ignored. Clay gave careful consideration to the letter, then answered it at length, approving the general plan and stating reasons why a Home Department seemed to him necessary. Rush declared himself too inexperienced in the business of the Treasury Department to have any decided opinion to offer. Barbour acknowledged that he would be glad to have pensions and Indian affairs off his shoulders as Secretary of War. Southard found his tasks as Secretary of the Navy not specially burdensome.[37]

That a bill was not only contemplated, but was actually in course of formulation at the time, would appear from Adams's reference on January 24 to "the proposed bill for the establishment of a Home Department," for the President added that "the duties to be assigned to it will be taken almost entirely from the Departments of State and of War."[38] But the evidence after this on the progress of the matter is scant. It is certain that no definite action on the subject was taken by Congress in 1826, although on May 22, the last day of the session, a report was made to the House and was placed on file.[39] The subject seems never again during

[37] *Senate Documents,* 21 Cong., 1 sess. (1829-1830), vol. II, No. 109, pp. 13. Here will be found the correspondence.

[38] *Memoirs,* VII, 109.

[39] Printed in *Senate Documents,* 21 Cong., 1 sess. (1829-1830), vol. II, No. 109. The Report omits the text of a bill in a way which leads one

Adams's term to have come before Congress. But Adams did not forget it, for as late as 1839, in a paper read before the New York Historical Society on "The Jubilee of the Constitution," he then deplored the absence of a Home Department. [40]

President Jackson, like his predecessor, Adams, was impressed by the justness of Madison's plea for an additional executive department. He gave the subject brief consideration in his first annual message of December, 1829. The State Department had from an early period, as he remarked, been overburdened with business owing to many complications in our foreign relations. These relations, moreover, had been very much extended because of large additions made to the number of independent nations. The remedy proposed, the establishment of a Home Department, had not met favorable attention from Congress "on account of its supposed tendency to increase gradually and imperceptibly, the already too strong bias of the federal system toward the exercise of authority not delegated to it." Accordingly, in view of the popular expression of opposition, he was himself disinclined to revive the old recommendation. Appreciating, however, the importance of somehow relieving the Secretary of State of larger burdens, he ventured to call the attention of Congress to the problem.[41]

to think that somehow the text might have been lost before the Report was printed.

[40] *The Jubilee of the Constitution*, A Discourse delivered at the request of the New York Historical Society, in the City of New York, on Tuesday, the 30th of April, 1839 (New York: 1839), p. 77.

[41] *Messages and Papers*, II, 461-462.

Congress was inclined to respond to the suggestion. They endeavored to reorganize the office of the Attorney-General—a matter that Jackson considered of paramount importance—and carried out some slight alterations in that office during the spring of 1830.[42] The debates on the matter in the Senate show clearly that Webster, Rowan of Kentucky, and Barton of Missouri all favored a Home Department. One thing was perfectly obvious at this time: the incongruity in having Indian affairs under the Secretary of War, the Patent Office in the State Department, and a Secretary of the Treasury who was obliged by law to consider and decide innumerable problems connected with the public lands.[43]

Just before his retirement from the Presidency Jackson put himself on record regarding the prosperous condition of the executive departments, referring to the ability and integrity with which these departments had been conducted.[44] Somehow Jackson's principal officers, it would seem, got on very well without a Home Department. But the topic of a Home Department cropped up in the newspapers occasionally after Jackson's term, for administrative burdens were constantly increasing and seemed to

[42] See *supra*, chapter VII, p. 173.

[43] *Register of Debates* (1829-1830), vol. VI, Pt. I, pp. 276, 323-324. A text-book of the time remarked: ''It is the opinion of many intelligent persons, that the labors of conducting the government could be more easily and correctly performed by the establishment of a Home Department. . . . .'' William Sullivan, *The Political Class Book* (Boston: 1831), p. 90.

[44] *Messages and Papers*, III, 259.

demand more careful differentiation than they had yet received.[45]

IV

President Polk followed Jackson's lead in more ways than one. Like Jackson he called attention in his first annual message of December, 1845, to the necessity of relieving the executive departments by redistributing various duties among them. The administrative organizations seemed to him in many places to be out of joint. He commented especially on the duties of a domestic nature which rested on the shoulders of the Secretary of State, and suggested that the Patent Office might well be transferred to the office of the Attorney-General. The tone of the recommendations was not robust and strong. The recommendations sounded as though Polk himself doubted whether, under the circumstances of trouble with Mexico over the Texas situation, Congress would be inclined to undertake measures of administrative reform.[46] No such measures at any rate were undertaken, for the war with Mexico soon absorbed attention and concentrated congressional effort on other matters. Yet the results of the war—particularly the acquisition of territory from Mexico—and the control of the Oregon country as the outcome of the treaty of 1846, were largely responsible for the ultimate attainment of a new department in 1849.

[45] *National Intelligencer*, October 21, December 8, 1841. The *Cincinnati Gazette* about this time was vigorous in its approval of the project for a Home Department.

[46] *Messages and Papers*, IV, 414.

Polk's Cabinet was carefully selected. It contained several men of marked ability: James Buchanan was Secretary of State; William L. Marcy was Secretary of War; and Robert J. Walker was Secretary of the Treasury. It was Walker who was largely responsible for arousing Congress to an appreciation of the vital need for the act, on the basis of which the Department of the Interior was organized in March, 1849.

Born in 1801 and educated in Pennsylvania, Robert J. Walker, while a young man, moved to Natchez, Mississippi, and there allied himself to some extent to southern interests. A lawyer by profession, he showed from early manhood a vigorous interest in politics and gained a leading position in advocating the candidacy of Andrew Jackson for the Presidency. Like Jackson he opposed nullification and the re-chartering of the United States Bank. He favored the Independent Treasury system. Although an owner of slaves, he could not approve many features of the slavery régime. Entering the national Senate from Mississippi at about the age of thirty-five, he was soon made chairman of the Senate Committee on Public Lands and engaged actively in the work of lawmaking. He was an indefatigable expansionist, first favoring the recognition of the independence of the Texas republic, and later, in 1844, arguing for its annexation to the United States. His fellow-citizens of Mississippi marked him as their choice for the Vice-Presidency in the campaign of 1844. His selection the next year by President Polk as head of the Treasury Department fostered ability already apparent and gave him new and unexpected opportunities to reveal unusual powers in constructive statesmanship. His first report as Secretary of the Treasury raised a storm of debate and led to the so-called Walker Tariff Act of 1846, of which he was in reality the framer. During his later life he acted for a brief time (1857) as governor of Kansas, then in a condition of turmoil. When the war broke out between the states in 1861, Walker stood loyally by Lincoln's administration and worked for it. He was for a time employed by the federal government as financial agent and expert on business that took him to Europe where he was able to negotiate some heavy loans for the Union cause. He died in Washington, in November, 1869.[47]

On December 9, 1848, after serving nearly four years at the head of the Treasury Department, Walker was moved to make certain definite recommendations to Congress in his last annual report, for the purpose not only of relieving the Treasury Department from burdens, but also of altering the administrative organization in such a manner as ultimately to promote—as he explained—the interests of the American people. His report was dated four days later than Polk's last annual message. There was a patriotic note in Walker's suggestions that could not have escaped even a casual reader. Indeed it seems fair to assume that the Secretary of the Treasury considered the report as his valedictory word to the American people, deliv-

[47] *Democratic Review* (February, 1845), XVI, 157-164; *Green Bag,* XV, 101-106; *American Historical Review,* X, 357; Appleton, *Cyclopaedia of American Biography,* VI, 329; Taussig, *Tariff History,* 5th ed., p. 114.

ered, as it was, from a position of marked prominence. His suggestions on administrative organization are worthy of careful attention, for behind them were ripe experience and association with men and measures of a momentous epoch. Inevitably they reflected the administrative deficiencies of an earlier time.

At the outset of his suggestions Walker was perhaps unduly deferential to the supposed wisdom of Congress in respect to any action that that body might be inclined to take. However, he began his considerations by asserting that the Treasury organization was defective and that its deficiencies made it peculiarly burdensome to any man at its head. In his view there was real danger lest the department might be broken down by the very weight of its own machinery.

Its varied and important duties [he declared], with the rapid increase of our area, business and population, can scarcely be all promptly and properly performed by any one secretary. Yet in detaching any of its duties from this department, the greatest care must be taken not to impair the unity, simplicity, and efficiency of the system . . . . there are important public duties having no necessary connexion with commerce or finance, that could be most advantageously separated from the treasury, and devolved upon a new department. . . . .[48]

This comment led Walker to the presentation of a positive plan for the new department which should be placed under a "head"—"to be called the Secretary of the Interior, inasmuch as his duties would be con-

[48] *Executive Documents*, 30 Cong., 2 sess. (1848-1849), II, Doc. 7, p. 35.

nected with those branches of the public service . . . .
associated with our domestic affairs. The duties of
this new department . . . . would be great and important, fully equal to those appertaining to the head of
any other department except the treasury. . . . .''[49]

In Walker's plan there were five definite propositions, all of which were involved later in the act of
1849. In the new department he would place, first, the
work of the General Land Office. Second, he would
relieve the Secretary of the Treasury of sundry duties
of supervision which had no necessary connection with
finance, but were concerned with the expenses of the
courts of the United States. Third, Indian affairs
should have a place in the new department. Fourth,
the Patent Office, taken from the supervision of the
State Department, should come under the Secretary of
the Interior. Finally, the Pension Office, a burden to
the War Department, should also find a place under
the new official.

On the subject of the Land Office, Walker was
especially detailed and informing. "The business of
the Land Office," he wrote, "occupies a very large
portion of the time of the Secretary of the Treasury
every day, and his duties connected therewith must be
greatly increased by the accession of our immense
domain in Oregon, New Mexico, and California,
especially in connexion with their valuable mineral
lands, their private land claims, and conflicting titles.
From all decisions of the Commissioner . . . . ,'' he
continued, "an appeal lies to the Secretary of the

[49] *Executive Documents,* op. cit., p. 37.

Treasury.'' Then he added this comment from his own experience:

I have pronounced judgment in upwards of five thousand cases, involving land titles, since the tenth of March, 1845. These are generally judicial questions . . . . requiring often great labor and research, and having no necessary connexion with the duties of the Treasury Department.[50]

Indian affairs called forth this statement:

The duties now performed by the Commissioner of Indian Affairs are most numerous . . . . and must be vastly increased with the great number of tribes scattered over Texas, Oregon, New Mexico, and California. . . . . These duties do not necessarily appertain to war, but to peace, and to our domestic relations with those tribes. . . . . This most important bureau, then, should be detached from the War Department, with which it has no necessary connexion.[51]

About two months after Walker's report had appeared, Samuel F. Vinton of Ohio, a leading Whig and chairman of the Committee of Ways and Means in the House, presented a bill approved by his committee for the purpose of organizing a Department of the Interior.[52] Vinton promptly acknowledged that it had been prepared by the Secretary of the Treasury at the special request of the committee. "The bill," he declared, "with one or two unimportant alterations . . . . was the bill as it came from the hands of the Secretary of the Treasury." Some time during the previous month of January it appeared that Vinton had

[50] *Ibid.*, p. 35.
[51] *Ibid.*, p. 36.
[52] February 12, 1849.

visited Walker and had then urgently requested him to prepare a bill.[53]

This notable origin of the measure aroused not a word of comment in the debates in the House. One of the less conspicuous Senators, however, was moved to remark that it should have been "a cabinet measure." Lack of co-operation on the part of the other principal officers tended in his opinion to condemn it.[54]

The House showed some opposition to the bill. Howell Cobb of Georgia, in the lead of the hostile elements, gave three reasons for opposing the bill. He dwelt at some length on the fact that no preceding Congress had ever been willing to sanction such a measure. He showed that a new department would increase considerably the federal patronage. Moreover, it was certain, he argued, to add "another cabinet officer to the Government."[55] But Cobb and his followers failed to convince. On February 15 the bill passed the House by one hundred and twelve yeas to seventy-eight nays.[56] This step had hardly been accomplished when John G. Palfrey of Massachusetts, the historian, moved to amend the title by striking out "Department of the Interior" and substituting for it "Home Department."[57] This suggestion of Palfrey, truly doctrinaire in view of the fact that there was no reference in the text of the bill to anything but a Department of the Interior, fixed the title in law with

---

[53] *Congressional Globe*, 30 Cong., 2 sess. (1848-1849), XX, 514.
[54] *Ibid.*, p. 687. Allen of Ohio, March 3.
[55] *Ibid.*, p. 516.
[56] *Ibid.*, p. 543.
[57] *Ibid.*, p. 544.

an incongruity that did not escape later comment. Both Ewing and Stuart, first and third Secretaries of the Interior, referred to the matter.[58]

The Senate discussions over the bill were vigorous and at times acrid. They were confined, however, to a single day and evening session, for the bill was not reported by Senator R. M. T. Hunter of Virginia until March 3, the last day of the Thirtieth Congress. Hunter was mild in his opposition by comparison with his colleague, Senator James M. Mason, grandson of Colonel George Mason, member of the Philadelphia Convention of 1787. Mason made quite the most bitter protest against the bill that the record of debate shows; and he was seconded in his position by John C. Calhoun. The leaders of the small Senate majority that favored the measure were Daniel Webster of Massachusetts and Jefferson Davis of Mississippi. Both these men argued ably and well. The bill passed the Senate by a vote of thirty-one yeas to twenty-five nays.[59]

The particular note sounded by the Senate opposition at different times in the course of the debate was first suggested by Hunter.[60] It was not a new note, for Jackson's quick ear had detected it as far back as 1829, and it was probably even then well known. It was the expression of fear of any tendency that seemed likely to increase, however imperceptibly, the bias of the federal system toward authority not clearly delegated. The proposal in 1849 to create a new

[58] See Note 2 at the end of this chapter.
[59] *Globe*, 30 Cong., 2 sess., p. 680.
[60] *Ibid.*, pp. 670 ff.

department—even though the move was really scarcely more than a readjustment of existing organization— aroused this fear in a manner not easy to understand. The fear was expressed in some variety of ways. "Mr. President," exclaimed Calhoun, "there is something ominous in the expression, 'The Secretary of the Interior.' This Government . . . . was made to take charge of the exterior relations of the States. And if there had been no exterior relations, the Federal Government would never have existed. . . . . Sir, the name 'Interior Department' itself indicates a great change in the public mind. . . . . Everything upon the face of God's earth will go into the Home Department."[61] Senator Niles of Connecticut felt that "the whole tendency of this Government is . . . . to foster and enlarge the executive power which is becoming a maelstrom to swallow up all the power of the Government."[62]

To Senator Mason the bill for the new department seemed a project destined to place industrial pursuits and other interior concerns under the management of the general government. He could not avoid the sectional note:

Are we to increase this central power? More especially are we who belong to the South—who have very little more interest in this country than to have the protection of our independence with the other States; from whom a great part of the revenue is drawn, and to whom very little of it is returned; who pay everything to Federal power, and receive nothing for it. . . . .

[61] *Globe*, 30 Cong., 2 sess., p. 672.
[62] *Ibid.*, p. 671.

A little further along he declared:

We have yet some hope, although it may be impaired by the experience of every day, that the State organizations will yet outlive the overshadowing influence of this Federal Government.[63]

Into this confusion of thought and juggling with words there came the clearer ideas of such men as Webster and Davis. "Why call this the Secretary of the Interior?" asked Webster in response to Calhoun's rhetoric about a title. "The impression seems to be that we are going to carry the power of the Government further into the interior. . . . . I do not so understand it. Where is the power? It is only that certain powers heretofore exercised by certain agents are to be exercised by other agents. That is the whole of it."[64] To Webster, grown old in active efforts for his country's welfare, his mind filled with recollections of the past, the historic aspect of the measure must have been deeply significant. "As far back as the time of Mr. Monroe," he said, "and up to this time, persons most skilled and of the most experience in the administration of this Government, have recommended the creation of some other department. . . . . Gentlemen can remember what . . . . Mr. Madison said on that subject." Then, in another vein, he added:

It is said, but not very conclusively, that we create offices from time to time, and make additions to salaries. . . . . Well, the country is increasing; the business of the Government is increasing; there is a great deal more work to be done. . . . . This bill may not be perfect. . . . . But the

[63] *Ibid.*, p. 672.
[64] *Ibid.*, p. 677.

popular branch of the Legislature has passed it.   It is here. It is my opinion that there is a general sense in the country that some such provision is necessary.[65]

Jefferson Davis was not forgetful of the force of an appeal to the past. He reminded his fellow Senators that several of the great Virginian Presidents were believers in the ideal of the bill. But perhaps his particular contribution to the debate was his reference in the following passage to the import of the bill to the "new States," among which Mississippi was at this time reckoned. "I feel a very peculiar interest in this measure," he asserted, "as every one who comes from a new State must feel." Then he said:

We are peopling the public lands; the inhabitants of the old States are the people of commerce. The Treasury belongs to us in common. The Secretaries of the Treasury must be taken from those portions of the country where they have foreign commerce, and therefore they are men who are not so intimately connected and acquainted with the relations and interests of the public lands in the new States.[66]

The implication was obvious that the interests of the new and the inland states were likely to be better guarded if the new department could be established.

To several Democrats the fact that a new cabinet officer would have to be appointed was a disturbing thought. "We are assuming that those who are to succeed us require more advisers than we have had; we are doing that thing which they ought to do, if they think it is required."[67]

[65] *Globe*, 30 Cong., 2 sess., p. 671.
[66] *Ibid.*, pp. 669-670.
[67] *Ibid.*, p. 670.

To the reader of the debates of 1849 the balance of argument seems strongly in favor of the measure. So thought the majority in both Senate and House. Late on the night of March 3 the bill was presented to President Polk for his signature. It was a long bill— too long to have received any very careful consideration from Polk during these last hours of his Presidency. "I had serious objections to it," wrote Polk several weeks later in his *Diary,* "but they were not of a constitutional character and I signed it with reluctance. I fear its consolidating tendency. I apprehend its practical operation will be to draw power from the states, where the Constitution has reserved it, and to extend the jurisdiction and power of the U. S. by construction to an unwarrantable extent. Had I been a member of Congress I would have voted against it."

In Polk's eyes the measure was inexpedient. It is altogether probable that, had he had more time, he would have vetoed it.[68] But fortunately the long struggle ended as it did. Three days later, on March 6, President Taylor sent to the Senate the name of Thomas Ewing of Ohio as first Secretary of the Interior. On March 8 Ewing, duly commissioned, entered upon his duties, taking his place as seventh member of the Cabinet.

V

The plan of an Interior Department in 1848-1849 was essentially a Democratic measure in its source. It was the direct result of the pressure of administrative

[68] *The Diary of James K. Polk during his Presidency,* IV, 371-372.

burdens. There is no evidence to show that general opinion outside administrative or congressional circles had anything whatever to do with it. It was certainly not the outcome of widespread demand or popular pressure.

The establishment of the department was mainly dependent upon a House of Representatives containing a small Whig majority (one hundred and seventeen Whigs and one hundred and eleven Democrats) and upon a Democratic Senate (thirty-six Democrats and twenty-two Whigs).[69] Circumstances and a few clearheaded men happily combined to enforce its need. The war with Mexico was over and settled. The new regions added to the national domain during Polk's term had increased or were likely to increase the burdens of administration to such an extent as to make the demand for a new administrative official and organization imperative.[70] The official, Secretary of the Interior Department, was conceived of as one who would naturally assume the rank and position of a cabinet member. His department was bound to increase the range of the federal patronage. Knowledge of these facts served inevitably in Congress to smooth the way of the measure among Whig partisans, for Taylor was about to take office as a Whig President in succession to a Democratic régime. Much was to be said in favor of the intrinsic merits of the plan. It would provide, as Webster pointed out, a necessary organization. The action of the Ways and Means

[69] *Globe*, 30 Cong., 2 sess., p. 516.
[70] See Note 3 at the end of this chapter.

Committee, together with the vote on the bill in the House, afforded some evidence that the public was ready to approve such a readjustment of administrative work as would facilitate the tasks of the federal government which were growing year by year more numerous and more complicated.

Though familiar to public men since the foundation period of the Constitution, and advocated more or less forcibly by such characters as Madison, Monroe, John Quincy Adams, and Andrew Jackson, the idea of a Department of the Interior was newly conceived and clearly formulated by an experienced and public-spirited Secretary of the Treasury from Mississippi. For the plan of organization Robert J. Walker has never received from any historian the credit that is his just due.[71] He voiced the need and launched the project more carefully than any statesman before him. But it must not be overlooked that his plan was skilfully and ably supported in a doubting Senate by two such leaders as Daniel Webster and Jefferson Davis.

[71] But see Schouler, *History of the United States*, V, 121.

NOTES

1. JUDGE AUGUSTUS B. WOODWARD (c. 1775-1827):

Attention has already been called in Chapter VI to Judge Woodward's pamphlet of 1809 entitled *Considerations on the Executive Government of the United States of America* (Flatbush, N. Y., pp. 87). In 1824 Woodward was again writing on various phases of administrative work and taking a particular interest in the project for a Home Department—a subject, it should be said, which was not even mentioned in his pamphlet of 1809. Articles of his which I have observed will be found in the files of the *National Journal* of Washington, D. C., as follows:

April 24, 1824. "On the Necessity and Importance of a Department of Domestic Affairs, in the Government of the United States."

May 29. "On the Distribution of the Bureaux in a Department of Foreign Affairs: Supplementary to the discussion on the necessity and importance of a Department of Domestic Affairs. . . . ."

May 27 to August 31. At intervals between these dates there appeared about a dozen articles on The Presidency. These, together with the two foregoing articles, were collected and printed in the form of a pamphlet entitled: *The Presidency of the United States,* by A. B. Woodward (New York: 1825, pp. 88). The copyright date of this rare pamphlet was May 21, 1825.

April 9, 1825. Letter from Willie Blount to Judge Woodward of Florida, dated March 14, 1825, approving Woodward's plan of a Department of Domestic Affairs. Woodward's reply.

May 21. Letter of Major H. Lee to Judge Woodward, dated April 14. Woodward's reply.

In the *National Intelligencer* of Washington, D. C., of April 23, 26, and 28, 1825, Woodward's two articles that had appeared the year before in the *National Journal* of April 24 and May 29 were reprinted with a brief editorial comment on April 28 in favor of his plans. In general, Woodward was opposed to what he termed the "cabinet system." His writings, however, do not leave the impression that he had any very definite or practical substitute to offer in its place. In 1824 he was appointed federal judge for the West District of Florida (*National Intelligencer*, February 26, 1825). The probable year of his death is given as 1827 in Appleton's *Cyclopaedia of American Biography*, VI, 606. He appears to have been interested in science as well as government. Charles Moore has thrown some light on an earlier phase of Woodward's career in a slight sketch entitled *Governor, Judge, and Priest: Detroit, 1805-1815. A paper read before the Witenagemote on Friday evening, October the Second, 1891* (New York: pp. 24). For some additional information about Judge Woodward, see T. M. Cooley's *Michigan* (Amer. Commonwealth Series, Boston: 1905), and D. G. McCarty, *The Territorial Governors of the Old Northwest* (Iowa City: 1910).

2. ACT TO ESTABLISH A "HOME DEPARTMENT" IN 1849:

The first Secretary of the Interior, Thomas Ewing, in his Report of December 3, 1849, wrote:

The department is named in the title "A Home Department"; but the body of the act provided that it shall be called "The

Department of the Interior.'' The title of the act, being the part last adopted in the process of enactment, is believed to express the intention of Congress as to the name. . . . .

Secretary Alexander H. H. Stuart suggested, in his Report of December 2, 1850, that Congress remove the ambiguity. But nothing was done until the revision of the statutes in 1873, when the department was properly entitled.

In respect to the incongruity between the title and the text of the act of 1849, I quote from a personal letter on the point sent to me under date of April 13, 1910, by Mr. Middleton Beaman, then librarian of the Law Library of Congress and the Supreme Court:

So far as I know, the title of the act of 1849 is the only instance in which the title ''Home Department'' is used in legislation. Examination of the indexes of the *Statutes at Large* from 1849 to 1873 discloses numerous instances of reference to this department as the ''Interior Department.'' . . . . The title of the original act cannot govern the usage, as the body of the act expressly declared that the department should be.called ''The Department of the Interior.'' By well settled rules of statutory construction the title of an act can have no weight except where the provisions of the act itself are ambiguous. I therefore am of opinion that the official designation has always been ''The Department of the Interior.''

3.   GROWTH OF THE NATIONAL DOMAIN :

The extent of the land acquisitions that were made to the United States in Polk's administration will be easily understood by the following table, taken from Professor T. N. Carver's article, ''Historical Sketch of American Agriculture,'' in L. H. Bailey's *Cyclopedia of American Agriculture* (1907 ff.), IV, 50:

1781–1802:	Cessions by the States .	819,815	square miles.
1803:	Louisiana Purchase . .	877,268	'' ''
1805:	Oregon	225,948	'' ''
1812:	West Florida . . .	9,740	'' ''
1819:	Florida	54,240	'' ''
1845:	Texas	262,290	'' ''
1846:	Region north of the Columbia River	58,880	'' ''
1848:	California and New Mexico	614,439	'' ''
1853:	Gadsden Purchase . .	47,330	'' ''

It should be noted that none of the land in Texas belonged to the public domain, and that much of the land in California and New Mexico had been granted to private individuals before these regions came under the jurisdiction of the United States.

CHAPTER XI

ESTABLISHMENT OF THE SECRETARYSHIP OF AGRICULTURE

NEAR the close of Mr. Cleveland's first term of service as President, almost exactly a century after the government was inaugurated under Washington, the Secretaryship of Agriculture was established by the law of February 9, 1889.[1] Reckoning from 1789, the Secretary of Agriculture was the sixth principal officer to be termed Secretary. The department over which the new official was to preside was the eighth to be characterized as "executive." Moreover, the Secretary of Agriculture was the eighth member to take a place in the President's Cabinet Council.

Since 1862 there had been a Department of Agriculture over which there had been an officer called a Commissioner, but it had not been known hitherto as an executive department. Its activity, however, had been steadily extending for many years, so that, under the rearrangements of 1889 and some later statutes, the Department was seeking the remotest regions of the earth for crops suitable to the areas reclaimed by the government; it was mapping and analyzing soils, fostering the improvement of seeds and animals, tell-ing the farmer when and how and what to plant, and making war upon diseases of plants, animals and insect pests.[2] From its origin in the epoch of the Civil

[1] 25 *Statutes at Large,* pp. 659 ff.
[2] Frederick J. Turner, "Social Forces in American History," in *American Historical Review* (January, 1911), XVI, 223.

War it was designed to promote the welfare of the American farmers, the industrial class on which the wealth of the nation inevitably rested.

It would be misleading to cite Hamilton's view, expressed in December, 1787, to the effect that the supervision of agriculture could never become one of the "desirable cares of a general jurisdiction,"[3] as at all widespread or generally acceptable at that time. Yet we may be sure that neither Hamilton nor any one of his great contemporaries could have appreciated the influence on institutions or the consequences of the westward movement of population, a movement beginning about the close of the American Revolution and continuing for more than a century, until the West had been largely colonized, and there was no longer any really describable frontier line. The "westward-moving tide of population" which has been characterized as "the greatest fact in American history"[4] tended to affect profoundly the whole course of domestic federal administration. In truth, it was probably the most fundamental factor among many that were making toward the establishment of a national Department of Agriculture. A great variety of circumstances aroused popular interest in such a Department. Once aroused and properly directed into effective channels, this interest gained more or less capable direction at Washington, and finally exacted from somewhat unwilling and preoccupied legislators, at a

[3] *The Federalist* (ed. Ford), No. 17, p. 104. December 5, 1787.
[4] T. N. Carver, "Historical Sketch of American Agriculture," in L. H. Bailey's *Cyclopedia of American Agriculture*, IV, 55.

critical moment of the Civil War, the desired organization.

At the outset attention should be called to two lines of effort, both of which had a perceptible and traceable influence in bringing about the establishment of the Department in 1862 and the Secretaryship in 1889. In the first place, certain statesmen—men like Washington who were themselves practically interested in problems of farming—were apt to foresee from the latter days of the eighteenth century the ultimate desirability of some form of central administrative organization, called variously by the names ''Board,'' ''Bureau,'' or ''Department,'' which might be established at the seat of government for the purpose of representing, understanding, and aiding local interests in farming. As time advanced, these men set themselves to work definitely for the object. In the second place, from an early period of our history there were to be found local or state organizations which were designed to aid and foster farming interests. Many circumstances tended to bring these different organizations, having similar aims, into co-operating groups until at length a large and fairly representative agricultural society was formed which made one of its leading aims the establishment of a federal Department of Agriculture. By 1840, or a little later, the subject was given new significance because of the widespread feeling that a proper disposition of the public lands was likely to have a marked effect in ameliorating social conditions. And this feeling undoubtedly had its influence, both in and outside

Congress, in enforcing the need of various legislative measures, notably those for a federal Department of Agriculture and the Homestead Acts.

I

During the colonial period King and Parliament had occasionally, but in rather desultory fashion, attempted to encourage certain kinds of agricultural industry. This accorded well with the theory of colonization, for ''the essential thing was that the colony produced commodities that the mother country would otherwise have to buy from foreigners. Hence greater stress was laid on colonies as sources of supply, than as markets for British manufactures.''[5] The colonial legislatures themselves, appreciating the ideal, sometimes encouraged such industries as the raising of indigo, mulberry trees for silk culture, hemp, flax, and other products especially desirable to the home country. In the latter part of the eighteenth century, when England became interested in manufacturing and was passing into the epoch known as the Industrial Revolution, it was still the ideal that the colonies should attend to agricultural pursuits, partly as a means of keeping their inhabitants diverted from manufacturing. To the colonists in America agriculture was bound to be a most precious interest.

In the latter part of 1789 President Washington was in correspondence with a certain Baron Pöllnitz, who seems to have had a farm for experimental purposes in the neighborhood of New York. In the early part of

[5] G. L. Beer, *British Colonial Policy, 1754-1765*, p. 135.

the next year, in the course of his first annual message
to Congress, Washington referred to agriculture as
a pursuit that should be encouraged along with commerce and manufactures.[6] Although the reference to
agriculture was rather casual, it apparently induced
Pöllnitz to commend to the President's attention the
subject of establishing an experimental farm under
the government's patronage. Washington replied
cautiously to the suggestion, saying:

I know not whether I can with propriety do any thing more
at present than what I have already done. I have brought
the subject in my speech at the opening of the present session
of Congress before the national legislature. It rests with
them to decide what measures ought afterwards to be adopted
for promoting the success of the great objects, which I have
recommended to their attention.[7]

After eight years of administrative experience, in
his last annual message, Washington once more
renewed the subject and recommended a central establishment or board of agriculture.[8] For the origin of
the conception of something akin to a department,
bureau or board of agriculture in the United States
the student need go no farther back than to the closing decade of the eighteenth century. This utterance
of President Washington on the subject in 1796 is
among the earliest that can be found. The idea
behind it was largely the outcome of certain definite
English precedents.

[6] *Messages and Papers,* I, 66.

[7] Sparks, *Writings of George Washington,* X, 68, 81. Letters of
December 29, 1789, and March 23, 1790.

[8] *Messages and Papers,* I, 202.

In 1793, through the indefatigable efforts of Sir John Sinclair, a young Scotch member of Parliament and a writer on agricultural topics, the government of Pitt agreed to the establishment of a Board of Agriculture. To Arthur Young, Sinclair's friend, the plan seemed in January, 1793, to be preposterous. "Pray, don't give Ministers more credit than they deserve," wrote Young to Sinclair. "In manufactures and commerce you may bet securely; but they never did, and never will do any thing for the plough. Your Board of Agriculture will be in the moon; if on earth, remember I am to be secretary."[9] About the middle of the following May the plan, perhaps through the favoring influence of the King behind it, was carried through Parliament. There was opposition. Such statesmen as Hawkesbury, Sheridan, Grey, and Fox felt that the measure might be a "job" for the purpose of placing patronage in the hands of the government.[10] But on August 23 the Board's charter was sealed. Sir John Sinclair was made president. Arthur Young, in accordance with his wish, was made secretary. The English Board of Agriculture, thus established in 1793, lasted until 1817, in which latter year the government declined to make further appropriations for it.

The organization of the English Board was this: It was to be composed, in the first place, of certain government officials and a number of lay coadjutors. This, as the central body, sent out to the farmers in all

[9] *The Correspondence of the Right Honourable Sir John Sinclair, Bart.* (2 vols., London: 1831), I, 407.

[10] *Parliamentary History*, XXX, 949 ff. May 15, 17, 1793.

parts of England lists of questions to be answered. Some competent person was chosen in every county, directed to draw up a survey of agricultural conditions there and to return it to the Board. Under such an arrangement the Board was enabled to appreciate the needs of the various counties. In the course of time, by means of numerous publications—called "Communications" from 1802 to 1806—the central Board furnished much information to the farmers. The information was of a kind to keep them in touch with foreign improvements and give to them the means of understanding new or advanced methods of agriculture. Moreover, the Board provided lectures in different places, and offered prizes for essays on various topics of importance. Account was taken in its publications of the statistics of population—a subject that was brought into prominence by the anonymous publication in 1798 of Malthus's *Essay on the Principle of Population*. When this first English Board of Agriculture went out of existence in 1817, there were numerous local organizations which were competent (if not actually designed) to carry on the educational work so well started. Among these were the Smithfield Club, the Highland Society, and the Bath and West of England Agricultural Society.[11]

Sir John Sinclair was an enthusiast in whatever he

[11] Besides references already cited, I have used in these paragraphs: R. H. Inglis Palgrave, *Dictionary of Political Economy* (1894 ff.), I, 156-157. *Dictionary of National Biography*, LII, 301-305. Art. "Sir John Sinclair" (1754-1835). This first Board is not to be confused with the present Board of Agriculture established in 1889, 52 & 53 Vict., c. 30.

undertook to do. He was, moreover, an indefatigable correspondent, constantly seeking intimacies with men who, he had reason to believe, would utilize his schemes or extend his ideas. With President Washington and his four successors Sinclair carried on correspondence, much of which has been preserved and rendered easily accessible. He took occasion also to address other well-known and influential Americans, among them John Jay, Richard Rush, William Pinkney, Richard Peters, Gouverneur Morris, and Colonel David Humphreys, most of whom had special interest in the promotion of agriculture. He was, of course, very much enlisted in the work of the English Board of Agriculture, of which he was president, first from 1793 to 1798, and again from 1806 to 1813. It was Sinclair who brought Washington to an understanding of the work of the English Board. He was influential, likewise, in inducing Washington to insert a paragraph regarding some such institution for the United States into his last annual message to Congress in 1796.

To an English correspondent Washington wrote, under date of July 15, 1797, as follows: "I have endeavored," he said, "both in a public and private character to encourage the establishment of Boards of Agriculture in this country, but hitherto in vain. . . . . Since the first establishment of the National Board of Agriculture in Great Britain, I have considered it as one of the most valuable institutions of modern times, and conducted with so much ability and zeal as it appears to be under the auspices of Sir John Sinclair, must be productive of great advantage to the Nation and to Mankind in General.'"[12]

In 1794 Washington, who had then been in correspondence with Sinclair for about two years, referred in an interested way to the plan of the English Board of Agriculture. He felt sure of its importance, but he knew that for the present, at any rate, the plan was not likely to be adopted in the United States.[13] Such a friendly reference, however, could not be overlooked or forgotten by the zealous young parliamentarian. Accordingly, it is not surprising that Sinclair, on hearing in the summer of 1796 of Washington's proposed retirement from the Presidency, expressed the hope that Washington would recommend to the American people "some agricultural establishment on a great scale, before you quit the reins of government. By that," continued Sinclair, "I mean a Board of Agriculture, or some similar institution, at Philadelphia, with societies of agriculture in the capital of each state, to correspond with it. Such an establishment would soon enable the farmers of America to acquire agricultural knowledge, and . . . . afford them the means of communicating what they have learnt to their countrymen . . . . it might be in my power, on various occasions, to give useful hints to America, were there any public institution to which they might be transmitted.'"[14]

This suggestion made an impression, for reference to it appeared in a letter of Washington written to

[12] *Writings* (ed. W. C. Ford), XIII, 406-407.
[13] Sinclair, *Correspondence*, I, 280 ff. II, 18-19.
[14] *Ibid.*, II, 6. Letter dated London, September 10, 1796.

Alexander Hamilton on November 2, 1796, while Washington had under consideration his last annual message to Congress. These were the President's words to Hamilton:

Since I wrote to you from Mount Vernon . . . . I received a letter from Sir John Sinclair . . . . on the subject of an agricultural establishment.—Though not such an enthusiast as he is, I am nevertheless deeply impressed with the benefits which would result from such an institution, and if you see no impropriety in the measure, I would leave it as a recommendatory one in the Speech at the opening of the Session . . . . it is in my estimation a great national object, and if stated as fully as the occasion and circumstances will admit, I think it must appear so . . . . whatever may be the reception, or fate of the recommendation, I shall have discharged my duty in submitting it to the consideration of the Legislature. . . . .[15]

The matter assumed sufficient importance for Washington to ask Hamilton and John Jay for their "joint opinion" on it.

About a month later President Washington's last message was delivered. Preceded by some general remarks on the primary importance of agriculture, there was a passage referring directly to the substance of Sinclair's suggestions. Institutions for promoting agriculture, remarked the President, grow up and are supported by the public purse. To what object, he asked, can the public purse "be dedicated with greater propriety"? Then he continued:

Among the means which have been employed to this end none have been attended with greater success than the establishment of boards . . . . charged with collecting and diffusing

[15] Washington, *Writings*, XIII, 326.

information, and enabled by premiums and small pecuniary aids to encourage and assist a spirit of discovery and improvement. This species of establishment contributes doubly to the increase of improvement by stimulating to enterprise and experiment, and by drawing to a common center the results everywhere of individual skill and observation, and spreading them thence over the whole nation. Experience accordingly has shewn that they are very cheap instruments of immense national benefits.[16]

On December 10 the Senate responded, indicating their interest in this particular project. A few days later, on December 16, the House named a committee of three to consider the matter. On January 17 following, this House committee recommended a Society for the Promotion of Agriculture, having a secretary who should be paid by the national government. It was planned that the Society should be established at the seat of government, its membership including Senators, Representatives, Judges of the Supreme Court, the three Secretaries of Departments, the Attorney-General, "and such other persons as should choose to become members agreeably to the rules prescribed." At the annual meeting this miscellaneous membership was to elect officers and "a Board, to consist of not more than thirty persons which shall be called 'A Board of Agriculture.' "[17] The Society was to be incorporated.

This plan for a Society and a National Board of Agriculture was crude and at the time impracticable. It was allowed to drop. "I am sorry," wrote Wash-

16 *Messages and Papers*, I, 202. December 7, 1796.
17 *Annals of Congress*, 4 Cong., 2 sess. (1796-1797), p. 1835.

ington to Sinclair on March 6, 1797, ". . . . that nothing *final* in Congress has been decided respecting the establishment of a National Board of Agriculture, recommended by me, at the opening of the session." There was no opposition to the measure among members of Congress, Washington thought. The plan fell through because of limited time and the pressure of more important business. He remarked in a consoling tone that he thought it "highly probable that next session will bring this matter to maturity."[18] But, while the original plan was probably forgotten, Washington's suggestion in his message of December, 1796, was referred to frequently and for many years after its first utterance.

II

Local associations for assisting farmers began to appear in the United States soon after the close of the Revolution. The year 1785 witnessed the commencement of the Philadelphia Society for Promoting Agriculture (incorporated in 1809), and the Charleston (S. C.) Society for the Promotion of Agriculture. By 1800 there were at least a dozen such organizations to be found here and there from the province of Maine southwards.[19] No one of these was destined to have greater usefulness, through the character of its membership as well as its publications, than the Massachusetts Society for Promoting Agriculture (1792). In 1803 the Society for Promoting Agriculture in Connec-

[18] Sinclair, *Correspondence,* II, 26.
[19] Bailey, *Cyclopedia of American Agriculture,* IV, 291.

ticut was started, later to be known as the New Haven County Agricultural Society. Five years afterwards, in 1808, the Pennsylvania Society of Agriculture was organized. The mere list might be considerably increased.

The Berkshire Agricultural Society in western Massachusetts was established chiefly through the energetic efforts and foresight of Elkanah Watson in 1810. Watson worked toward this object from the time that he purchased a farm in Pittsfield in 1807. It appears, from his account of the matter, that in the autumn of that year he exhibited a pair of merino sheep *"under the great elm tree in the public square, in Pittsfield."* Soon afterward he addressed the farmers in that region for the purpose of getting them interested in the breeding of merinos, and incidentally conceived of the plan of an agricultural society. Arousing his neighbors to the importance of agriculture and cattle-breeding by a series of small agricultural exhibits and cattle shows, he finally succeeded in starting the Berkshire Society. The annual exhibitions gradually brought the Society into prominence. Watson lost no opportunity to extend its influence by writing and speaking of it, so that the Berkshire Society became the model of many similar organizations in numerous states. By 1817 the Massachusetts legislature was willing to assist the organization. Already the Society had become a powerful factor in the industrial life of western Massachusetts.[20]

[20] Elkanah Watson, *History of the Rise, Progress, and Existing Condition of the Western Canals in the State of New York . . . . together* ·
with the Rise, Progress, and Existing State of Modern Agricultural

In the long epoch of peace which succeeded the war of 1812 American agriculture (like other forms of industry) experienced changes which amounted to a profound transformation. It passed from its old basis of self-sufficiency into a great and prolonged commercial stage in which its products were primarily intended for world-wide markets. The transformation was the result of many factors, chief among which were the rapid expansion of population westwards, the development of a public land policy, the growth of southern cotton, the application of science and invention to farm products, and the development—especially remarkable after 1830—of transportation. Under the spell of this process agricultural societies sprang up in many states of the Union: there were district societies, county societies, and state societies to be found in the East, the South, the Middle and even the Far West. In 1852 it was estimated that there were some three hundred active organizations in the thirty-one states and five territories.[21] And by the opening of the Civil War, nine years later in 1861, such organizations probably reached nearly a thousand in number—so notable was the decade 1850-1860 for agricultural progress.[22]

Societies, on the Berkshire System . . . . (Albany: 1820), pp. 116-125, 133 ff., 179 ff. I have used in this account D. J. Browne's "Progress and Public Encouragement of Agriculture in Russia, Prussia, and the United States" appearing in *Executive Documents,* 35 Cong., 1 sess. (1857-1858), IV, No. 30, pp. 1-50.

[21] *Journal of the United States Agricultural Society* (Washington, D. C., August, 1852), I, iii.

[22] B. P. Poore declared in January, 1860, that there were 941 agricultural organizations on the books of the United States Agricultural Society of Washington. *The Quarterly Journal of Agriculture* (Washington, April, 1860), VIII, 26.

By that time, too, many state boards of agriculture had been formed, especially in the northern states. As early as 1791 New York had shown a very progressive spirit in beginning a series of annual reports on agriculture; and early in 1820 had made provision for a state board of agriculture, including appropriations for its farming interests.[23]

There were influences working toward interstate organizations of agricultural societies and interests from an early date. Cattle fairs had been known in colonial times.[24] In Wethersfield, Connecticut, a fair for the display and sale of farming products was held in October, 1784. Legal provision was made by the authorities of the City of Washington in 1804-1805 to encourage the organization of fairs for the exhibition of cattle and merchandise. Within those two years there are records of three fairs held in Washington. The "Arlington Sheep-Shearing"—organized yearly for a series of years previous to 1812 on the estate of George W. P. Custis in northern Virginia— was a sort of fair. In fact, at least as early as 1810, Custis had outlined a project for a national agricultural organization which was to be partly sustained by government funds. The project, it may be presumed, reflected vaguely President Washington's ideal of a national board of agriculture.

The first careful organization of an interstate nature

[23] E. Watson, *op. cit.*, pp. 152 ff. Watson exerted himself vigorously for the attainment of a board of agriculture in New York, the state in which he resided after 1815.

[24] *Journal of the United States Agricultural Society*, III, 29. Passage cited from the *Maryland Gazette* of September 8, 1747.

was the Columbian Agricultural Society. This Society, sustained by the private subscriptions of such patrons as Charles Carroll of Carrollton, John F. Mercer, Custis, and Joel Barlow, was definitely planned in November, 1809. It went out of existence in the winter of 1812 after having held six semi-annual exhibitions in Georgetown. It brought together at regular intervals products from the District, Maryland, and Virginia, in the shape of cattle, horses, sheep, and wares.[25]

While the war of 1812 interrupted commerce, it had only a slight effect upon agriculture. Cotton, sugar, and tobacco became more and more important crops after 1815 in the South. In the North and Middle West mixed farming made rapid advances. But when, in 1816, Elkanah Watson conceived the idea of petitioning Congress for a National Board of Agriculture planned in accordance with President Washington's suggestion advanced twenty years earlier, he was almost sure to be disappointed. Watson's petition, sanctioned by and presented in the name of the Berkshire Association for the Promotion of Agriculture and Manufactures, was brought before the House of Representatives on January 29, 1817. Nearly a month later, on February 21, a bill providing for the establishment of such a Board was read twice. That was the end of the matter.[26]

Congress, hurrying towards the close of its session, was distinctly opposed to any increase of administrative machinery and was striving to contract govern-

[25] *Ibid.*, VII, 105-124. See also *Report of the Commissioner of Agriculture* for 1866, pp. 516 ff.

[26] *Annals of Congress*, 14 Cong., 2 sess. (1816-1817), pp. 767-768, 1018.

ment appropriations. Moreover, the country was hardly prepared for such a novel institution as a National Board of Agriculture. Watson himself was quite aware of the reasons for the failure of the project when he wrote of it a year or so later and commented: "The diffusion of agricultural societies, in all the states, will prepare the way. They will soon see the importance and necessity of such an institution, to take a lead, especially in drawing from foreign countries, through our consuls, all that can promote agriculture and the arts in America....."[27]

III

From an early period the government's consuls abroad reported to the State Department much information valuable to American farmers. Rare plants and seeds were frequently forwarded, and occasionally animals, as when, for example, William Jarvis, consul at Lisbon, sent to America in 1810 a large flock of merino sheep.[28] Under date of March 26, 1819, the Secretary of the Treasury, William H. Crawford, addressed a circular letter to the American consuls asking them to procure from abroad useful seeds and plants as well as inventions. Crawford assured them that the collectors of the different ports of the United States would cheerfully co-operate in this interesting and beneficial undertaking, thus becoming distributors of any collections of plants and seeds which might be consigned to them. "At present," he concluded, "no

[27] E. Watson, *op. cit.*, pp. 204 ff.
[28] C. H. Greathouse, *Historical Sketch of the U. S. Department of Agriculture* .... (Washington: 1907, 2d revision), p. 7.

expense can be authorized, in relation to these objects. Should the result of these suggestions answer my expectations, it is possible that the attention of the national legislature may be attracted to the subject, and that some provisions may be made, especially in relation to useful inventions. . . . .'' Crawford's plan was certainly among the very first practical national measures for the promotion of American agriculture.[29]

About a year after Crawford's letter was written, Congress created a Committee on Agriculture, presumably for the purpose of devising ways and means for the encouragement of farming.[30] Congress occasionally authorized the printing of some report or treatise pertaining to the subject for general distribution. But for years agricultural interests were looked after in desultory fashion until the Patent Office was reorganized in 1836. At that time there came into the new position—that of Commissioner of Patents—a man who appreciated the situation, particularly with respect to the lack of order and regularity in supplying information to the farmers, and who set deliberately about improving it. The first Commissioner of Patents was the son of Oliver Ellsworth, once Chief-Justice of the Supreme Court—Henry L. Ellsworth of Connecticut, who served in the office from 1836 to 1845.

From April, 1790, when the first law providing for patents was enacted, the State Department had been the repository for all patent records. At first Con-

[29] E. Watson, *op. cit.*, pp. 205-206.

[30] *Annals of Congress*, 18 Cong., 1 sess. (1823-1824), pp. 1686, 1690. The Committee on Agriculture was created on May 3, 1820.

gress entrusted the granting of letters patent to the Secretary of State, Secretary of War, and the Attorney-General. But in February, 1793, the privilege of granting patents was confined to the Secretary of State with the approval of the Attorney-General. In the course of years a clerk in the State Department, officially known as Superintendent of Patents, was authorized. And this was the arrangement until 1836 when the Patent Office was organized as a bureau in the State Department. Inasmuch as a very large proportion of patents involve improvements in implements of agriculture or in processes for tilling the soil, the Patent Office was bound to form a center of interest to the farmers, especially as by law the Commissioner of Patents was obliged to report such statistics of agriculture as he might collect.[31]

Henry L. Ellsworth was a man of ideas. Trained at Yale College, where he was graduated in 1810, he entered for a time into the profession of law, practicing in Hartford, Connecticut. He was interested even in his younger days in the problems of farming, for he acted as secretary of the Hartford Agricultural Society long before he entered the government service. He saw something of life on the frontier and was for a while resident commissioner among the Indian tribes in Arkansas. In his first report as Commissioner of

[31] 1 *Statutes at Large*, pp. 109 ff., 318 ff., 5 *ibid.*, pp. 117 ff. W. C. Robinson, *The Law of Patents for Useful Inventions* (3 vols., 1890), I, 76 ff. Gaillard Hunt sketches the early history of the Patent Office in ''The History of the Department of State,'' printed in *The American Journal of International Law*, October, 1909, III, 909-912.

Patents he spoke of "the aid which husbandry might derive from the establishment of a regular system for the selection and distribution of grain and seeds of the choicest variety for agricultural purposes."[32] Largely through his influence the next year (1839), Congress was induced to make a puny appropriation of one thousand dollars—its first—for aiding agricultural interests. In the winter of 1841, becoming interested in the formation at Washington of the Agricultural Society of the United States, Ellsworth headed a committee of that organization in petitioning Congress in August, 1842, for a portion of the Smithson bequest, for the purpose of promoting agriculture throughout the Union. The petition was tabled.[33] Then in January, 1843, Ellsworth recommended in his annual report an agricultural bureau, although, he argued, even an agricultural clerkship might be made of much service to the farming interests.[34] As the years passed, his annual reports were more and more widely read and sought for; and Congress lent its aid in distributing them.

That Ellsworth actually succeeded in making a government document interesting, will be obvious from a passage under date of March 31, 1845, taken from John Quincy Adams's *Memoirs*. "I became immersed this morning," wrote Adams, "in the annual report of the Commissioner of the Patent Office, Henry L. Ells-

[32] *Senate Documents*, 25 Cong., 2 sess. (1837-1838), II, No. 105, pp. 4-5.

[33] W. J. Rhees, *The Smithsonian Institution:* Documents relative to its Origin and History (1901), I, 238-239. *Infra*, Appendix C, p. 402.

[34] *Senate Documents*, 27 Cong., 3 sess. (1842-1843), III, No. 129, p. 3.

worth—a document which he has rendered so interesting that at the recent session of Congress the House ordered twenty-five thousand extra copies of it to be printed for circulation by the members. He has for a succession of years been improving it from year to year, till it forms a volume of five hundred pages, and a calendar of mechanical and agricultural inventions and discoveries more sought after than any other annual document published by Congress. Ellsworth has turned the Patent Office," declared Adams, "from a mere gim-crack shop into a great and highly useful public establishment." The conscientious old statesman, lured by Ellsworth's skill, thus concluded:

I read the report this morning. It consumed an hour of time, and diverted me from my prescribed and appropriate employment; further, it seduced me to turn over for another hour and more the subsequent pages and the appendix. . . . . As I proceeded, I found continual instigation to further enquiry, and was finally obliged to break off so as not to lose the whole day.[35]

With small appropriations from Congress for the purpose of distributing seeds, carrying on investigations, and collecting agricultural statistics, and an annual report filled with information for the farmers of the country, the Patent Office by 1845 had really assumed in many respects the functions of an agricultural bureau. In fact, as Edmund Burke, successor to Ellsworth, pointed out, "the Patent Office is now [1846] regarded as the general head and representative of the useful arts and the industrial interests of

[35] XII, 188-189.

the country.'' Burke's special suggestion was this: that ''it might be employed in collecting the statistics of all the great branches of national industry—agricultural, manufacturing, commercial and mining.''[36]

Here and there the thought of centralizing farming interests at Washington was taking shape and finding expression. A southern writer, for example, in De Bow's *Commercial Review,* a publication that endeavored to represent agricultural and industrial matters of the South and West, contributing an article on ''Agriculture of Louisiana'' in May, 1847, remarked that a ''national board of agriculture, comprising great intelligence, sagacity and judgment, which should have the whole subject of American production, agriculture, manufactures, and commerce before it, could do more to indicate the true policy for each section to pursue, than can be acquired in any other way. This,'' continued the writer, ''was the favorite plan of our illustrious Washington, and has been sedulously cherished and ably advocated by many of our most intelligent statesmen since.''[37]

President Zachary Taylor, himself from Louisiana, was the first President after Washington who made a definite recommendation in his annual message approving some sort of central administrative organization for agriculture. The recommendation, appearing in December, 1849, follows:

No direct aid has been given by the General Government to the improvement of agriculture except by the expenditure

[36] *Senate Documents,* 29 Cong., 1 sess. (1845-1846), VI, No. 307, p. 17.
[37] III, 413. The author was R. L. Allen of New Orleans, La.

of small sums for the collection and publication of agricultural statistics and for some chemical analyses, which have been thus far paid for out of the patent fund. This aid is, in my opinion, wholly inadequate. To give to this leading branch of American industry the encouragement which it merits, I respectfully recommend the establishment of an agricultural bureau, to be connected with the Department of the Interior. To elevate the social condition of the agriculturist, to increase his prosperity, and to extend his means of usefulness to his country, by multiplying his sources of information, should be the study of every statesman and a primary object with every legislator.[38]

Although Congress took no action on Taylor's recommendation, the passage in the message brought the subject once more into prominence at an epoch when both local and national authorities were to become satisfied that a bureau or department of agriculture was a necessary addition to the organization of the central government. To get such an organization established was one of the many notable tasks of the next momentous decade.

IV

The more sensational episodes of the decade 1850-1860, influencing party politics and attracting widespread popular attention, have naturally enlisted the interest of historical writers concerned with the affairs of that time. These episodes have been emphasized somewhat to the neglect of certain quiet, persistent, and normal social and industrial forces which, pushing

[38] *Messages and Papers*, V, 18.

ahead under the steady impetus of developing resources and western expansion, were making for various administrative and institutional changes of consequence. After 1830 the stream of foreign immigrants into the United States began noticeably to expand. The census of 1850 indicated that 1,713,-250 newcomers had entered the country within a decade. Many of these were destined to take up lands in the West. Between 1850 and 1860 the influx of foreigners, attracted by the discovery of gold and alluring opportunities of various kinds, reached in numbers to 2,598,214; and there was only a slightly diminished number of foreign arrivals during the decade opened by the Civil War. By 1850 the South was conscious of having lost ground in the great struggle toward industrial improvement. The North and the West on the other hand were becoming more and more prosperous, and were equally conscious of the fact.

No writer has hitherto referred in any but the briefest way to the establishment at Washington in 1852 of the United States Agricultural Society. Inasmuch as this Society was the means of arousing local interests in agriculture and focusing them on the problem of general moment—the problem of obtaining from Congress the establishment of a Bureau or Department of Agriculture in the national government—it may be well to examine briefly its history, for the Society had a marked influence in the matter of the legislation of 1862 which finally determined that a Department of Agriculture should be organized.

Efforts to form combinations of agricultural organizations go back, as we have seen, at least to the first
decade of the nineteenth century. The Columbian
Agricultural Society for the Promotion of Rural and
Domestic Economy, established at Georgetown, D. C.,
in 1809 and lasting for three years, was the first carefully constituted project of the kind, and might possibly have gained a place of influence, had it not been
for the War of 1812. Nothing of a similar nature can
probably be discovered until the Agricultural Society
of the United States was organized at Washington in
December, 1841. Designed as a medium of communication with agricultural societies throughout the Union,
the Society planned definitely to work for the establishment in the District of Columbia of a school of agriculture (including lectures on many scientific subjects),
an experimental farm, a periodical, and regular exhibitions or fairs. At the very outset, it determined to
petition Congress for the purpose of obtaining for its
objects the Smithson bequest, concerning the proper
disposition of which there was at the moment much
doubt. In some respects its aims were a duplication
of those of the National Institute for the Promotion of
Science, an organization already a year or so old in
1841; and consequently were not favored by certain
influential men in Washington. On the other hand the
Society enlisted the active interest of H. L. Ellsworth,
Commissioner of Patents, and of such leading Senators
as Dixon H. Lewis of Alabama, and Robert J. Walker
of Mississippi. John Stuart Skinner of Maryland,
well known as the editor of the first agricultural paper

established in the United States,[39] Edmund Ruffin of
Virginia, and Amos Kendall of Kentucky were connected with the Society in official capacities. Hon.
James Mercer Garnett of Virginia, who had served his
state in Congress and had acted for some twenty years
as president of the Fredericksburg Agricultural
Society, was chosen first and only president of the new
organization.

The Agricultural Society of the United States held
but one regular session after its start, the session of
May 4-5, 1842. There was not the slightest evidence
of enthusiasm about it. The tabling of the Society's
petition for the Smithson bequest by Congress in the
following August was the last incident in the Society's
history of which there is record. The time for such a
society had not come. But its failure lay partly in the
fact that it was largely the result of political forces;
it was neither representative of many agricultural
societies nor sufficiently disinterested in its aims to
make a widespread appeal to the farming class. It
expressed a clear demand for government aid to agriculture. Moreover, there cannot be the least doubt that
many of its members would have approved heartily of
petitions that had already begun to be addressed to
Congress asking for annual government reports on
agricultural conditions in this country and abroad, or
would have favored the demand for a national department of agriculture that was just beginning to be
heard.[40]

[39] ''The American Farmer.'' Baltimore, April 2, 1819-1862.
[40] *National Intelligencer,* November, 1841,—May, 1842. Garnett's

By the middle of the century the time for making
sporadic efforts on behalf of government aid for agriculture was nearly over. In 1850 the legislature of
Pennsylvania put itself on record as favoring a
National Board of Agriculture.[41] But nothing came of
the suggestion. At length, on May 20, 1852, through
the co-operation of a group of men actively interested
in various local agricultural boards and societies scattered principally over the northeastern states—men
keenly appreciative of the practical truth that public
improvements are brought about by voluntary association and combined effort—a call was sent out for
a National Convention of Agriculturists to meet at
Washington, D. C., on the 24th and 25th of the following June, for the purpose of forming a national agricultural society. In response there assembled in
Washington upwards of one hundred and fifty delegates who projected and organized the United States
Agricultural Society. Hon. Marshall P. Wilder of
Boston, one of the foremost projectors of the plan, a
well-to-do merchant, very accomplished as a farmer
and public spirited as a citizen, was chosen first presi-

address was printed in this paper on December 21, 1841. The list of
officers will be found printed on December 20, and again, as altered at
the May session, on May 11, 1842. On January 10, 1840, Joseph L.
Smith memorialized Congress, asking for an annual report on Agriculture. *Senate Documents*, 26 Cong., 1 sess. (1839-1840), III, No. 61. On
February 3 following, J. L. Smith and others petitioned for a Department of Agriculture. *Ibid.*, IV, No. 181. The *National Intelligencer* of
October 24, 1842, and January 21, 1843, throws some additional light
on the movement for a Department of Agriculture at this early time.

[41] *Senate Miscellaneous Documents*, 31 Cong. 1 sess. (1849-1850), I,
No. 107.

dent, and served as such until 1858. Vice-presidents were named—a long list, including one representative name from every one of the thirty-one states and five territories, as well as from the District of Columbia; and such other officers as were essential to maintain the active work of a large and truly representative society.

The Society as thus organized was a natural development of state and local institutions which for years had been gaining strength and working toward certain common ideals. Inevitably it drew to itself many of the leading farmers in the United States, and for ten years (1852-1862) expressed through its *Journal* the views on national and local affairs of the most enlightened and influential farming organizations in the country. From the very outset the Society tried to focus public attention on the proper solution of the problem of government aid for the farmers. At every annual meeting it presented such evidence of agricultural progress as could be discovered; and it discussed regularly, or urged the special project of, the establishment of a national Department of Agriculture with a cabinet officer at its head.

Presidents Fillmore, Pierce, and Buchanan appeared at one time or another at the annual meetings of the United States Agricultural Society. Such heads of departments as Webster, Secretary of State, Alexander H. H. Stuart of Virginia, Robert McClelland of Michigan, and Jacob Thompson of Mississippi, Secretaries of the Interior, and James Guthrie of Kentucky, Secretary of the Treasury, occasionally attended. By

1862 the Society had on its rolls as honorary members the five living ex-Presidents of the United States, as well as President Lincoln. Many Senators and Representatives served as regularly qualified delegates to its sessions. Among its active members may be named such men as Stephen A. Douglas of Illinois, Justin S. Morrill of Vermont, Isaac Toucey of Connecticut, George E. Waring, Jr., and Horace Greeley of New York, William Pitt Fessenden of Maine, Robert W. Barnwell of South Carolina, Tench Tilghman of Maryland, and James D. B. De Bow of Louisiana.

Beginning with an exhibition of horses at Springfield, Massachusetts, in the autumn of 1853, the Society conducted a series of eight annual fairs, the others taking place at Springfield, Ohio (1854), Boston (1855), Philadelphia (1856), Louisville (1857), Richmond, Virginia (1858), Chicago (1859), and Cincinnati (1860). These fairs, always extending over a period of several days, were carefully planned, largely attended, and served as a means of bringing together from all parts of the country interesting specimens of grain, seeds, fruit, cattle, horses, and agricultural machinery. On these field occasions the Society was addressed by men of such standing as Edward Everett, Robert C. Winthrop, Caleb Cushing, ex-President Tyler, and Senators Douglas and Crittenden.

From the very beginning the United States Agricultural Society had prestige, and was sure to have influence, for it was altogether an important as well as a unique organization—a remarkable expression, in its way, of the fact characterizing the decade before the

Civil War that agriculture had at length become fashionable.[42] In order to pass judgment on the significance of the Society in relation to the movement toward the establishment of a national Department of Agriculture, the reader should bear in mind two sets of factors that mark the decade before the War.

First, notwithstanding the crisis of 1857, the decade revealed great agricultural prosperity and development. Without entering into the detailed statistics of the decade, it may be said that the national wealth was more than doubled. So were the values of farms and farm property. There was a decrease in the production of sugar-cane. But such leading staples as corn, wheat, cotton, and wool increased enormously. The mileage of railroads was more than tripled. And Congress, aware of the growing importance of agriculture and doubtless influenced by knowledge of the fact, raised the annual appropriations for agriculture from $5,000 in 1853 to $10,000 in 1854. From 1854 to 1860 inclusive, these appropriations averaged yearly slightly less than $47,000, indicating the legislative trend of the epoch.[43]

Second, in government circles there was throughout the decade a decided inclination in favor of establishing a Bureau of Agriculture, a plan which would have taken the work of collecting agricultural statistics from the charge of the Commissioner of Patents and have placed it under an official directly responsible to

[42] "Agriculture has at length become *fashionable.*" B. P. Poore's opening sentence of an article in the *Journal of the United States Agricultural Society* for 1854 (ed. W. S. King, Boston: 1855), II, 138.

[43] See Note 1 at the end of this chapter.

the Secretary of the Interior. At least two efforts toward this end were recorded within the decade: (i) an effort in Congress in 1853;[44] and (ii) a project of Buchanan's Secretary of the Interior (Jacob Thompson of Mississippi) in 1859 to place Hon. Thomas G. Clemson in direct charge of a Bureau.[45] But although Clemson acted for a time as "Superintendent of Agricultural Affairs" in the Patent Office, neither effort was successful.

Some other pieces of evidence afford further indication of government interest in the problem of organization. In 1857 D. J. Browne of the Patent Office, as the result of a trip abroad made for the purpose of investigating certain phases of European agriculture, printed a report in which he described public methods of encouraging agriculture in Russia and Prussia, and gave perhaps the earliest careful résumé of what the United States government had done up to that time for the American farmers, together with a historical sketch of American agriculture from its beginnings.[46] In the spring of the next year the House Committee on Agriculture was considering a bill which provided for a National Board of Agriculture.[47] In 1860 Clemson, then in charge as superintendent of the agricul-

---

[44] *Journal of the U. S. Agricultural Society* for 1854, II, 28.

[45] *Quarterly Journal of Agriculture* (January, 1860), VII, 377. *Ibid.*, (April, 1860), VIII, 34, 51, 55-56, 169. [This is the later title of the organ of the U. S. A. Society. See Note 3 at the end of the chapter.]

[46] *Executive Documents*, 35 Cong., 1 sess. (1857-1858), IV, No. 30, pp. 1-50.

[47] *Transactions and Monthly Bulletin of the U. S. Agricultural Society* for 1858 (ed. B. P. Poore), March Bulletin, VI, 11.

tural division of the Patent Office, presented in his report a concise statement of the facts about agricultural departments, bureaus, and boards as he understood them to be in England, France, Spain, Belgium, Austria, Russia, and Prussia. His division of the Patent Office he did not hesitate to characterize as an "embryotic organization," a mere expedient which should be altered, he thought, in a way to give it the independent standing of a Department. Such a Department, he declared, "should know no section, no latitude, no longitude. It should be subservient to no party other than the great party of production."[48]

From the moment of its organization in June, 1852, to its last annual meeting of any consequence in January, 1862, the United States Agricultural Society recorded itself time and again as favorable to the establishment of a Department of Agriculture with a Secretary of cabinet rank and position at its head. The protagonist of a Department in the Society, determined, persistent, and never allowing any opportunity for the presentation of his favorite view to be lost, was a certain Charles B. Calvert of Maryland. Graduated at the University of Virginia in 1827, Calvert had been president of the Maryland Agricultural Society, and had devoted himself heart and soul to the promotion of farming interests. Serving his state in the legislature as a comparatively young man for brief terms, he was finally elected a Representative to the Thirty-seventh Congress (July 4, 1861-March 4, 1863) where

---

[48] *House Executive Documents*, 36 Cong., 2 sess. (1860-1861), No. 48, p. 11.

he acted as a member of the House Committee on Agriculture. He died in 1864.[49]

When, in 1852, the business committee of the Society recommended that the Society should work for the establishment of a national Department or Bureau of Agriculture, Calvert at once opposed the bureau ideal. To the attitude of Senator Douglas and others opposing either a department or a bureau, on the ground that either would provide places for politicians, and that occupants of such places would be removed at every change of administration, Calvert replied that he "would like to have a politician, a Cabinet Minister, at the head of agriculture. If this were the case, politics would be the better for it."[50] At the first annual meeting in February, 1853, he gained, after some opposition, the unanimous vote of the Society in favor of a memorial to Congress "to establish . . . . a *Department of Agriculture,* the head of which . . . . shall be a Cabinet Officer."[51] The next year he opposed before the Society a bill, then under consideration by a committee of Congress, which provided for a bureau. Others at that time came to his assistance, notably the eminent chemist, Professor James J. Mapes. "Talk of an Agricultural Bureau," declared Mapes, "and what would it amount to? He had no notion of the farming interest of the country being sifted down to a well-hole at the bottom of a Patent Office. . . . . An

[49] C. Lanman, *Biographical Annals of the Civil Government of the United States* (Washington: 1876), pp. 65-66.

[50] *Journal of the U. S. Agricultural Society,* I, 13-18.

[51] *Ibid.,* I, No. 2, pp. 15 ff.

Agricultural Department is absolutely necessary.'' For the second time the Society declared itself unanimously for a Department.[52] In 1855 Calvert deprecated further efforts to gain any legislation from Congress. He suggested that the time was ripe for ''the agriculturists of the whole country to meet in convention, and determine for themselves what legislation is necessary for their protection.''[53] Impracticable as the idea was, it was no more so than the proposition of B. B. French of Washington, D. C., who in the autumn of the same year propounded as a solution of difficulties that the farmers of the country should elect the head of a Department of Agriculture.[54] ''When a Cabinet Minister represents agriculture,'' said Calvert in 1856, ''the farmer will be appreciated by the Government. . . . until . . . . such a representative takes his seat in the Cabinet, the hope . . . . that the Government will regard agriculture as its chief bulwark and cherish its advance accordingly, is fallacious.''[55]

In 1857, and again in 1858, President Marshall P. Wilder of the Society voiced in his annual addresses the Calvert view. Once more, in 1857, the Society voted in accordance with this view to memorialize Congress, asking for a Department ''with a Cabinet Minister at its head.'' In spite of the financial disturbance of 1857, Wilder believed in 1858 that the time was near when the national government would come

[52] *Ibid.*, II, 28-29.
[53] *Ibid.*, III, 17-18.
[54] *Ibid.*, III, 179.
[55] *Ibid.*, IV, 67.

more effectively than ever to the aid of the farming interests.[56]

Notwithstanding overshadowing political issues already threatening to destroy the stability of the national governmental structure, there were signs favorable to Wilder's hopeful mood. Congress had appropriated in 1857 $75,000 for agriculture. Morrill was making headway with his Land Bill which, if successful, would donate millions of acres to the states to provide colleges for the benefit of agriculture and the mechanic arts. A committee of Congress had under advisement the project of a National Board of Agriculture. In 1859 an Advisory Board of Agriculturists met at the request of the House Committee on Agriculture and, after discussion, made a report which recommended the creation of a Department with a cabinet officer at its head. This report was apparently suppressed in 1860, its specific recommendation having become known and having aroused in some parts of the country opposition.[57] The sectional issues loomed large and were inevitably reflected in the United States Agricultural Society, tending to divide the members into groups. But Calvert held persistently to his original views, and at the four annual meetings, from 1859 to 1862, was regularly recorded as urging his favorite project.[58]

At the annual meeting of the Society in 1860, Joseph

[56] *Journal*, V, 24, 29, 66. *Transactions*, etc., for 1858, VI, 10.

[57] *Quarterly Journal of Agriculture*, VIII, 36-39. Other facts in the paragraph may be discovered in the Society's periodical, VI-VII, *passim*.

[58] *Journal of Agriculture*, VII, 18. *Quarterly Journal*, VIII, 55. *National Intelligencer*, January 12, 1861. *Journal*, X, 21 ff.

C. G. Kennedy, famous in his day as a statistician, and superintendent of the eighth census, left an interesting estimate on record as to the influence of the United States Agricultural Society. "Having resided at this capital ever since the period of your organization as a society," he said, "and having carefully observed the effects of its influence upon the Government and the country, I can say from personal knowledge that, unknown perhaps to the most prominent and useful members of the association, and to those upon whom its effects have fallen, the society has been silently but surely working a revolution in the feelings of those charged with the direction of public affairs, and each successive administration appears to realize more and more the claims of agriculture upon its attention, and the necessity of complying with the general demand for official recognition of the importance of an interest heretofore much neglected. . . . . The only question of doubt appears now to be, not the propriety of doing something, but how in a just and liberal spirit can the power of the ruling authority . . . . be best exerted to lend a helping hand to the support and elevation of the great mainstay of our national prosperity." It was Kennedy's view that the feeling among the people as well as in government circles would go on gathering strength "until we have what other Governments have found it necessary to organize, a department devoted principally to the interests of agriculture."[59]

Almost the last vigorous utterance from an organization whose work was practically over in 1862 came

[59] *Journal*, VIII, 31-32.

from President W. B. Hubbard's address at the annual meeting of that year in which he urged the farmers of the country to give their Representatives in Congress no rest ''until a Secretary of Agriculture, representing your combined interests, has a potential voice in the Cabinet of your President of the United States.''[60] Just two days before this address a bill had been introduced into the House of Representatives, on January 7, providing for the establishment of an Agricultural and Statistical Bureau. After being read twice, it was referred to the House Committee on Agriculture, which included in its personnel Charles B. Calvert of Maryland.[61]

V

David P. Holloway of Indiana, Commissioner of Patents in 1861, had a long series of considerations in his report for that year which led him by a roundabout way to the conclusion that Congress ought to create a Secretary of Agriculture, Commerce, and Manufactures, or (in other words) a Minister of Industry. His first idea had been to recommend merely a Commissioner of Agriculture, impressed as he was by the fact that three-fourths of the people were engaged in farming. But almost everybody else, he reflected, was a laborer of some sort. Such foreign countries as France, Italy, and Prussia had succeeded in combining Agriculture, Commerce, and Manufactures under one headship, thus gaining economy, unity, and efficiency

[60] *Journal*, X, 13-14.
[61] *Congressional Globe*, 37 Cong., 2 sess. (1861-1862), Pt. I, pp. 218, 855-856.

of administration. Why should the United States not do so? He failed to detect any constitutional difficulties in the way of such a project. Let the proposed Secretary or Minister of Industry be placed over a "Department of the Productive Arts." "We are," he wrote, "in the midst of a great revolution, not only social and political, but industrial and economical. Thus far the best efforts of the great minds of the nation have necessarily been directed mainly to the consideration of the former; but the day is fast coming when the latter will command the attention that is its due." First of all, he knew, the rebellion must be crushed out. Its political consequences alone will call for the wisest statesmanship. But there are to be economic consequences. There will be a vast debt of many millions which will weigh heavily on all the productive interests. "These interests," he concluded, "must be recognized, fostered, and organized, that they may be equal to the burden and the extinguishment of this debt."[62]

Holloway's view was more advanced than that of his superior, the Secretary of the Interior, Caleb B. Smith, as presented in his annual report of November 30, 1861. "I feel constrained," said Smith, "to recommend the establishment of a Bureau of Agriculture and Statistics, the need whereof is not only realized by the heads of departments, but is felt by every intelligent legislator."[63] Smith's suggestion would seem to be the true

[62] *Senate Executive Documents*, 37 Cong., 2 sess. (1861-1862), V, No. 39, pp. 5-10, *passim*.

[63] *Senate Documents*, 37 Cong., 2 sess. (1861-1862), I, No. 1. Report of the Secretary of the Interior, pp. 451-452.

source of Lincoln's recommendation to Congress in his
annual message, three days later, of an "agricultural
and statistical bureau." The matter is chiefly interesting as the first recommendation of an agricultural
bureau in a presidential message since Taylor's in
1849. It brought the subject into prominence. It was
otherwise not notable, for the idea of some such organization had been familiar enough to Congressmen and
others for years past. Indeed, there were doubtless
not a few who would have agreed heartily with Senator Foster of Connecticut when, a few months later, he
declared that he would not have chosen this time to
create either a Bureau or a Department. "We are
engaged," he remarked, "in a struggle for national
existence, and we need all our energies to be directed
to that object and to that alone."[64]

But action on the subject, to which Lincoln had once
more drawn public attention, was soon called for, inasmuch as several bills providing for an agricultural
organization were introduced into Congress. Between
January 7, 1862, the date of the introduction of a bill
providing for an Agricultural and Statistical Bureau,
and February 11 following, the House Committee on
Agriculture determined to recommend, not the plan of
a Bureau which was Lincoln's suggestion, but that of
a Department in charge of a Commissioner who should
be appointed by the President. The bill was disposed
of in the House of Representatives with great speed on
February 17, winning almost the unanimous approval

[64] *Globe*, op. cit., Pt. I, p. 1756. *Messages and Papers*, VI, 52-53.

of that body.[65] The way had been carefully prepared by means of a report signed by all the members of the Committee, a report which contained an admirable sketch of administrative progress toward the object of the bill since the time when Ellsworth had been placed in charge of the Patent Office by Jackson in 1836. "It may be asked," wrote the Committee, "why not have a minister of commerce, of manufactures, as well as a minister of agriculture? In reply to this, the Committee would state that in most countries these interests are represented in the Government by a distinct bureau or minister. But there is this also to be considered. The commercial and manufacturing interests being locally limited and centralized, can easily combine and make themselves felt in the Halls of legislation and in the Executive Departments of the Government. . . . . New York and Lowell have often more immediate influence in directing and molding material legislation than all the farming interest in the country. Agriculture clad in homespun is very apt to be elbowed aside by capital attired in ten-dollar Yorkshire. Every government in Europe . . . . has an agricultural department connected with it.'"[66]

Such comments suggested at the very outset the question of class legislation, and indirectly the constitutionality of the measure. Congress, however, was peculiarly free at the time from extremists of all sorts. There were no states-rights advocates to rise up, as Calhoun and Mason had done in the discussions of 1849

[65] *Globe,* p. 857. The vote was 122 yeas and only 7 nays.
[66] *Ibid.,* pp. 855-856.

over the creation of a Department of the Interior, and
object to the erection of an agricultural bureau or a
department as a step taken by the central government
to exercise overbearing or unwarrantable dominance
over the states. That fear found at any rate no
spokesman, although Senator Cowan at a later time
expressed his belief that the bill was unconstitutional.[67]
Some difficulties presented themselves in the Senate.
These were, however, of an adjustable kind. The problems propounded concerned chiefly the relations of the
proposed organization: Should there be a Bureau in the
Interior Department? Or, on the other hand, should
there be a separate Department with a cabinet officer
at its head? Efforts for both Bureau and Department
could be cited from the immediate past. The arrangement of the pending bill was something of a departure
from precedent.

The petition of the United States Agricultural
Society, asking for an independent Department, was
referred to in the Senate discussion. The president of
that Society had himself been before the Senate Committee to urge the creation of a Department, convinced,
however, that it should be disconnected ''from any of
the Departments of the Government whose chief was
appointed from political considerations.''[68] This point
of view, together with opposition against arranging for
a Secretary who should go at once into the Cabinet,
affords the probable clue to the result that at the head
of the new Department there was placed a Commis-

[67] *Globe,* op. cit., pp. 2014-2017, *passim.*
[68] *Ibid.,* p. 2015.

sioner. Like much legislation that is enduring, the arrangement was a compromise—an attempt to satisfy in part the more advanced advocates such as Calvert, and the conservatives who were, at least in administrative circles, numerous.

The objection to a cabinet officer, although voiced but once in the House by John E. Phelps of Missouri,[69] drew out much comment in the Senate. "If we make it a Department," argued Senator Foster, "there will be a necessity for a greater amount of expenditure; for the head of the Department of Agriculture will naturally consider himself somewhat slighted if he does not have a salary equal in amount to that of other heads . . . . with a seat in the Cabinet."[70] Senator John P. Hale of New Hampshire asserted that "the great anxiety to have agriculture elevated to a Department . . . . and finally to a seat in the Cabinet, for that is what it looks to, does not come from the men . . . . that lean upon their plow-handles; but it comes from the men who want them to take their hands off the plow-handle and vote for them at the ballot box. . . . . Now there are seven heads of Departments, with places in the Cabinet . . . . this Agricultural Department will soon furnish another."[71] "I know people shake their heads," observed Senator J. F. Simmons of Rhode Island, one of the chief spokesmen for the bill. "Senators seem to be determined to regard this measure as one proposing an independent Department headed by and by with a

[69] *Ibid.*, p. 2098.
[70] *Ibid.*, p. 1756.
[71] *Ibid.*, p. 2014.

cabinet officer. I do not know of any possible reason for apprehending it."[72]

Signed by President Lincoln on May 15, 1862, the bill became law. Hon. Isaac Newton of Pennsylvania, previously in charge of the agricultural division of the Patent Office, was named as Commissioner—the first of a series of six such officials—and entered upon his duties on July 1 following.

The sources of law-making opinion are often not easy to discover. But the evidence thus far gathered in this chapter has missed its object, if it does not indicate that the conviction which gained possession of Congress in 1862 and created an independent Department of Agriculture was the result of hard effort, persistent agitation, and widespread expression of views favorable to some such measure. In fact, the movement of thought had for years been directed to this end, influenced much, as of course it was, by the rapid growth of the country in population, resources, and wealth. The time had come when a Department of Agriculture could be exacted from Congress, notwithstanding the obvious fact that our political structure was being shaken to its foundations.

VI

The Fiftieth Congress (December 5, 1887-March 3, 1889) was deluged with petitions and memorials asking that the grade of the Department of Agriculture be raised to "executive" rank in order that a Secretary

[72] *Globe,* op. cit., p. 2015.

might thus be obtained to represent farming interests in the Cabinet. Many bills were drafted in response to such appeals. The agitation, however, was by no means new. For a period of many years Congress had been the recipient of similar petitions and appeals. Bills for the purpose of meeting such demands had heretofore been prepared; they had occasionally passed the ordeal of one or the other House, but were eventually lost through opposition. The so-called Hatch bill which was finally passed in a modified form and signed by President Cleveland in February, 1889, had run a long course under various guises since February, 1881. In brief, the problem of raising the grade of the Agricultural Department had occupied at times the attention of several Congresses for a period of fully eight years.[73]

By the spring of 1888 there was a very widespread impression, clearly recognized in Congress, that something ought to be done to satisfy the persistent efforts on the part of farmers' associations to get "represented in the Cabinet" of the President. The more conservative Congressmen were still inclined to think that an Agricultural Bureau would serve all important purposes. Accordingly they protested mildly against the movement as likely to lead to paternalism and centralization. The most serious objections were voiced by Senators O. H. Platt of Connecticut, and

[73] *Congressional Record*, XIX, 4479, 9303. Representative W. H. Hatch of Missouri on October 8, 1888, related the history of various measures from February 7, 1881, their starting point in the third session of the 46th Congress.

William E. Chandler of New Hampshire, the latter
once Secretary of the Navy in President Arthur's
Cabinet. "If a new department is to be created,"
argued Platt on June 4, 1888, "it ought to be a department which should embrace within its purview all of
the great business interests of the country. There is
no reason," he continued, "why those people interested in agriculture should be represented in the Cabinet, and those who are interested in manufactures, or
mining, or transportation, or commerce, should not
be." Labor, from Platt's standpoint, could on no
account be overlooked. Several speakers, following
out the same line of thought, were inclined to favor a
new department which should be termed a "Department of National Industries."[74]

Senator Chandler, though favoring in some ways
the movement for an executive Department of Agriculture, reminded his colleagues of an argument
against it that he had urged some years before. "The
present members of the President's Cabinet," he
declared on September 20, "are at the head of political
departments of the Government. They are all political; they are all in some way connected with and essential to the political government of the country. But
agriculture is in no sense an essential of political
government. The fostering of agriculture is not a
necessary part of government." Still further to illus-
trate his position, Chandler remarked that the Departments of State, Treasury, War, Navy, Justice, Interior, and the Postal Establishment were "political."

[74] *Record*, XIX, 4876, 8686 ff., 8804 ff.

He was convinced that the creation of an executive Department of Agriculture would be a distinct breach in tradition—an opening for many dangerous possibilities in the future. Where the process of executive "establishments" might end, were the farmers to gain their object, no man could say.[75]

These views of Senators Platt and Chandler, while not essentially new, were forcibly presented. Chandler's position was clearly that of a constitutional lawyer, and was based upon the technical language of the law. In the eyes of some of the stricter constructionists in the Senate it appeared reasonable. Platt was viewing the problem from a broader standpoint, interested in the possible claims of all classes, and somewhat fearful of anything that had the semblance of class legislation. However, Congress as a body failed to be determined or concluded by them.

Senator Plumb of Kansas did not hesitate to answer Chandler. He refused to see any reasonable distinction between "political" and "non-political" departments. The Cabinet did not, he contended, cover "the entire scope of proper administration." "We have," he continued, "now a Department of Labor. Experience with that department may prove after a time that it is desirable to make the person who presides over that department also a secretary . . . . while I can appreciate . . . . the feeling which the Senator from New Hampshire has derived no doubt from his experience in the Cabinet of President Arthur, that when you have got a good thing it is well to have it at pretty

[75] *Ibid.*, pp. 8778, 8801 ff.

close quarters and distributed among a very few persons, to make the crowd as small and therefore as select as possible, yet that idea is opposed to the republican theory of government.'' The only question—the real question, as he conceived the problem—was simply whether the agricultural interest ''is of sufficient importance in itself . . . . to warrant the Congress of the United States in practically requiring the President to take into his councils . . . . the person who presides over the Department of Agriculture.''[76]

There were occasional expressions of opinion to the effect that the Cabinet was already large enough. ''Perhaps in a multitude of counsellors there is safety,'' said Senator Platt, ''but,'' he added, ''. . . . the chief executive office is one which a great many advisers will only hamper.''[77] There were various references in the long course of the debates to the practices of foreign countries in administering to the needs of the farming classes. But these can have had little or no influence on the final solution of the matter.[78] The second session of the Fiftieth Congress witnessed the settlement of the subject. The President approved the bill on February 9, 1889. The Department of Agriculture was raised to the grade of an Executive Department with a Secretary over it of cabinet rank. On February 11 President Cleveland nominated Hon. Norman J. Colman of Missouri, who had acted as Commissioner of Agriculture since April,

---

[76] *Record*, XIX, 8805.

[77] *Ibid.*, p. 4876.

[78] *Ibid.*, pp. 4480 ff., 8803.

1885, to the new Secretaryship, and Colman's nomination was confirmed by the Senate on February 13.[79]

Once more, as in 1862, the desired end was attained through force of many circumstances aided by persistent and well-directed popular effort and thought. Although the final result was not equivalent to a National Board of Agriculture which Washington and his contemporaries a century earlier had wished to establish, the Department of Agriculture was intended to accomplish the work of such a Board, and very much besides.

[79] *Ibid.*, XX, 1398, 1399, 1413, 1764. Mosher, *Executive Register*, p. 251. By a curious coincidence the British Board of Agriculture dates from the same year, 52 & 53 Vict., c. 30.

NOTES

1. APPROPRIATIONS FOR AGRICULTURE: 1850-1865; 1900-1912:

The following figures are taken from a much more elaborate table which will be found on page 91 of Mr. Charles H. Greathouse's "Historical Sketch of the U. S. Department of Agriculture: its Objects and Present Organization" printed as Bulletin 3 of the United States Department of Agriculture (Washington: 1907, pp. 97). Through the courtesy of Mr. Greathouse, I have obtained and added the annual figures through 1912.

FISCAL YEAR	AMOUNT APPROPRIATED	FISCAL YEAR	AMOUNT APPROPRIATED
1850	$ 5,500.00	1900	$ 3,006,022.00
1851	5,500.00	1901	3,304,265.97
1852	5,000.00	1902	3,922,780.51
1853	5,000.00	1903	5,015,846.00
1854	10,000.00	1904	5,025,024.01
1855	50,000.00	1905	6,094,540.00
1856	30,000.00	1906	7,175,690.00
1857	75,000.00*	1907	9,932,940.00
1858	63,500.00	1908	9,447,290.00
1859	60,000.00	1909	11,672,106.00
1860	40,000.00	1910	12,995,036.00
1861	60,000.00	1911	13,487,636.00
1862	64,000.00	1912	16,900,016.00
1863	80,000.00		
1864	199,770.00		
1865	112,304.00		

* Including deficiency appropriation.

The annual appropriations were increased to upwards of $1,000,000 in 1888. They have ranged from about $3,000,000 in 1900 to nearly $17,000,000 in 1912, steadily increasing during the period, except for a very trifling falling off in 1908.

2. LAST MEETING OF THE UNITED STATES AGRICULTURAL SOCIETY IN 1881:

In a paper contributed to the Annual Report of the Commissioner of Agriculture for 1866 (pp. 525-526), the curious reader will find a statement by Ben: Perley Poore about the Society as it then existed. The statement is given in the course of a sketchy "History of the Agriculture of the United States." What seems to have been the last meeting of the Society was recorded in a pamphlet, now very rare, entitled "Proceedings of the 29th Annual Meeting of the United States Agricultural Society, January 12, 1881" (Washington: 1881. Pp. 24). A copy of this pamphlet may be seen in the Library of the Department of Agriculture in Washington. The author was Major B. P. Poore, who was first appointed secretary of the Society in 1856.

It appears that a mere handful of aged members attended the meeting held in the parlor of the Ebbitt House. Hon. John Merryman of Maryland presided, while Major Poore acted as secretary, first reading the minutes of the twenty-eighth annual meeting. President Merryman reviewed the early history of the Society, dwelling with special pride on the fact that it was the only "National Agricultural Association ever chartered by the Congress of the United States"

(April 19, 1860), and reflecting that it was a realization of the National Board of Agriculture recommended by George Washington. Moreover, he took pride in the fact that the Society had urged the establishment of a Department of Agriculture "until the desired result was attained." The record thus continues:

During the war the officers and members of the United States Agricultural Society were estranged. Some wore blue uniforms and some gray, and were conspicuous on hard-fought fields or languished in military prisons. The society was, however, kept alive, and the annual meetings prescribed by the constitution were regularly held. Messrs. Tilghman of Maryland; Hubbard of Ohio; French and Corcoran of the District of Columbia; and Frederick Smyth of New Hampshire were successively chosen presidents. The Secretary was annually re-elected, and on the death of the Treasurer, Mr. Wm. M. French of New Hampshire, now a sojourner at Washington, was chosen.

Asked what the future of the organization should be, the members indicated their desire to continue it. Merryman was named as president. Vice-presidents to the number of forty-three were selected from most of the states, among them being Alexander H. Stephens of Georgia, Cassius M. Clay of Kentucky, Dr. G. B. Loring of Massachusetts, and General Burnside of Rhode Island. A resolution of congratulation was framed to be sent to Hon. Marshall P. Wilder, then living, and regarded as the founder of the Society. "The meeting was not largely attended," commented Secretary Poore, "as no new annual or life members have been admitted since 1860, and those who joined before that time are generally too far advanced in life to go far from their homes. It was, in fact, a re-union of veteran agriculturists, and the meeting of old friends and co-laborers was cordial and interesting.'' It was voted to arrange a program for the thirtieth annual meeting which should be held at the Department of Agriculture on Wednesday, January 11, 1882, at ten a.m. There is no record of any such meeting.* The simple truth seems to be that the puny gathering of 1881 was the last feeble but dignified gasp of an organization that had been in its day, before the Civil War, powerful and really effective.

3. THE PUBLICATIONS OF THE UNITED STATES AGRICULTURAL SOCIETY:

These consisted of ten volumes. The only set—not quite complete—that I have ever seen is in the Library of Congress.

Volume I. *The Journal of the United States Agricultural Society.* Washington: 1852 ff.
No. 1. August, 1852. Pp. 144. Introd. signed by Daniel Lee, July, 1852. (Lee was at one time editor of the ''Genesee Farmer'' of Rochester, N. Y.)
No. 2. Pp. 160. Ed. by J. C. G. Kennedy.
Nos. 3-4. Pp. 279. Ed. by Wm. S. King.

Volume II. *The Journal of the United States Agricultural Society for 1854.* Ed. by William S. King. Boston: 1855. Pp. 256.

* On July 26, 1881, the Commissioner of Agriculture, G. B. Loring, sent an invitation to a large number of agriculturists over the country to assemble in Washington, D. C., at a convention in January, 1882. See *Proceedings of a Convention of Agriculturists,* held in the Department of Agriculture, January 10 to 18. Washington: 1882. Pp. 204.

Volume III. *The Journal of the United States Agricultural Society for 1855.* Ed. by W. S. King. Boston: 1856. Pp. 263.

Volume IV. *The Journal of the United States Agricultural Society for 1856.* Ed. by Wm. S. King. Boston: 1857. This consists of Pt. I, pp. 82 (Boston: 1856) and pp. 272.

Volume V. *The Journal of the United States Agricultural Society for 1857.* Ed. by Ben: Perley Poore. Washington: 1858. Pp. 282.

Volume VI. *Transactions and Monthly Bulletin of the United States Agricultural Society for 1858.* Ed. by Ben: Perley Poore. Washington: 1859. Pp. 104. The "Monthly Bulletin" consisted of 11 nos. (February-December, inclusive). The number for August is wanting in the volume in the Library of Congress. The others contain 8 pages each except the number for November, which has 12 pages.

Volume VII. *The Quarterly Journal of Agriculture* (outside cover). Inside title: *The Journal of Agriculture:* comprising the Transactions and the Correspondence of the United States Agricultural Society for 1859. Ed. by Ben: Perley Poore, Secretary, Washington: 1860. This volume consisted of "Transactions," etc., pp. 88.
No. 1. April, 1859. Wanting.
No. 2. July, pp. 104.
No. 3. October, pp. 92.
No. 4. January, 1860, pp. 104.

Volume VIII. *The Quarterly Journal of Agriculture.* Ed. by Ben: Perley Poore. Washington: 1860.
No. 1. April, 1860.
Nos. 2-4. Wanting.

Volume IX. Wanting.

Volume X. *The Quarterly Journal of Agriculture.* Ed. by
Ben: Perley Poore. Washington: 1862.
No. 1. February, 1862, pp. 76.
No other numbers to be found—probably the last regular
issue of the periodical.

There is a stray pamphlet to be found in the Library
of the Department of Agriculture entitled:

*Proceedings of the 29th Annual Meeting of the United States
Agricultural Society, January 12, 1881.* Washington:
1881. Pp. 24.
This pamphlet was apparently edited by Major B. P.
Poore, and is undoubtedly the last actual record of the
remnant of the Society. For some account of the meeting, see above Note 2.

Attempts to discover a complete file of the periodical
outside Washington have proved unsuccessful. The
Boston Public Library contains a few scattered numbers of the *Journal.*

CHAPTER XII

ESTABLISHMENT OF THE SECRETARYSHIP OF COMMERCE AND LABOR

ON February 14, 1903, President Roosevelt signed the bill which provided for the creation of the Executive Department of Commerce and Labor with a Secretary at its head to be known as the Secretary of Commerce and Labor.[1] Mr. George B. Cortelyou of New York was at once appointed to the new Secretaryship, entering upon his duties two days later in temporary headquarters at the White House. In the following June permanent offices were formally opened in the New Willard Building on Fourteenth Street in Washington, and administrative work was there fully begun on July 1.[2] The Secretary of Commerce and Labor thus became the ninth member of the President's Cabinet.

The act of 1903, like that which created the Department of the Interior in 1849, provided in part for a readjustment of administrative burdens, particularly those resting upon the shoulders of the Secretary of the Treasury. It relieved likewise the Secretaries of State and of the Interior of some of their duties, coordinating, adjusting, and focusing under one direction a large variety of work. There had been a slow but gradually swelling undercurrent of popular opinion

[1] 32 *Statutes at Large*, pp. 825 ff.
[2] *Organization and Law of the Department of Commerce and Labor* (Washington: 1904. Document No. 13), p. 22.

and effort making for some such organization for
many years, certainly traceable with some degree of
clearness since the close of the Civil War. Numerous
circumstances had aided the movement. Problems of
commercial regulation had confronted the national
government from the beginning. Notwithstanding the
fact that local organizations of craftsmen can be discovered as far back in American history as the latter
part of the eighteenth century, large national labor
organizations did not assume the proportion of a
momentous and compelling national factor demanding
recognition in government administration until after
the Civil War.

I

The problem of establishing satisfactory trade regulations with foreign countries and between the states
was at the very foundation of the movement which
forced a re-organization of the national form of government in 1787 and led to the general acceptance of
the Constitution in the following year. The problem
was carefully considered and discussed in many of its
phases during the formative period of the government.
It came prominently forward in the sessions of the
Philadelphia Convention. In Gouverneur Morris's
plan for a Council of State as presented to the Convention on August 20, arrangement was there made
for a "secretary of commerce and finance." When,
however, the plan had passed the ordeal of committee
discussion, no such officer appeared—there was to be

simply a secretary of finance.[3]   A few years later, in
Morris's "Notes on the Form of a Constitution for
France," a "minister of commerce" was mentioned.[4]
The Federalist revealed the interest of both Hamilton
and Madison in the general problem.[5]   Among many
suggestions of the period it is worth while to call
attention to two—those of Pelatiah Webster and
Alexander Hamilton.

Pelatiah Webster, out of his mercantile experience,
and because of a natural taste for speculating over the
solution of various industrial problems, afforded his
readers sundry reflections on the subject of government regulation of trade.   Referring in 1783 to merchants and manufacturers as a class, he wrote: "I
could wish that Congress might have the benefit of that
extensive and important information, which this body
of men are very capable of laying before them . . . .
the merchants are not only *qualified to give the fullest
and most important information* to our supreme legislature, concerning the state of our trade . . . . but are
also the most likely to do it *fairly* and *truly* and to
forward . . . . every measure which operates to the
convenience and benefit of our commerce. I
therefore humbly propose . . . . that they shall be permitted to form a *chamber of commerce,* and [that]
their advice to Congress be demanded and admitted

[3] Elliot, *Debates,* V, 446, 462.   Now that Mr. Max Farrand's *The
Records of the Federal Convention of 1787* (New Haven: 1911.   3 vols.)
is available, any one can refer to the discussions over commerce easily
by means of the copious index in volume III.

[4] J. Sparks, *Life of Gouverneur Morris,* III, 481 ff.

[5] P. L. Ford's edition, especially No. 42, pp. 275 ff., and No. 60, pp.
400 ff.

concerning all bills before Congress as far as the same may affect the trade of the States."[6]

In the concluding paragraphs of Hamilton's celebrated "Report on Manufactures" there occurred a reference to a Board, the functions of which should involve looking after the proper distribution of any surplus arising from duties. A portion of the public income was "to constitute a fund for the operation of a board to be established for promoting arts, agriculture, manufactures, and commerce. Of this institution," said Hamilton, "different intimations have been given in the course of this report." Briefly summarized, the plan was this: the Board, consisting of three or more government officials, was to be authorized to spend money for the sake of inducing artists, manufacturers, and skilful artisans to come to this country from abroad, or to draw forth by means of prizes all sorts of useful mechanical inventions and practical discoveries. Voluntary contributions might be received, it was suggested, from any one interested in aiding these objects. The Board was, finally, to make an annual report to Congress of all receipts and expenditures.[7]

Neither Webster's nor Hamilton's plan was carefully worked out. Both plans were merely suggestive of possible methods of solving administrative problems arising from the requirements of trade, commerce, or industries of various kinds. They were symptomatic

[6] *Essays* (1791), pp. 215-217. See also pp. 199, 202, 218-219, 232, 248, 251, 254.

[7] *American State Papers, Finance,* I, 144.

of a period when men were groping toward effective administration.

To Congress the Constitution had entrusted power to regulate trade and commerce. The Treasury Department chiefly, but also the State Department through its consular and foreign commerce bureaus, were concerned in carrying out such regulations in these matters as Congress might authorize. In the course of time the Department of the Interior (1849) and that of Agriculture (1862) were to come to the rescue, in certain particulars, of both State and Treasury Departments. Moreover Congress, through gradual development of a system of standing committees, was thus to find a means whereby it might place itself in a position to understand and appreciate the most vital needs of the nation. The historic factors that lay behind the appearance of all the Secretaryships up to 1889 have already been examined and set forth. As to the standing committees very little need be said. Beginning with provisions for two such committees in 1795—the Committee of Commerce, Manufactures, and Agriculture, and the Committee of Ways and Means— Congress gradually added to them or sub-divided them so that, among a good many additional committees, note may be taken of the Committees on Manufactures (1819), on Agriculture (1820), on Railways and Canals (1831), on Appropriations (1865), on Banking and Currency (1865), on Mines and Mining (1865), on Education and Labor (1867), on Labor (1883), and on Interstate and Foreign Commerce (1891).[8] By means of

8 L. G. McConachie, *Congressional Committees* (1898), pp. 349 ff.

such committees Congress put off the necessity of providing separate departments of administration for these various objects, and kept at the same time within its reach and control many of the subjects which might seem better provided for under the specific direction of separate departments with principal officers in charge.

II

Not far from the middle of the nineteenth century efforts on the part of organizations closely concerned with various industries began to be made for the purpose of having established at the seat of government either bureaus or independent departments which should collect, preserve, and distribute accurate information about specific industries, and at the same time aid Congress in formulating the best sorts of legislation. It was felt keenly, after the establishment of the Department of Agriculture in 1862, that the farmers had gained a peculiar advantage over other classes of workers. Inasmuch as the farmers were represented by a Department and Commissioner of Agriculture, it was not clear why the merchants, the manufacturers, the miners, and organized labor generally should not be granted similar representation in the national administration. From about the close of the Civil War attempts to bring about some such consummations form a pretty clearly defined movement. From 1864 to 1902 the list of appeals to Congress in the shape of resolutions and bills on behalf of Departments of Commerce, Manufactures, Mines and Mining, Industries, Navigation, and Labor is prodi-

giously large. There were those who thought that
bureaus might serve every purpose. But far the
greater number of bills were formulated for the sake of
obtaining departments or, as occasionally they were
specifically termed, Executive Departments.[9] All these
appeals were characteristic of an epoch of increasing prosperity, rapidly accumulating wealth, and the
growth of industrial organization.

A glance at the trend of effort—at least so far as
that trend was revealed by congressional proceedings
—indicates unmistakably that plans for a Department
of Commerce or a Department of Commerce and
Manufactures were most frequently presented to Congress, and occasionally gained some consideration.
Behind the effort for such a Department were very
persistent expressions of opinion favoring it which
came from commercial conventions, the National Board
of Trade, and other organizations of business men.[10]
The demand was echoed in political platforms. It was
made at various hearings by witnesses before the
Industrial Commission (1898-1901).[11] It was admirably and forcibly formulated at length in President
Roosevelt's first annual message of December, 1901.[12]

[9] A conveniently arranged and sufficiently full bibliography of legislative proceedings in Congress anticipating the Department of Commerce
and Labor will be found in the volume already cited, *Organization and
Law of the Department of Commerce and Labor*, pp. 13-21.

[10] Conventions at Detroit (1865) and at Boston (1868). The National
Board of Trade memorialized Congress in 1874. *Ibid.*, pp. 19, 21.

[11] *Report* (Washington: 1900 ff.), IV, 177. VII, 15. IX, lxxiv.
XIX, 575 ff.

[12] *Messages and Papers*, Supplement (1899-1902). Ed. by G. R.
Devitt, p. 323.

The establishment of the Interstate Commerce Commission in 1887 probably had a tendency to delay the outcome of the effort, for that attempt to eradicate the transportation evil of rebates occupied time and sapped the energy of commerce committees of Congress.

Labor was almost as persistent an applicant for administrative recognition within the period as Commerce or Manufactures—first striving to obtain a Bureau, and later (beginning early in the ninth decade) harassing Congress for a Department headed by a cabinet Secretary. By 1888 Labor appeared to be close to the attainment of its goal, for, in the first place, Congress granted it the Bureau of Labor in June, 1884, in the Department of the Interior.[13] Soon after the termination of the great Southwestern strike on the railroads in 1886, the Knights of Labor, then at the very acme of their career as an influential labor factor, had hopes that President Cleveland would succeed in obtaining a Commission of Labor that might in future reduce the probability of such unfortunate occurrences as strikes. Cleveland was induced to draft a recommendation to Congress on the subject under date of April 22, 1886.[14] But the project, notwithstanding executive assistance, failed to mature.

For many years, as we have seen, the farmers of the country had been eager to have the Department of Agriculture raised to the dignity and importance of

---

[13] June 27. 23 *Statutes at Large,* pp. 60 ff.

[14] *Messages and Papers,* VIII, 394-397. Cf. *Congressional Record,* XXXV, 1000 ff. (January 27, 1902.)

an Executive Department. When that subject was at length forced upon Congress, attempts were made to have action taken on behalf of other industrial interests, notably those of Organized Labor. Why, it was asked, should there not be a Secretary of Labor as well as of Agriculture? Congress was, however, in no mood to admit the claims of Labor to such rank. As a sort of sop to Cerberus, the Bureau of Labor was taken from the Department of the Interior and given an independent footing as the Department of Labor by an act of June 13, 1888.[15] The matter was thus disposed of greatly to the chagrin of many laboring men. Hon. Carroll D. Wright continued his sway as Commissioner of Labor. He was not the kind of man to satisfy the average labor organization, although as a trained statistician he proved eminently useful to the government during a long term of service. With all his ability and knowledge of industrial conditions, the laboring men protested that Wright could never speak with authority for the wage earner.[16]

After 1889, with a shrewd sense of the force of the movement backed by merchants, manufacturers, and others, Labor tagged close behind or travelled occasionally in company with Commerce, hoping thus to gain its object. As illustrations of this truth, it is worth noting that in 1896, 1897, and again in 1901 bills providing for a Department of Commerce, Labor, and Manufactures were introduced into Congress.[17]

---

[15] 25 *Statutes at Large,* pp. 183 ff.

[16] *Congressional Record,* XXXV, 1000.

[17] *Organization and Law of the Department of Commerce and Labor,* pp. 19, 21.

III

As one considers the years 1898-1903 with especial reference to the final outcome, and keeps in mind impressions which reveal themselves in the debates in Congress, three factors appear to have had marked influence—a compelling force—on the movement toward the creation of a new department. There was, first of all, the war with Spain in 1898, resulting in various acquisitions of territory to the United States. New administrative problems arose almost immediately, and called for more effective federal organization. This factor hardly calls for any detailed examination. In the second place, there was very great complexity in the general industrial situation, a situation clearly and forcibly set forth in the Roosevelt message of 1901. Consolidation of great business interests had been advancing rapidly. The Northern Securities merger attracted widespread attention as an effort to combine certain railroads in a way directly opposed to public welfare. But it was only one of the more conspicuous illustrations of the whole movement toward industrial combination. Third, the strike of the anthracite coal miners in 1902, coming at a time when there was a maturing conviction that something should be done to adjust the claims of the wage earning classes, was a factor in the industrial situation that assumed considerable political importance. Some attention to the Roosevelt message and to the debates in Congress over the passage of the law will serve to bring these two latter factors into perspective, and reveal their bearing.

Devoting a long section of his first annual message to a careful consideration of social and highly complicated industrial conditions which confronted the nation at the very outset of the twentieth century, President Roosevelt made a vigorous plea for improving the machinery of government in such a way as might provide in future for more careful and effective legislation on all matters which directly concerned the public welfare. In general he advocated, first, greater publicity—a knowledge of industrial and social facts obtained, if necessary, by due process of law. In the second place, he advocated, on the basis of such knowledge, increased governmental supervision and regulation of all corporate interests of an interstate nature which were certain to affect, for better or worse, the general welfare. As one means to the contemplated ends, Mr. Roosevelt made this tangible proposal: "There should be created," he said, "a Cabinet officer, to be known as Secretary of Commerce and Industries, as provided in the bill introduced at the last session of the Congress. It should be his province to deal with commerce in its broadest sense; including among many other things whatever concerns labor and all matters affecting the great business corporations and our merchant marine. The course proposed," he continued, "is one phase of what should be a comprehensive and far-reaching scheme of constructive statesmanship for the purpose of broadening our markets, securing our business interests on a safe basis, and making firm our new position in the international industrial world; while scrupulously safeguarding the rights of wage worker and capitalist, of investor and private citizen, so as to secure equity as between man and man in this Republic. With the sole exception of the farming interest,'' he added, ''no one matter is of such vital moment to our whole people as the welfare of the wage workers. If the farmer and the wage worker are well off, it is absolutely certain that all others will be well off too.''

This passage, attracting attention, met generally with favorable comment. The special proposal, moreover, was in line with a long train of effort which, as we have seen, was making for some such office. The interests of both Commerce and Labor were emphasized together as standing on the most intimate footing. Indeed, in the whole history of the growth of Executive Departments, it may be doubted whether there had ever been made a more timely or effective plea than was Mr. Roosevelt's in the winter of 1901. It touched Congress to the quick at the very climax of public effort for a new Department.

Several bills under various titles, but all designed to provide for a new Department, were introduced into either the House or the Senate within the first few days after the opening of the Fifty-seventh Congress in December, 1901.[18] For more than ten years— ever since, in fact, Senator Frye of Maine had projected a plan for a Department of Commerce and introduced it into the Senate on January 15, 1891—one bill after another had appeared and been shelved. But Frye was remarkably persistent; he got a bill into the

[18] *Congressional Record,* XXXV, 51, 53, 95, 125, 128.

Fifty-fifth Congress on March 18, 1897, and won a hearing for his project in the Fifty-sixth Congress. The bill of Senator Nelson of Minnesota which called simply for a Department of Commerce and was introduced on December 4, 1901—the day after the Roosevelt message had been delivered—was in all essentials equivalent to Senator Frye's most recent plan. It was destined, furthermore, after sundry alterations, to win the approval of President Roosevelt and Congress in February, 1903, and accordingly became law. But its passage through both the Senate and the House was slow and hampered by difficulties.

Late in January, 1902, the Senate decided to recognize Labor in the title, thus characterizing the projected department as the Department of Commerce and Labor.[19] The decision was not made without an effort that threw an interesting light on the whole course of the project.

According to the plan, the Department of Labor, which had stood on an independent footing since 1888 under supervision of a Commissioner, was to be merged in the new Department as the Bureau of Labor, still retaining a Commissioner who was, however, to be subject to the Secretary of Commerce and Labor. Evidence was produced in the Senate to indicate that the old and enfeebled organization known as the Knights of Labor approved the new arrangement and merger. A Department of Commerce and Labor, containing a Labor Bureau, seemed to them preferable to an independent Department of Labor which (as they

19 *Congressional Record*, XXXV, 912, 1051.

phrased it) had from the beginning been conducted "as a personal asset of the Commissioner." To the Knights of Labor the new measure appeared to be a step toward an executive Department of Labor having a Secretary of cabinet rank at its head.[20] The American Federation of Labor, on the other hand, declined to favor any such plan. In the eyes of the Federation it looked like a step backward, for it seemed to reduce the Bureau of Labor to virtually its original status of 1884, when it had first been placed under the Department of the Interior. The efforts of Organized Labor to secure the independent Department of 1888 were apparently to count for nothing. "Questions often arise in the official family of the President," declared Mr. Samuel Gompers in a letter introduced into the Senate discussion, "in which justice, fair dealing, ethics, and the law and its administration must frequently be under consideration, and," he added, "unless there is some representative of the workers competent to speak in their name, to advocate their cause, to convey to the executive head and his advisers the laborers' side of labor's contention, he and they must be deprived of valuable and far-reaching information."[21]

These two opposing points of view opened the way to much discussion, some of it futile and clearly inspired by political bias or partisan considerations. The dominant majority refused to be distracted from its position that the projected department was a real

[20] *Ibid.*, XXXV, 1000-1001.
[21] *Ibid.*, XXXV, 863.

necessity, and declined to favor Labor, whether organized or unorganized, as an element that could fairly claim to be differentiated as a class from the other elements involved. As Senator Hanna declared with force, the commercial and industrial interests of the country had for a long time been demanding a department. These interests were really one and included labor of all kinds. Moreover, he urged, the interests of capital and labor were so intimately related as really to be identical and mutual.[22]

Almost a full year elapsed before the bill was brought before the House of Representatives—a year peculiarly memorable because of the great disturbance to industry which was the result of the strike of the anthracite coal miners. Discussion was opened in the House on January 15, 1903, by Representative James R. Mann of Illinois who, with a remarkably clear understanding of the whole course of departmental history, helped to bring the House to an intelligent consideration of the measure. Two days later, on January 17, the bill passed its last ordeal, and was quickly adjusted by conference committees in a way to meet the approval of both Congress and the President.[23]

Representative Mann, calling attention to the efforts that had been made for years past to get commercial, manufacturing, mining, labor, and even educational interests represented in the Cabinet, reminded his colleagues that only two new Executive Departments

22 *Congressional Record*, XXXV, 914.
23 *Ibid.*, XXXVI, 549, 858 ff., 929-930, 945-946, 1398, 1446, 1465-1467, 2008, 2036, 2188.

—Interior and Agriculture—had been created within a century. "The original .... Executive Departments," he asserted, "were each created because of a necessity and propriety which was apparent. The Interior Department was created because at the time it seemed very desirable to relieve some of the other departments of what were to them excrescences, and also to create an official adviser to the President who would give particular attention to the growth and development of our country internally." Here the speaker dwelt on the distinction between the establishment of the Department of Agriculture in 1862 and that of its predecessors. Its establishment was a clear departure from the previous policy of the government. The Department of Agriculture was not, he showed, essential to the administration of the government, although it had proved in the course of years to be immensely useful. Primarily it was a center for research and scientific investigation. That its success had much to do with the persistent demands of such other interests as Commerce and Manufactures for departmental recognition, he had no doubt. Many industrial interests had increased since that day to such a degree of importance that they, as well as Agriculture, could reasonably ask for recognition in the federal government. The Department of Commerce and Labor would afford a means of carrying on scientific research, the results of which could be used by all classes of the people, indeed by all the people "upon even terms." Investigations, he said, which "are now carried on in secret by the employees of some of the great corpora-

tions and used exclusively for the benefit of those corporations" should be placed under the direction and
supervision of the new Department. One of its chief
functions would be to furnish reliable statistics on all
sorts of home industries; and thus it would unify much
statistical work.[24]

In urging that the Bureau of Labor should be placed
in the new Department, Mann reminded the opponents
of the plan that a "statement or recommendation in
the annual report of one of the Cabinet officers is likely
to attract some attention; but the opinion or recommendation of the head of a branch of the service not
connected with one of the general departments is apt
to be overlooked—not from design, not from thought-
lessness . . . . but from lack of time and endurance."[25]

Turning to the example of foreign countries, Mr.
Mann directed attention to the British Board of Trade
as in some respects analogous to the projected department. The British Board he regarded as having been
influential in bringing about British supremacy in the
world's commerce. He reminded his hearers that such
countries as Germany, France, Belgium, Russia, Spain,
and several others had found it feasible to arrange for
special ministries which gave careful attention to just
such work—administrative and statistical—as the bill
contemplated.[26]

In view of the necessity of administrative enlargement and of popular approval for such enlargement,

---

[24] *Congressional Record*, XXXVI, 858-860 (*passim*).
[25] *Ibid.*, XXXVI, 862.
[26] *Ibid.*, XXXVI, 860.

the speaker was convinced that the time had come for the creation of another department. More than one department, however, could not wisely be organized. More than one new cabinet official should not be thrust on the President. ''The President's Cabinet is extra-constitutional. It . . . . exists voluntarily and by force of custom. It has become the custom, however . . . . when a department is created and the head thereof is denominated 'Secretary' . . . . to consider him as a cabinet officer. There is, of course, nothing to prevent the President from requesting the head of any other department to attend the meetings of . . . . the Cabinet. But the force of custom as it now exists is very strong. No departure from it is likely to soon occur. The meetings of the Cabinet necessarily exercise a tremendous influence upon the policies of the Executive. A department which is represented in the Cabinet is thereby given a great advantage . . . . It never has been the policy of the President to unduly extend the size of his Cabinet. To add greatly to its numbers would destroy its efficiency. It never has been the policy, therefore, of Congress to easily create a new head of an executive department who, under the custom, would be entitled to the courtesy of a seat in the Cabinet.''[27]

Mr. Mann's careful and illuminating speech furnished at the very outset a foundation of facts that tended in all probability to abbreviate the succeeding debate. But a factious minority felt bound to express itself against the measure. It was claimed, in the first place, that Labor, although not actually left out of the

[27] *Ibid.*, XXXVI, 858-859.

proposed department, was really subordinated and, by being confined to a mere Bureau, would be stripped of its existing dignity of an independent department.[28] It was easy for Representative Richardson of Alabama to cite the Democratic platform of 1900, which had declared for a Department of Labor, and to contrast it with the Republican platform of the same year which had declared for a Department of Commerce. He argued that the measure before the House had been drawn upon Republican lines and favored the commercial as differentiated from the labor class. "If," said the same speaker, alluding to very recent events, "there had been a secretary of labor in the Cabinet of the President having authority to speak for labor and to confer with the President, the President could have avoided the necessity of inviting Mr. Mitchell and other labor leaders to join the coal operators with him in conference in an effort to adjust the differences of the great anthracite coal strike. More than that," he continued, "had there been such a secretary then by the President, the creation of the Strike Commission, admitted to be unauthorized by law, would have been avoided."[29] "Your Secretary of Commerce," asserted Representative C. F. Cochran of Missouri, "will be drawn from classes and your Department of Commerce will be dominated by influences interested solely in increasing trade and the profits of traders."[30] Another speaker objected that

[28] *Congressional Record*, XXXVI, 864.
[29] *Ibid.*, XXXVI, 867.
[30] *Ibid.*, XXXVI, Appendix, p. 145.

there was no reference of any consequence to Labor. The new Department, he contended, was misnamed: "So far as labor is concerned in this country, it is not recognized." The plan was simply one more effort to centralize all the interests of the people.[31]

Limited by such views, the minority struggled obstinately to force Congress to make a clear difference in the bill between the interests of Capital and Labor. They refused to be satisfied by anything short of two departments—a Department of Labor and a Department of Commerce, each with its Secretary of cabinet rank. What in substance they wanted would have virtually forced Congress to declare officially that "the best the statesmanship of the future can hope to do is to give these two classes a fair field and no favors and let them fight it out."[32]

IV

The Department of Commerce and Labor could have been established for no partisan ends. It was intended primarily as a means of affording reliable information to the people of the entire country on such subjects as trade, commerce, labor, and various sorts of industries. Incidentally it relieved the overburdened Treasury Department of numerous charges. Among various transfers, it took over the Bureau of the Census from the Interior Department; and it relieved the Department of State of the Bureau of Foreign Commerce, the latter being made part of the Bureau

[31] Ibid., XXXVI, 875.
[32] Ibid.

of Statistics. The Bureau of Corporations and the Bureau of Manufactures were distinctly new creations in the Department. Much statistical and scientific work of the government was actually placed in the Department, and could be so placed at the discretion of the President in accordance with growing needs.[33]

In the whole course of the debates, very little was said as to the constitutionality of the proposed department, although there were casual reflections on the subject here and there. The Department of Commerce and Labor was not, strictly speaking, essential to the administration of the federal government. Behind the movement for it there were many industrial and social factors which were likely to be greatly benefited by its creation. It came chiefly as a result of the intelligent recognition that government knowledge and supervision of those factors was necessary to the maintenance of the general welfare. The measure was clearly akin to the act which established the Department of Agriculture in 1862. It too marked the departure in administrative policy which that act had first revealed.

For a great many years there had been an intelligent prejudice against enlarging the Cabinet. This prejudice had asserted itself even as far back as 1849 when the plan of a Department of the Interior was under discussion.[34] It appeared in 1862, and was still more

[33] 32 *Statutes at Large,* p. 825. Professor John A. Fairlie devotes a chapter (XVI) to the Department of Commerce and Labor in his volume entitled *The National Administration of the United States of America* (1905), pp. 230-247.

[34] *Supra,* chapter X, p. 284.

pronounced in 1888-1889.[35] In 1903 Mann's intelligent
outline of the growth of the Cabinet, from the very
beginning under Washington, probably tended to
reduce the force of any such argument against the
establishment of the new Department. At any rate
Mr. Mann indicated very directly that he had pondered
carefully the problem and would himself disapprove
of much enlargement of the Cabinet. There was very
little opposition to the bill that could have rested on
the basis of this prejudice. Nevertheless the old
prejudice is very likely to reappear in connection with
any future attempt to establish an additional executive department, for there is good reason to believe
that the Cabinet cannot now be enlarged without
seriously interfering with its usefulness as a consultative body.

[35] *Supra,* chapter XI, pp. 333, 338.

CHAPTER XIII

CONCLUSIONS

IN the world of political progression no government, it is safe to say, can ever rest on quite its original plan. Experience, and circumstances beyond the knowledge and control of one generation or set of men make succeeding generations constantly sensible of new wants, and force them to adopt political devices which may help to satisfy such wants. "We must follow the nature of our affairs," said Edmund Burke, "and conform ourselves to our situation. If we do, our objects are plain and compassable."[1] The fabric and the administrative machinery of government rest on the written laws. But the laws, as Burke very well understood, reach but a very little way. Administration, to be effective, must often depend on practices of which the written laws take little or no account. Behind the laws there are assumptions which give room for the exercise of individual judgment and discretion essential to their proper execution. The field of political practices and devices has always been large and ill defined. The student of history who would enter it can never do so by an easy road, for the various practices and devices within its bounds can seldom be seen or determined at a glance.

[1] *Works*, II, 357. Speech in the House of Commons on February 11, 1780.

I

The President's Cabinet is, and from the outset of its existence has been, a political device not directly accounted for in the statute laws or in the Constitution. It came into being as one result of the discretionary power with which the makers of the Constitution intended to endow the chief magistrate. It was created by President Washington in the opening years of our government under the Constitution in response to a demand of the President for a board of qualified assistants and confidential advisers, a demand so fundamental and natural as to be felt, but not anywhere at that time definitely formulated or at all clearly expressed.

This board of assistants summoned by the first President was akin in structure, if not also in functions, to some of the colonial Councils of State—occasionally called Privy Councils—and to the English Cabinet Council, the particular institution from which the President's Cabinet, by popular analogy, was named.[2] As early as 1783 Pelatiah Webster had conceived a similar board and termed it the Council of State in connection with his design for altering the government of the Confederation. It would, indeed, perhaps be fair to say that Webster's Council of State foreshadowed the later Cabinet.[3] At any rate, a board of administrative officials or heads of departments as advisers to the President was foreseen as a possibility several years later, at the epoch of the Conven-

2 *Supra,* pp. 78 ff., 89-96, 135-139, 150, 155-158.
3 *Supra,* pp. 62-63.

tion of 1787, by a few of the more discerning statesmen then hard at work on the problem of establishing
an efficient chief magistrate who should have control
over a national system of administration. This possible board was first termed the "Cabinet Council" in
1787 by Charles Pinckney of South Carolina in a passage to be found in his *Observations on the Plan of
Government submitted to the Federal Convention.*[4]
But such a board was not made practically assured
until the first Congress, during the spring and summer
of 1789, had arranged the statutes which provided for
four principal offices—three Secretaryships and the
Attorney-Generalship; and until the Senate had in
September of that year ratified Washington's appointments to those offices.[5]

As time elapsed, and the volume as well as the diver-
sity of presidential and administrative tasks increased,
five other offices were so arranged by the laws as to
make it not only practicable but likewise desirable for
the President to increase the original board from four
to nine confidential assistants. Thus the President's
Cabinet originated, and was formed, and grew into the
institution which we know to-day. But the process of
growth was slow, extending over a period of more than
a century.

With the establishment of the Secretaryship of the
Navy in 1798[6] and the Secretaryship of the Interior in
1849,[7] together with the admission of the Postmaster-

4 *Supra,* pp. 90-94.
5 *Supra,* pp. 97 ff., 110-119.
6 *Supra,* chapter VIII.
7 *Supra,* chapter X.

General into the President's circle of regular advisers in 1829,[8] the Cabinet reached a stage of maturity, if not of political completion in its growth, by about the middle of the nineteenth century, that is to say, after an existence of nearly sixty years. The occupants of the seven great offices, which by that time composed the Council, were officers necessary to any vigorous and efficient central system of administration. From the standpoint of centralization it was certainly desirable that such officers should be intimate with the President and his trusted advisers in matters of public policy. While five out of the seven offices had been more or less definitely arranged by the statutes of 1789 or a little later, the two remaining offices, the Secretaryships of the Navy and the Interior, were foreseen at that early day as likely in the course of years to become essential to a well-managed and vigorous government. When these latter two Secretaryships were created—relieving the older principal offices of various tasks, and meeting the pressure of new administrative needs—their creation completed the original ideal of an American secretariat, the ideal (let us say) of the decade, 1780-1790.

Within the third quarter of the nineteenth century sundry legislative enactments aided what may be called the process of cabinet unification, although none of the enactments, it should be added, took any direct account of the Cabinet. An act of March 3, 1853, placed the seven officials then forming the Council for the first time on an equal footing in the matter of sala-

[8] *Supra,* chapter IX.

ries.[9] This was the culmination of a series of occasional efforts, traceable from a much earlier date, to
bring the salaries of the principal officers into uniformity.[10] Again, between 1870 and 1874, several
alterations and various re-adjustments were made in
the laws affecting the principal offices in ways to show
that the statutes were being shaped into some degree
of conformity with political practices of which they
took no express account.

The statutes of 1789, it may be recalled, had provided for only two "executive" departments—the
Departments of State and War.[11] The Department of
the Navy was an "executive" department from the
date (1798) of its establishment; so likewise was the
Department of the Interior from 1849. The law on
the basis of which the Treasury Department had been
originally organized contained certain peculiarities of
language and intent which gave ground for the contention that the Secretary of the Treasury might be
regarded as not only within the range of congressional
control but also of congressional direction. President
Jackson, however, assumed that the Secretary of the
Treasury was, to all intents and purposes, an executive official and, at least in matters involving presidential policy, strictly subject to the direction of the
chief magistrate. Jackson, moreover, acted on the
basis of this interpretation of the law, and accordingly
established a precedent which could not be overlooked

9 See Appendix A, p. 396.
10 *Supra*, pp. 105, 159, 161, 163, 169 ff., 173 ff., 178.
11 Chapter IV, *supra*, p. 100.

in future by his successors. When the statutes were revised in 1873 and approved the next year, the law at length defined the Treasury Department as an "executive department."[12] From 1789 to 1870 the Attorney-General occupied an "Office." By the act of June 22, 1870, he became head of the "executive department" of Justice.[13] By the provisional law of 1789 the Post-master-General, while placed under the general direction of the President, was regarded as an official in charge of the "Post-Office." In the slow process of elaborating legal phraseology the Post-Office of 1789 was viewed as an "Establishment" (1810), as a "Department" (1825), and finally as an "Executive Department" (1874). But years before the clear enactment of 1874 the Post-Office Department was considered, by construction, as an executive department, and the Postmaster-General as "an executive officer of the United States."[14] It was the revision of the statutes in 1873 which finally disposed of the incongruous title of the Department of the Interior.[15]

Thus the revision of the statutes in 1873 was largely an attempt to re-shape and make consistent a great amount of legislation which had been lagging behind the needs of the times, or was to some extent outgrown. The officials of the Cabinet were henceforth all heads

[12] *Supra,* pp. 100-105.

[13] *Supra,* chapter VII, 187 ff.

[14] *Supra,* chapter IX, 231-232. The quotation is from Benjamin F. Butler's opinion of June 19, 1837, printed in *United States* vs. *Kendall* (1837). Butler was Attorney-General under Jackson and Van Buren from 1833 to 1838.

[15] *Supra,* chapter X, Note 2, p. 289, for remarks on the "Home Department."

of "executive" departments, and strictly so recognized in the statutes.

Meantime Congress had been forced to establish the Department of Agriculture in 1862, a new and independent department having a Commissioner at its head who should be appointed by the President. The Commissioner was required to report in writing annually to Congress and to the President. The general design of the Department contemplated the acquisition, and diffusion among the people, of "useful information on subjects connected with agriculture in the most general and comprehensive sense of that word." Furthermore, the Department was "to procure, propagate, and distribute among the people new and valuable seeds and plants."[16]

The establishment of the Department of Agriculture in the second year of the Civil War marked a notable variation, if not a new phase, of administrative progress and development. While the ideal of some such department was by no means new at that time, for it may be faintly traced from the closing years of the eighteenth century and with considerably greater clearness and consistency from about 1840, yet it was not regarded by the makers of the Constitution as essential to the government. The Secretaryship of Agriculture, in a word, was not involved in what I have chosen to call the original ideal of an American secretariat. Again, the Department of Agriculture is not and never has been primarily a political department. It was originally conceived as a department concerned

[16] 12 *Statutes at Large,* pp. 387 ff.

with the education of the farming classes. Its chief function has always been to supply careful information, and so to instruct and aid the farmers. Its establishment was a clear recognition by the national government of the importance of certain industrial and social factors to the general welfare of the country. The organization of the Department was exacted from Congress at a critical period as the result largely of a very persistent and intelligent popular demand. After an existence of twenty-seven years under a Commissioner, the Department of Agriculture was given the standing in law of an "executive" department in 1889. It was then, for the first time, provided with a Secretary who went at once by custom into the Cabinet as its eighth member.[17]

In 1888 the Department of Labor—an outgrowth of the Bureau of Labor of 1884, which had been a subdivision in the Interior Department—was authorized by law. This, like the Department of Agriculture, was an independent department. It followed, in this respect, accordingly, the precedent of the earlier establishment of 1862. Moreover, it too came as the result of popular pressure and demand. Fifteen years later, in 1903, the Department of Labor was reduced to the status of a bureau in the newly created executive Department of Commerce and Labor. With the establishment of this last executive department in charge of the Secretary of Commerce and Labor, provision was made for the ninth principal officer who was given the customary cabinet place and rank. Thus, since

[17] Chapter XI, *supra*, pp. 292 ff.

1849, two executive Secretaryships have been formed; and both of them have been largely the result of well-directed and widespread popular demand.[18]

When, in February, 1907, the term *cabinet* was for the first time in our history consciously introduced into the statute law of the United States,[19] the Cabinet was known to consist of nine principal officers, all of whom were heads of executive departments, and seven of whom were called Secretaries. Since 1903 there have been no independent departments in our government not recognized as "executive," although our administrative history has revealed in the past two such departments with commissioners not of cabinet rank or place at their heads. Just what constitutes an executive department has, so far as I know, never been definitely determined. This, however, is clear: Whenever a department has been created since 1789, and has been placed in charge of a principal officer termed a *Secretary,* it has been assumed for upwards of a century—in fact, ever since the establishment of the executive Department of the Navy in 1798—that such Secretary would become as a matter of course a member of the President's Cabinet Council. The first Secretaries of the Navy, of the Interior, of Agriculture, and of Commerce and Labor (Messrs. Stoddert of Maryland, Ewing of Ohio, Colman of Missouri, and Cortelyou of New York) were made members of the Cabinet so soon as they were commissioned to their respective positions. In brief, the practice of Presidents in inviting

18 Chapter XII, *supra*, pp. 346 ff.
19 *Supra*, pp. 156 ff.

new Secretaries into the Council has been invariable and in strict accord with this old assumption. The practice has established a custom that, it is certain, could not be broken in future without arousing comment and calling for explanation or justification.

Although the term *cabinet* has made its way into the federal law, it is by no means clear that this unique usage would be interpreted by the courts as any recognition of the well-established political device which the term characterizes. When first the term came into popular vogue, it was the designation of a board of four presidential assistants summoned at convenient times for the purpose of helping the President by advice to carry out or to accomplish effectively his duties. To-day the term characterizes a similar and enlarged board, now and for many years past called together regularly for the same general purpose on Tuesdays and Fridays during the sessions of Congress, and occasionally—depending solely upon the wishes of the President—at other times.

II

The President's Cabinet as a political device was at the outset an experiment. It came into existence naturally, and so very easily that its advent was unheralded—neither commented on nor explained. Although it was some years before it assumed the guise and the attributes of an institution, such a board had not been unforeseen. It called, however, for no special justification until it had proved to a measurable degree its utility, and was somewhat generally appreciated or understood.

As early as March, 1788, Alexander Hamilton expressed himself as strongly opposed to such a board if it were to be made a constitutional device: forced, that is to say, by law on the President, and certain— as he conceived it—to restrain the President by giving advice which he would be obliged to follow. Hamilton, nevertheless, was perfectly clear in his view that the administrative officers should be regarded as "the assistants or deputies of the chief magistrate." These assistants, he believed, should derive their office from the President's appointment, "at least from his nomination, and ought to be subject to his superintendence."[20] He might have added that confidence between the President and his deputies was an essential element in the relationship. At any rate the debates in the first Congress of 1789 make it evident that by that time this element was not overlooked in the statutory arrangements of the principal offices.[21]

In 1792, after experience in the capacity of special adviser to President Washington, Hamilton remarked that the energy and success of the new government must depend on the union and mutual deference subsisting between the principal officers, and on the conformity of their conduct with the views of their chief, the President.[22] Eight years later, in 1800, he set forth briefly the opinion that any efficient chief magis-

---

[20] *The Federalist* (ed. Ford), No. 70, pp. 466 ff. No. 72, pp. 481-482. March 15 and 19, 1788.

[21] Chapter IV, *supra*, pp. 98 ff.

[22] Chapter VI, *supra*, p. 135.

trate would find it useful, if not necessary, to consult his principal officers or—as he then termed them—"his constitutional advisers."[23] This latter statement, taken into consideration with earlier reflections, is good enough ground for reckoning Hamilton as among the number of American statesmen who at that time justified the Cabinet in theory as well as in practice. In the first quarter of the nineteenth century it is not difficult to discover in scattered sources—in congressional debates, in the writings of Jefferson, Judge Augustus B. Woodward, and other American publicists—evidence of an understanding, if not always approval, of the device.

There have been, from the beginnings, three clear ideals underlying the conception of the American Presidency. Without them, indeed, it is hardly conceivable that a board of presidential counsellors such as the Cabinet could originally have been formed, and gradually have been increased to its present size. There was, first, the ideal of unity in the executive power. There was, second, the ideal of the responsibility of the President to the people for the proper and faithful execution of the laws. There was, third, the ideal of allowing the President a limited but generous political discretion in his task of supervising, directing, and removing—if necessary—his assistants, the principal officers. The first of these was perhaps the most fundamental, the outgrowth of experience. But all of them may be easily illustrated by passages taken from early and authoritative sources.

[23] *Ibid., supra,* p. 140.

"I clearly concur in opinion," wrote Hamilton in *The Federalist,* ". . . . with a writer[24] whom the celebrated Junius pronounces to be 'deep, solid, and ingenious,' that 'the executive power is more easily confined when it is ONE'; that it is far more safe there should be a single object for the jealousy and watchfulness of the people; and, in a word, that all multiplication of the Executive is rather dangerous than friendly to liberty.'"[25]

"It is evidently the intention of the constitution," declared Madison, speaking in the first House of Representatives on June 16, 1789, "that the first Magistrate should be responsible for the executive department; so far, therefore, as we do not make the officers who are to aid him in the duties of that department responsible to him, he is not responsible to his country."[26]

"By the constitution of the United States," said Marshall in 1803, "the president is invested with certain important political powers, in the exercise of which he is to use his own discretion, and is accountable only to his country in his political character and to his own conscience. To aid him in the performance of these duties, he is authorized to appoint certain officers, who act by his authority, and in conformity with his orders. In such cases," continued the Chief-

---

[24] De Lolme.

[25] P. 474. March 15, 1788. Cf. Amos Kendall's statement: "The executive is an unity. The framers of the Constitution had studied history too well to impose on their country a divided executive." June 24, 1837. 5 Cranch, *Reports of Cases . . . . in the United States Circuit Court of the District of Columbia,* p. 197.

[26] *Annals of Congress,* I, 480.

Justice, "their acts are his acts; and whatever opinion may be entertained of the manner in which executive discretion may be used, still there exists, and can exist, no power to control that discretion. The subjects are political . . . . the decision of the executive is conclusive."[27]

These three formulations of the ideals of executive unity, executive responsibility, and executive discretion, written in the early years of our government by three of the foremost students of the Constitution, reveal with admirable precision the important ideals at the basis of the general conception of the American Presidency. It was these three ideals which helped markedly toward the development of that office in consistency and efficiency. While it is true that these ideals were gravely endangered in Jackson's second term, especially in 1833 and 1834, when controversy raged over the question of the President's right to remove his Secretary of the Treasury, William · J. Duane, and of the relation of that Secretaryship to the President;[28] and while the three ideals were temporarily shattered under President Johnson by the passage of the Tenure of Office Act of March 2, 1867, and by the Senate's arrogant claim of a right to destroy Johnson's discretion in removing an obnoxious cabinet official, the Secretary of War, Edwin M. Stanton;[29] never-

[27] *Marbury* vs. *Madison* in 1 Cranch, *Reports* (2d ed., New York: 1812), p. 165.

[28] See Jackson's "Protest" of April 15, 1834, in *Messages and Papers*, III, 69 ff for a telling argument against his persecutors. *Supra*, chapter IV, 103 ff.

[29] Grover Cleveland presented a discerning view of this whole subject in its historic relations in his essay entitled "The Independence of the

theless, it is also true, I believe, that these three ideals may be said to have stood the test of upwards of one hundred and twenty years of government under the Constitution. For Jackson carried the day against his opponents; and with the modification of the Tenure of Office Act in 1869, and its final repeal in 1887, the Presidency was restored once more to its pristine prerogatives and powers.

Aware of his responsibility to the people, entrusted, as he knew himself to be by the Constitution and the laws, with abundant discretion, aided by experience and circumstances in bringing his assistants into co-operation, Washington soon discovered as President that the method of asking for the opinions or advice of his qualified assistants "in writing" was as a rule impracticable and unnecessary. He listened to oral advice or counsel as a matter of course. But in business of general importance he found the method of summoning a council at convenient times both natural and effective. Accordingly, within a few years after the opening of his Presidency, he adopted the method. It appealed to his successors as useful, and was followed by all of them with more or less regularity. Thus in the course of time the practice of cabinet councils assumed an institutional character. The Cabinet, in brief, achieved a distinct place in history.

Executive,'' in *Presidential Problems* (1904), pp. 3-76, *passim.* The legal aspect of the subject was commented on by W. M. Evarts in 12 *Opinions of the Attorneys-General*, pp. 439, 446. The Supreme Court expressly declined to pass judgment on the constitutional question of the President's power of removal, although it quoted at length from the legislative and judicial history of the subject in the case of *Parsons* vs. *United States* (1896). See 167 *U. S. Reports*, pp. 334-335, 340 ff.

It requires no great familiarity with the lore of cabinet meetings as these meetings are revealed in three such records as the *Memoirs* of John Quincy Adams, the *Diary* of President Polk, and the fragmentary *Diary* of Gideon Welles as thus far available,[30] to discover how comparatively seldom written opinions have hitherto been demanded from the cabinet associates of various Presidents. Washington was probably much more inclined to depend for advice upon such opinions than were any of his successors. "At each meeting of the Cabinet," wrote Polk on September 23, 1848, "I learn from each member what is being done in his particular Department, and especially if any question of doubt or difficulty has arisen. I have never," he added, "called for any written opinions from my Cabinet, preferring to take their opinions after discussion, in Cabinet & in the presence of each other. In this way harmony of opinion is more likely to exist."[31] While this illuminating statement should be taken only in its applicability to a single administration, it has been generally true since Washington's day that written opinions have been exceptional as a mode of taking advice.[32] Moreover, it has not been the

[30] *Atlantic Monthly*, February-November, 1909 (The War period: July 13, 1862-April 22, 1865). *Ibid.*, February, 1910-January, 1911 (The period of Reconstruction: April 21, 1865-April 17, 1869). For comment on the untrustworthiness of this precious record as printed thus far, see *The Nation* (New York) XC, May 12, 1910. The Diary is now (September, 1911) promised for publication in several volumes.

[31] *Diary*, IV, 131.

[32] Based on much scattered evidence, but largely on the sources cited in the narrative. These three sources alone afford materials on approximately 740 separate cabinet meetings. Polk's *Diary* yields evidence on about 365 meetings of the Cabinet held during his term, yet his records

practice of President Taft thus far to ask for written opinions on questions of policy.[33]

III

As related to the theory of the Cabinet, attention may be directed at this point to a problem of presidential practice which arose early in the history of the institution. There is some evidence to show that President Washington was inclined, for several years after the opening of his Presidency, to call upon Vice-President John Adams for both written and oral opinions on matters of policy. On at least one occasion (April 11, 1791) Adams was summoned to a meeting of the Secretaries at the President's suggestion. At the time Washington was absent from Philadelphia, then the temporary seat of the national government. He assumed, it may be inferred, that during his absence and in view of the fact that the Senate was not in session, the Vice-President would be the proper person to consult with the Secretaries. Jefferson believed that this appearance of the Vice-President at a cabinet session was unique. Whether this was true or not, Jefferson's avowed conception of the vice-presidential office—first expressed in 1797—as being an office constitutionally limited to legislative functions, would hardly have permitted him, while he acted as Vice-President to John Adams, to take any part

do not begin until August 26, 1845; they close with the entry of June 2, 1849, some months after Polk's retirement from office.

[33] Private letter to the author, dated February 7, 1911, from the Secretary of War, Jacob M. Dickinson, who has since resigned his place.

in "executive consultations."[34] We may be reasonably certain, moreover, that during his own Presidency Jefferson never thought of inviting the Vice-President to sessions of the Cabinet for this, if for no other, reason. As late as 1825 Judge Woodward, a shrewd observer of executive practices, asserted that it had been the "uniform course" up to that time to exclude the Vice-President from the Cabinet.[35]

Close scrutiny of much printed cabinet data since 1825 has failed thus far to reveal a single authenticated instance of a Vice-President in attendance at a cabinet meeting. President Polk, who was throughout his four-year term on a friendly footing with Vice-President George M. Dallas, consulted Dallas freely on many matters of policy which came at one time and another before the regular sessions of the Cabinet. The Vice-President was asked occasionally to read portions of Polk's messages, in their less mature stages, and to make suggestions on these and other subjects. But, although Polk's *Diary* indicates that the President sometimes invited outsiders into cabinet meetings,[36] it gives not a single record of Dallas's presence at such meetings.

Within recent years there has arisen a popular impression that Vice-President Hobart, known to have been on intimate and friendly terms with President McKinley, was at times admitted to sessions of the Cabinet. In referring to the intimacy between Hobart

[34] *Supra,* pp. 124 ff.
[35] *Supra,* pp. 144 ff.
[36] *Diary,* I, 161. II, 47-48, 132-133, 264-265, 272-273, 432, 486. III, 168, 261. IV, 125, 196-197.

and McKinley, Mr. Hobart's biographer has this to say:

> They were both friends and confederates. So certain was the President of the loyalty and good judgment of his colleague, that the latter was consulted in all questions of general policy. . . . . It may be safely said that no measure of importance was discussed with the Cabinet of which the Vice-President was not cognizant; and that members of the Cabinet, as well as the President, freely took counsel with him. The unusual title given him in some of the papers in recognition of his influence was "Assistant President."[37]

The passage here cited gives no authority to the view that Hobart attended sessions of the McKinley Cabinet. He may have done so. A good many Presidents have at different times invited outsiders into cabinet meetings. It is reasonable to suppose that on occasions in the past it has been deemed a matter of simple wisdom and political discretion for a President to summon a friendly Vice-President into a session of the Cabinet. Mr. McKinley seems to have consulted Vice-President Hobart very much as Polk consulted Vice-President Dallas. The evidence does not allow us at present to say anything more determinate. Here the matter must rest until some one who was a member of the McKinley Cabinet chooses to speak plainly. What is certain is this: that from the beginning of the government the rule—the all but "uniform course"—has been to exclude the Vice-President from the Council.

In several of the early projects for an executive council, notably in Ellsworth's project of August 18,

37 David Magie, *Life of Garret Augustus Hobart* (1910), pp. 168-169.

1787, the "president of the Senate" was to be found.[38] The Constitution, however, finally left the Vice-President in a somewhat anomalous place: he is not a member of the Senate, although he presides over that body; and he has no vote on any matter unless the Senate is equally divided.[39] Inasmuch as the Constitution did not expressly forbid the Vice-President to take part in executive business, the President was left at liberty to consult him if he chose to do so, while still shouldering the whole responsibility for his acts.

It is presumably well that President and Vice-President should be always members of the same party, as indeed they have had to be ever since the Twelfth Amendment went into effect, for the Vice-President should understand and appreciate the party principles of the man whom he may be called upon suddenly to succeed. But appreciation of principles is one thing; the sort of intimacy which should exist between a President and a close adviser is quite another. It was undoubtedly fortunate that Polk and Dallas remained in close touch and on terms of peculiar intimacy during Polk's trying administration. Such instances of intimacy, however, have been few and very infrequent in the history of the two offices.[40] The Vice-President represents no Department. With his nomination to office the President has, as a rule, nothing whatever to do. He occupies no such powerful position as the Speaker of the House of Representatives. While

[38] *Supra*, chapter III, p. 75.
[39] Article I, sec. 2.
[40] The three well-known intimacies are those of Jackson and Van Buren, Polk and Dallas, and McKinley and Hobart.

there have been a few men of great eminence in the
Vice-Presidency in the past, nevertheless the office has
been generally regarded as rather undesirable. Indeed,
it has been deliberately declined or has gone begging on
at least three separate occasions.[41] What a man can
accomplish in it must depend not alone on circumstances often beyond control, but also on such factors
as the candidate's party position, his political sagacity,
and his personal force—all of these factors sure to
affect his capacity to guide and influence the Senate.

To force the Vice-President into the Cabinet would
seem, from the preceding considerations, to be as
unwise as it is really unnecessary. To do so, would
be to limit the discretionary power of the President
and to interfere with the unity of the executive—a
limitation and an interference that would tend to alter
two of the great ideals that have been recognized for
years as at the very basis of the American Presidency.
At all events, such helpful influence as the Vice-
President can exert on matters involving executive policy has been heretofore exerted outside the
Cabinet.[42]

[41] Senator Silas Wright of New York declined an almost unanimous
nomination in 1844 on the Polk ticket. Senator Benjamin Fitzpatrick of
Alabama declined a similar nomination to run on the Douglas ticket in
1860. In 1884 the convention of the Anti-Monopoly party—a party that
had had no prior history and did not last—nominated Benjamin
F. Butler of Massachusetts for President. Leaving the settlement of
the nomination for Vice-President to its national committee, that body
finally determined to adopt General Alanson M. West of Mississippi,
candidate of the National or Greenback party, for the second position.
E. Stanwood, *History of the Presidency*, pp. 213-214, 286, 423.

[42] The Vice-Presidency has been much discussed in the newspapers of
late years. As a topic it was brought into special prominence by Mr.

IV

The Senators have frequently been termed the "constitutional counsellors" of the President from the earliest days of the government. In a somewhat different sense the principal officers have likewise been termed "constitutional counsellors" or "constitutional advisers" by careful writers. The Vice-Presidents have never been so called or so considered.

Hamilton, as I have pointed out more than once,[43] referred to the principal officers or heads of departments in 1800 as "constitutional advisers." In his "Opinion" of March 8, 1854, Attorney-General Cushing, writing of Washington's principal officers, asserted that those officers "were the immediate superior ministerial officers of the President, and his constitutional counsellors during the whole period of the administration."[44] Once more, in his "Opinion" of August 31, 1855, Cushing, directing attention to the statement in the Constitution that the President may require in writing the advice of his principal officers, declared that for that reason "those officers are sometimes characterized, and not improperly, as 'constitutional advisers' of the President."[45] In a special

W. J. Bryan's declaration in midsummer, 1908, that he proposed to admit his running-mate, John W. Kern, into the Cabinet, should he be elected to the Presidency in the following November. Long before this declaration, Mr. Bryan had discussed the subject in the first number of his paper, *The Commoner* of January 23, 1901. For editorials on the subject, see the *New York Times*, June 13, and July 17, 1908; *The Sun* (New York), July 19, 1908; and the *Hartford Courant*, July 3, 1908.

[43] *Supra*, pp. 5, 140, 379.
[44] 6 *Opinions*, p. 330.
[45] 7 *Opinions*, p. 460.

message to the Senate of December 12, 1867, President Johnson referred to his cabinet officers as "constitutional advisers."[46] Hamilton was perhaps writing rapidly, *currente calamo,* and took some liberties with language. Cushing and Johnson, on the other hand, wrote deliberately—they intended that their words should be taken literally. In any case, this usage of language, although it has been objected to,[47] rests upon a perfectly rational theory of the advisory function.

It is true that the principal (or cabinet) officers were not, like the Senate, created by the Constitution. The principal offices are statutory. The statutes attempted to define the duties of their chief officers or heads. But one duty the statutes have never defined— the notable duty obligatory upon every head of a department to give advice to the President when asked to do so—for the sufficient reason that that duty has been imposed upon the heads of departments, whatever their number, by the Constitution itself. The exaction of such an obligation was left to the discretion of the President. When once the President called for an opinion, it must be forthcoming, for it is required

[46] *Messages and Papers,* VI, 585.

[47] *E. g.* Senator Lodge says: "The members of the Cabinet are often loosely spoken of as constitutional advisers of the President. They are, as a matter of fact, nothing of the sort. They are not created by the Constitution, but by the laws. . . . . The Constitution contemplates the establishment of executive departments, and says that the President may require the opinion in writing of the heads of such departments, but these departments can exist only by the pleasure of Congress, and the President is not bound to consult their chiefs." The Senate, he concludes, is "constitutional"; the Cabinet is "statutory." *A Frontier Town,* etc. (1906), p. 73.

by the fundamental law that it should be. On such an occasion, argued President Johnson in his special message already cited, the head of a department "acts under the gravest obligations of law, for when he is called upon by the President for advice it is the Constitution which speaks to him. All his other duties are left by the Constitution to be regulated by statute, but this duty was deemed so momentous that it is imposed by the Constitution itself."[48]

Two ideas in respect to the Cabinet—the idea of unity of opinion and the idea of mutual confidence—appeared and were to some extent developed in Johnson's message. Both ideas, moreover, have been more or less recurrent in the course of the history of the theory of the American Presidency. Indeed, they were alien neither to Hamilton's nor to Cushing's thought of the principal offices.[49]

Unity of opinion, according to President Johnson, is absolutely essential to the executive upon great questions of public policy or administration. He thus elaborated his thought:

I do not claim that a head of Department should have no other opinions than those of the President. He has the same right, in the conscientious discharge of duty, to entertain and express his own opinions as has the President. What I do claim is that the President is the responsible head of the Administration, and when the opinions of a head of Department are irreconcilably opposed to those of the President in grave matters of policy and administration, there is but one result which can solve the difficulty, and that is a severance

[48] *Messages and Papers*, VI, 587.
[49] *Supra*, pp. 110, 135, 140, 182.

of the official relation. This in the past history of the Government has always been the rule, and it is a wise one, for such differences of opinion among its members must impair the efficiency of any Administration.[50]

To define all the relations existing between the heads of departments and the President would be a matter of great difficulty. The legal relations have been well enough defined by the statute laws which created the different principal offices. The principal officers, however, were placed by the Constitution in the position of assistants and advisers to the President. Accordingly, beyond the defined legal relations there are others not expressed, but necessarily attendant upon these. This was Johnson's view:

Chief among these is mutual confidence. This relation is so delicate that it is sometimes hard to say when or how it ceases. A single flagrant act may end it at once, and then there is no difficulty. But confidence may be just as effectually destroyed by a series of causes too subtle for demonstration. As it is a plant of slow growth, so, too, it may be slow in decay. . . . .[51]

President Johnson's special message to the Senate of December, 1867, remains one of the most remarkable contributions to the political theory of the Presidency that can be found in the whole range of American state papers. In respect to the theory of the Cabinet, it was discerning and illuminating. The basic ideals of the Presidency—executive unity, executive responsibility, and executive discretion—were underlying Johnson's thought. For them he was contend-

[50] *Messages and Papers,* VI, 589.
[51] *Ibid.,* VI, 592-593.

ing. They must be sustained by all his principal officers. An officer who refused to sustain them, it must be the President's privilege—his right—to dismiss. The sense of subordination of all the principal officers to the President had long since come to exist partly by construction of the constitutional duty of the President to take care that the laws be faithfully executed, and partly by the analogies of statutes. In the very nature of things there must be corporate conjunction on matters of policy, a board of advisers subject in all matters of doubt to one determining will.[52]

V

The Cabinet's usefulness as an advisory board has of course varied from time to time in the past in accordance with the different personal elements of which it has been composed. John Adams, Madison, Jackson, Tyler, Buchanan, Lincoln, Johnson, and Grant as Presidents all experienced more or less serious difficulties with their cabinet advisers. It is well enough known that both John Adams and Jackson were at times much disinclined to consult the body on matters of large and general importance. The Cabinet, however, could not be ignored for long by any of the Presidents. The twenty-six Cabinets of American history—reckoning to the close of President Roosevelt's administration in March, 1909,—have all con-

[52] I have used here several ideas derived from Caleb Cushing's two "Opinions" already cited.

tained a nucleus or coterie of able, experienced, and well-qualified men. These men could fairly claim and obtain consideration from their chiefs, the twenty-six Presidents who appointed them, as co-ordinate factors in the work of assisting in executive tasks. For the truth is that great measures for the country's welfare, often accredited to individual men, are seldom attained without the active efforts and earnest co-operation of many minds.

APPENDIX

TABLE A

Salaries of President, Vice-President, and Principal Officers: 1789–1909*

Years	President	Vice-President	Secretary of State	Secretary of the Treasury	Secretary of War	Attorney-General	Secretary of the Navy	Postmaster-General	Secretary of the Interior	Secretary of Agriculture	Secretary of Commerce and Labor
1789	$25,000	$5,000	$3,500	$3,500	$3,000	$1,500	$	$1,500	$	$	$
1791						1,900					
1792								2,000			
1794								2,400			
1797						2,400					
1798							3,000				
1799			5,000	5,000	4,500	3,000	4,500	3,000			
1819			6,000	6,000	6,000	3,500	6,000	4,000			
1827								6,000			
1830						4,000					
1849									6,000		
1853		8,000	8,000	8,000	8,000	8,000	8,000	8,000	8,000		
1862										3,000†	
1873	50,000	10,000	10,000	10,000	10,000	10,000	10,000	10,000	10,000	4,000	
1874		8,000	8,000	8,000	8,000	8,000	8,000	8,000	8,000	3,000	
1881										3,500	
1882										4,000	
1883										4,500	
1884											3,000§
1888											5,000
1889										5,000	
1903										8,000	
1907											8,000
1909	75,000	12,000	12,000	12,000	12,000	12,000	12,000	12,000	12,000	12,000	12,000

*Taken chiefly from the so-called Dockery Report. *House Reports,* 53 Congress, 1 Sess. (1893). II. Report No. 49.
†Commissioner of Agriculture to 1889. §Commissioner of Labor to 1903.

NOTES TO TABLE A

THE SALARY OF THE SECRETARY OF STATE (1909-1911)

By a somewhat unusual circumstance in 1909, the salary of the Secretary of State was temporarily reduced to its previous grade of $8,000, in order to allow Hon. Philander C. Knox, member of the federal Senate from Pennsylvania, 1905-1911, to take office as Secretary of State in President Taft's Cabinet. In accordance with the Constitution, Article I, section 6, paragraph 2:

> No senator or representative shall, during the time for which he was elected, be appointed to any civil office under the authority of the United States which shall have been created, or the emoluments whereof shall have been increased, during such time; and no person holding any office under the United States shall be a member of either house during his continuance in office.

The Legislative, Executive and Judicial Appropriation Act of February 26, 1907 (34 *Statutes at Large*, p. 993) fixed the annual compensation of heads of executive departments for the fiscal year ending June 30, 1908, at $12,000. When Mr. Knox accepted the portfolio of Secretary of State a special act of Congress was passed repealing the above act in so far as the same related to the annual compensation of the Secretary of State, fixing the compensation of that position at the rate of $8,000 (Act of February 17, 1909. 35 *Statutes at Large*, chap. 137, p. 626). On March 5, 1911, the annual compensation of the Secretary of State was placed on the $12,000 basis. The Deficiency Appropriation Act of March 4, 1911 (36 *Statutes at Large*, chap. 240, pp. 1289, 1290) provided additional compensation for that position for the period from March 5, 1911, to June 30, 1911, of $1,288.89, and the Legislative, Executive and Judicial Act of March 4, 1911

(36 *Statutes at Large,* chap. 237, p. 1186) provided $12,000 as the salary for the fiscal year ending June 30, 1912. The salary of that place is now consequently the same as that of the other heads of executive departments.

The case is not without precedent. For a discussion of it, the reader may be referred to the debates in the *Congressional Record* of February 11, 13, 15, etc., 1909.

THE PRESIDENT'S PERQUISITES

From the beginning the President has had, besides a salary, certain perquisites. As early as September 24, 1789 (1 *Statutes at Large,* ch. xix, 72) the President was to have "the use of the furniture and other effects, now in his possession, belonging to the United States." The next year the law (*Ibid.,* ch. xxviii, 130) made provision for the appointment of commissioners with power to purchase land in the District of Columbia partly for the purpose of a building for the President. The Act of April 24, 1800 (2 *Statutes at Large,* ch. xxxvii, 55) provided:

> That for the purpose of providing furniture for the house erected in the city of Washington, for the accommodation of the President of the United States, a sum not exceeding fifteen thousand dollars be expended, under the direction of the heads of the several departments of state, of the treasury, of war, and of the navy.

"An Act to provide for the Traveling Expenses of the President of the United States" (June 23, 1906. 34 *Statutes at Large,* ch. 3523, p. 454) arranges:

> That hereafter there may be expended for or on account of the traveling expenses of the President . . . . such sum as Congress may from time to time appropriate, not exceeding twenty-five thousand dollars per annum, such sum when appropriated to be expended in the discretion of the President and accounted for on his certificate only.

By the Deficiency Appropriation Act of March 4, 1909 (35 *Statutes at Large,* ch. 298, sec. 1, p. 908), provision was made for the appropriation for a housekeeper for the Executive Mansion, at the rate of $1,000 per annum, from March 4, 1909, to June 30, 1910.

TABLE B

Table to indicate the States of the Union from which the Principal Officers have been chosen between 1789 and 1909.*

SECRETARIES OF STATE

New York	7	Ohio	2
Virginia	6	Maryland	1
Massachusetts	5	Kentucky	1
Pennsylvania	3	Louisiana	1
Delaware	2	Georgia	1
Illinois	2	South Carolina	1
Maine	2	Michigan	1
Indiana	2	New Jersey	1

SECRETARIES OF THE TREASURY

New York	7	Minnesota	1
Pennsylvania	7	Connecticut	1
Ohio	5	Tennessee	1
Kentucky	4	Delaware	1
Massachusetts	3	New Hampshire	1
Georgia	2	Mississippi	1
Maryland	2	Illinois	1
Maine	2	Iowa	1
Indiana	2		

* The statistics here set forth have been chiefly compiled from Robert B. Mosher's *Executive Register.* The lists of Cabinets as printed in such books as the newspaper almanacs are quite unreliable.

SECRETARIES OF WAR

New York	8	Iowa	2
Massachusetts	5	Louisiana	1
Pennsylvania	5	Mississippi	1
Ohio	5	Kentucky	1
Virginia	3	Minnesota	1
Tennessee	3	Vermont	1
Georgia	2	West Virginia	1
South Carolina	2	Michigan	1
Illinois	2		

ATTORNEYS-GENERAL

Pennsylvania	7	South Carolina	1
Massachusetts	6	Maine	1
Maryland	6	Connecticut	1
Virginia	4	Missouri	1
Kentucky	4	Oregon	1
Ohio	4	Arkansas	1
New York	3	Indiana	1
Georgia	2	California	1
Delaware	1	New Jersey	1
Tennessee	1		

SECRETARIES OF THE NAVY

Massachusetts	6	South Carolina	1
Virginia	5	Indiana	1
Maryland	4	West Virginia	1
New York	4	Louisiana	1
North Carolina	4	Alabama	1
New Jersey	3	Illinois	1
New Hampshire	2	California	1
Pennsylvania	2	Michigan	1
Connecticut	2		

POSTMASTERS-GENERAL

New York	5	Vermont	1
Kentucky	4	Maine	1
Tennessee	4	Ohio	1
Pennsylvania	4	Virginia	1
Wisconsin	4	Iowa	1
Connecticut	3	Michigan	1
Maryland	3	West Virginia	1
Indiana	2	Massachusetts	1

SECRETARIES OF THE INTERIOR

Ohio	4	Virginia	1
Missouri	4	Illinois	1
Michigan	2	Colorado	1
Mississippi	2	Wisconsin	1
Indiana	2	Georgia	1
Iowa	2	New York	1
Pennsylvania	1		

SECRETARIES OF AGRICULTURE

Missouri	1	Nebraska	1
Wisconsin	1	Iowa	1

SECRETARIES OF COMMERCE AND LABOR

New York	2	California	1

TOTAL APPOINTMENTS TO PRINCIPAL OFFICES FROM THE STATES

1. New York	37*	18. Michigan	5
2. Pennsylvania	29*	19. Maine	4*
3. Massachusetts	26*	20. Delaware	4
4. Ohio	21*	21. Mississippi	4
5. Virginia	20*	22. North Carolina	4
6. Maryland	16*	23. California	3*
7. Kentucky	14*	24. New Hampshire	3*
8. Tennessee	9	25. West Virginia	3
9. Indiana	8*	26. Vermont	2
10. Connecticut	7*	27. Louisiana	2
11. Illinois	7	28. Minnesota	2*
12. Iowa	7	29. Alabama	1
13. Georgia	6*	30. Colorado	1
14. Wisconsin	6*	31. Nebraska	1
15. Missouri	6	32. Oregon	1
16. South Carolina	5*	33. Arkansas	1
17. New Jersey	5		

* NOTE: The figures in this tabulation will be misleading unless the reader observes that certain individuals, holding two (rarely three) cabinet offices, have been reckoned two or three times, in accordance with the facts. No account has been taken of the Postmasters-General prior to

STATES NOT REPRESENTED IN THE PRINCIPAL OFFICES:

1789-1909

Rhode Island	Montana
Florida	Idaho
Texas	Washington
Oklahoma	Wyoming
Kansas	Utah
South Dakota	Nevada
North Dakota	

C

THE SMITHSONIAN INSTITUTION AND THE CABINET

The Smithsonian Institution was organized for the purpose of administering a bequest to the govern-

1829, when first the office was recognized as carrying cabinet rank. The following names will make the figures clearer:

1. NEW YORK: B. F. Butler, W., Atg.; J. C. Spencer, W., Tr.; W. L. Marcy, W., St.; W. M. Evarts, Atg., St.; G. B. Cortelyou, C. and L., Pmg., Tr.; E. Root, W., St.
2. PENNSYLVANIA: R. Rush, Atg., Tr.; J. S. Black, Atg., St.
3. MASSACHUSETTS: T. Pickering, W., St.; S. Dexter, W., Tr.; D. Webster, St. (*bis*); R. Olney, Atg., St.; W. H. Moody, N., Atg.
4. OHIO: T. Ewing, Tr., Int.; E. M. Stanton, Atg., W.; A. Taft, W., Atg.; J. Sherman, Tr., St.
5. VIRGINIA: E. Randolph, Atg., St.; J. Monroe, St., W.; A. P. Upshur, St., N.; J. Y. Mason, N., Atg., N.
6. MARYLAND: R. Smith, N., Atg., St.; R. B. Taney, Atg., Tr.; C. J. Bonaparte, N., Atg.
7. KENTUCKY: J. J. Crittenden, Atg. (*bis*); J. Holt, W., Pmg.
9. INDIANA: H. McCulloch, Tr. (*bis*); W. Q. Gresham, Pmg., Tr.*
10. CONNECTICUT: I. Toucey, Atg., N.
13. GEORGIA: W. H. Crawford, W., Tr.
14. WISCONSIN: W. F. Vilas, Pmg., Int.
16. SOUTH CAROLINA: J. C. Calhoun, W., St.
19. MAINE: J. G. Blaine, St. (*bis*).
23. CALIFORNIA: V. H. Metcalf, C. and L., N.
24. NEW HAMPSHIRE: L. Woodbury, N., Tr.
28. MINNESOTA: W. Windom, Tr. (*bis*).

* Mr. Gresham was commissioned as Secretary of State (1893-1895) from Illinois—his third cabinet appointment.

ment of the United States by the will of James Smithson of London, a distinguished chemist and mineralogist, who died in Genoa, Italy, in 1829. It has, consequently, always occupied a peculiar relation to the government. Founded, after some opposition, "for the increase and diffusion of knowledge," it was first organized in Washington, D. C., by a law approved on August 10, 1846 (9 *Statutes at Large,* p. 102). The supervising and advisory body denominated an "Establishment" and placed over the Board of Regents—a body not wholly distinct from that Board —was to consist of the following members: the President of the United States, the Vice-President, the six principal officers (all the cabinet officers of that day), the Chief-Justice of the Supreme Court, the Commissioner of Patents, the Mayor of the City of Washington "during the time for which they shall hold their respective offices, and such other persons as they may elect honorary members." In the course of years this original law was found to be quite out of accord in some respects with the development of national administration. In the first place, the Secretary of the Interior, provided for by the law of March 3, 1849, had become the superior of the Commissioner of Patents. Again, there was no "Mayor" of Washington after 1870. Finally, another Secretaryship—that of Agriculture—was established by the law of February 9, 1889.

Down to March 12, 1894, the date of a change in the original law of 1846, only a single Secretary of the Interior—Columbus Delano of Ohio, serving in that office from 1870 to 1875 under President Grant—had acted as an honorary member of the Establishment, elected, as he was, in 1872. The statute of March 12 provided:

That the President, the Vice-President, the Chief-Justice, and the heads of the Executive Departments are hereby constituted an establishment by the name of the Smithsonian Institution, etc. (28 *Statutes at Large*, p. 41).

By this change in the law, the Secretaries of the Interior and Agriculture became *ex officio* members of the Establishment, so that to-day, with one additional Secretaryship, that of Commerce and Labor arranged for by the law of February 14, 1903, all the cabinet officers are included in the Establishment of the Smithsonian Institution.

For all details of this matter, see William J. Rhees's *The Smithsonian Institution.* 2 vols. Washington: 1901.

D

List of Authorities

The list of titles here printed includes every book, pamphlet, or magazine article that has been directly cited in the notes of these Studies, together with titles of a very few volumes not so cited. I have not found it possible, for example, anywhere in the notes adequately to indicate my indebtedness to two such works as Professor Dicey's *Law and Public Opinion* and Professor Sidgwick's *Development of European Polity,* for I have not been conscious of their direct bearing upon my theme. I have, on the other hand, gone to them frequently for stimulus; and I am sure that they have helped me here and there to formulate my thought. I have intentionally ignored in this list the usual and well-known bibliographical aids, although a few aids not so well known have been included. Some readers may derive assistance from Mr. Appleton P. C. Griffin's *Select List of Books on the Cabinets of England and America* (Washington: 1903). It has not seemed worth while to include Congressional Documents, especially as these have been carefully referred to in the foot-notes whenever they have been serviceable, notably in Chapters VII-XI.

ADAMS, HENRY: *History of the United States* [1801-1817]. 9 vols. New York: 1889-1891.

ADAMS, JOHN: *Works* . . . . with a Life of the Author, Notes, and Illustrations. By his Grandson, Charles Francis Adams. 10 vols. Boston: 1856.

ADAMS, JOHN QUINCY: *Memoirs* . . . . comprising portions of his Diary from 1795 to 1848. Ed. by Charles Francis Adams. 12 vols. Philadelphia: 1874-1877.
The Jubilee of the Constitution, A Discourse delivered at the Request of the New York Historical Society, in the City of New York, on Thursday, the 30th of April, 1839. New York: 1839.

ALGER, GEORGE W.: "Executive Aggression." In *Atlantic Monthly,* November, 1908. cii, 577-589.

ALLEN, GARDNER W.: *Our Naval War with France.* Boston: 1909.
Our Navy and the Barbary Corsairs. Boston: 1905.

A[LLEN], R. L.: "Agriculture of Louisiana." In DeBow's *Commercial Review of the South and West* (New Orleans), May, 1847. iii, 412-419.

ANDREWS, CHARLES M.: ''British Committees, Commissions, and Councils of Trade and Plantations, 1622-1675.'' In *Johns Hopkins University Studies* (1908), xxvi.

ANSON, SIR WILLIAM R., ed.: *Autobiography and Political Correspondence of Augustus Henry, Third Duke of Grafton, K. G.* London: 1898.
The Law and Custom of the Constitution. Part II. The Crown, 2d ed. Oxford: 1896.

APPLETON'S *Cyclopaedia of American Biography.* Ed. by James Grant Wilson and John Fiske. 7 vols. New York: 1887-1900.

ATTORNEY-GENERAL OF THE UNITED STATES: ''Contrast between Duties of the . . . . and those of the Law Officer of the British Crown.'' Note in 38 *American Law Review,* November-December, 1904. Pp. 924-925.

AUCOC, L.: *Le Conseil d' Etat avant et depuis 1789.* Paris: 1876.

BACON, FRANCIS: *The Essays or Counsels, Civil and Moral.* Ed. by S. H. Reynolds. Oxford: 1891.

BAGEHOT, WALTER: *The English Constitution.* Reprinted from the ''Fortnightly Review.'' London: 1867.

BAKER, WILLIAM S.: *Washington after the Revolution, 1784-1799.* Philadelphia: 1898.

BALDWIN, JAMES F.: ''Antiquities of the King's Council.'' In *English Historical Review,* January, 1906. xxi, 1-20. ''Early Records of the King's Council.'' In *American Historical Review,* October, 1905. xi, 1-15. ''The Beginnings of the King's Council.'' In *Transactions of the Royal Historical Society* (1905). xix, n. s. 27-59. ''The King's Council from Edward I to Edward III.'' In *Eng. Hist. Review,* January, 1908. xxiii, 1-14. ''The Privy Council of the Time of Richard II.'' In *Amer. Hist. Review,* October, 1906. xii, 1-14.

BALDWIN, SIMEON E.: *Modern Political Institutions.* Boston: 1898.

See especially chap. iv, "Absolute Power an American Institution," pp. 80-116.

BANCROFT, GEORGE: *History of the Formation of the Constitution of the United States of America.* 4th ed. 2 vols. New York: 1884.

BEER, GEORGE L.: *British Colonial Policy, 1754-1765.* New York: 1907.

[BENTHAM, JEREMY]: *A Fragment on Government;* being an Examination of What is Delivered, on the Subject of Government in General, in the Introduction to Sir William Blackstone's Commentaries. London: 1776.

BISHOP, JOEL P.: *New Commentaries on the Criminal Law.* 8th ed. 2 vols. Chicago: 1892.

BLACKSTONE, SIR WILLIAM: *Commentaries on the Laws of England.* 4 vols. Oxford: 1765-1769.

BOLINGBROKE, FIRST VISCOUNT: *Works.* 15 vols. London: 1798.

BOLLES, ALBERT S.: *Financial History of the United States.* Vol. i, 1774-1789. New York: 1879.

BROWN, WILLIAM G.: *The Life of Oliver Ellsworth.* New York: 1905.

BROWNE, DANIEL J.: "Progress and Public Encouragement of Agriculture in Russia, Prussia, and the United States." In *Executive Documents,* 35 Cong., 1 sess. (1857-1858), iv, No. 30, pp. 1-50.

BRUCE, PHILIP A.: *Institutional History of Virginia in the Seventeenth Century.* 2 vols. New York: 1910.
Illuminating glimpses of the colonial Attorneys-General.

BRYCE, JAMES: *The American Commonwealth.* New and revised ed. 2 vols. New York: 1910.

BUCHANAN, JAMES: *Works.* . . . . Ed. by John Bassett Moore. 12 vols. Philadelphia: 1907-1911.

BURKE, EDMUND: *Works.* . . . . Revised ed. 12 vols. Boston: 1866.

BUTTERFIELD, KENYON L.: "Farmers' Social Organizations." In L. H. Bailey's *Cyclopedia of American Agriculture,* iv (1909), 289-297.

Calendars of State Papers, Domestic Series [1603-1641]. 22 vols. London: 1857 ff. *Ibid.* [1690-1695], 4 vols. London: 1898-1906.

CARVER, THOMAS N.: "Historical Sketch of American Agriculture." In Bailey's *Cyclopedia of Amer. Agriculture,* iv, 39-70.

CHITWOOD, OLIVER P.: "Justice in Colonial Virginia." In *Johns Hopkins Univ. Studies* (1905), xxiii.

CLARENDON, EARL OF: *The Life of Edward, Earl of Clarendon.* By Himself. 2 vols. Oxford: 1857.
The History of the Rebellion and Civil Wars in England. New ed. 8 vols. Oxford: 1826.

CLARK, DAVIS W.: *The Problem of Life;* a Funeral Discourse on the Occasion of the Death of Hon. John McLean, LL. D. . . . . Preached in Cincinnati, April 28, 1861. Cincinnati: 1861.

CLARKE, WILLIAM: *The Clarke Papers.* Selections . . . . ed. C. H. Firth. 4 vols. Camden Society and Royal Historical Society. London: 1891-1901.

CLEVELAND, GROVER: *Presidential Problems.* New York: 1904.
Useful especially for the first essay, "The Independence of the Executive," pp. 3-76.

COLEMAN, MRS. ANN MARY: *Life of John J. Crittenden,* with Selections from his Correspondence and Speeches. 2 vols. Philadelphia: 1871.

COMMERCE AND LABOR: *Organization and Law of the Department.* Washington: 1904. (Document No. 13.)

CONNECTICUT: *Public Acts for 1897.* Hartford: 1898.

CONWAY, MONCURE D.: *Omitted Chapters of History disclosed in the Life and Papers of Edmund Randolph.* New York: 1888.

COOLEY, THOMAS M.: *Michigan.* Boston: 1905. American Commonwealth Series.
Useful for comments on the career of Judge A. B. Woodward.

[COOPER, JAMES F.]: *Notions of the Americans:* Picked up by a Travelling Bachelor. 2 vols. London: 1828.

For an estimate of this work, see *James Fenimore Cooper.* By Thomas R. Lounsbury. Boston: 1883, pp. 100 ff. Amer. Men of Letters.

Cox, HOMERSHAM: *The British Commonwealth:* or a Commentary on the Institutions and Principles of British Government. London: 1854.

The Institutions of the English Government; being an Account of the Constitution, Powers, and Procedure, of its Legislative, Judicial, and Administrative Departments. London: 1863.

CUSHING, CALEB: *Memorial of.* . . . . Newburyport: 1879.

''Office and Duties of Attorney-General.'' In 5 *American Law Register* (Philadelphia), December, 1856, pp. 65-94.

CUSTIS, GEORGE W. P.: *Recollections and Private Memoirs of Washington* by his adopted Son; with a Memoir by his Daughter . . . . and Notes by B. J. Lossing. New York: 1860.

[DE LOLME, JEAN L.] : *Constitution de l'Angleterre.* Amsterdam: 1771.

For sketch of the author, see *Dictionary of National Biography,* xiv, 325-327.

The Constitution of England; or, an Account of the English Government. New ed. with Life and Notes by John MacGregor, M. P. Bohn's Library. London: 1853.

DICEY, ALBERT V.: *Introduction to the Study of the Law of the Constitution.* 5th ed. London: 1897.

Lectures on the Relation between Law and Public Opinion in England during the Nineteenth Century. London: 1905. *The Privy Council.* London: 1887.

Dictionary of National Biography. Eds. Leslie Stephen and Sidney Lee. 68 vols. London: 1885-1904.

Dictionary of Political Economy. Ed. by R. H. Inglis Palgrave. 3 vols. London: 1894-1899.

i, 156-157, for a brief account of the English Board of Agriculture, 1793-1817.

Documentary History of the Constitution of the United States of America. 1786-1870. 5 vols. Washington: 1894-1905.

DRAKE, FRANCIS S.: *Memorials of the Society of the Cincinnati of Massachusetts.* Boston: 1873.

DUPRIEZ, L.: *Les Ministres dans les principaux Pays d'Europe et d'Amérique.* 3e éd. 2 vols. Paris: 1892-1893.

EASBY-SMITH, JAMES S.: *The Department of Justice:* its History and Functions. Washington: 1904.

ELLIOT, JONATHAN, ed.: *The Debates in the Several State Conventions, on the Adoption of the Federal Constitution . . . .* Together with the Journal of the Federal Convention. 2d ed. 4 vols. Washington: 1836.
A supplementary volume (v), Washington: 1845, contains the Debates in the Philadelphia Convention together with Madison's "Diary."

EVELYN, JOHN: *Memoirs. . . . .* comprising his Diary, from 1641 to 1705-06. Ed. by W. Bray. New ed. 5 vols. London: 1827.

EVERETT, EDWARD, and JOHN MCLEAN: "Letters between . . . . relating to the Use of Patronage in Elections." In *Proceedings of the Massachusetts Historical Society.* 3d ser. i, 359-393. February Meeting, 1908.

FAIRLIE, JOHN A.: *The National Administration of the United States of America.* New York: 1905.

FARRAND, MAX: "Compromises of the Constitution." In *Amer. Hist. Review,* April, 1904. ix, 479-489.
(Ed.) *The Records of the Federal Convention of 1787.* 3 vols. New Haven: 1911.

FINLEY, JOHN H., and JOHN F. SANDERSON: *The American Executive and Executive Methods.* New York: 1908. Amer. State Series.

FIRTH, CHARLES H.: "Clarendon's 'History of the Rebellion.'" In *Eng. Hist. Review,* January, 1904. xix, 26-54.
The House of Lords during the Civil War. New York: 1910.

FISH, CARL R.: *The Civil Service and the Patronage.* New York: 1905. Harv. Hist. Studies, ix.

FORCE, PETER, ed.: *American Archives.* A Documentary History of the North American Colonies. 4th ser. March 7, 1774-July 4, 1776. 6 vols. 5th ser. July 4, 1776-September 30, 1783. 3 vols. Washington: 1837 ff.

FORD, PAUL L., ed.: *Essays on the Constitution of the United States,* published during its Discussions by the People, 1787-1788. Brooklyn: 1892.

Pamphlets on the Constitution of the United States, published during its Discussions by the People, 1787-1788; with Notes and a Bibliography. Brooklyn: 1888.

The Federalist. A Commentary on the Constitution of the United States by Alexander Hamilton, James Madison, and John Jay. New York: 1898.

"Pinckney's Draft of a Constitution." In *Nation,* June 13, 1895. lx, 458-459.

FORD, WORTHINGTON C.: *George Washington.* Memorial ed. 2 vols. New York: 1900.

W. C. F. *et al. Report to the President by the Committee on Department Methods: Documentary Historical Publications of the United States Government.* Dated November 24, 1908. Washington: 1909.

A general survey in brief compass of the official printed and MS. materials of Colonial and United States history in possession of the Government.

The United States and Spain in 1790. . . . . Brooklyn: 1890.

Valuable for "opinions in writing" given to President Washington.

FOXCROFT, [MISS] H. C.: *The Life and Letters of Sir George Savile.* 2 vols. London: 1898.

FRY, WILLIAM H.: "New Hampshire as a Royal Province." New York: 1908. *Columbia Univ. Studies.* xxix.

GARDINER, SAMUEL R., ed.: *Constitutional Documents of the Puritan Revolution, 1628-1660.* Oxford: 1889.

History of the Great Civil War, 1642-1649. 3 vols. London: 1886 ff.

GARNETT, JAMES M.: *Biographical Sketch of Hon. James Mercer Garnett* . . . . with Mercer-Garnett and Mercer Genealogies. Richmond: 1910.

GIBBS, GEORGE, ed.: *Memoirs of the Administrations of Washington and John Adams;* ed. from the Papers of Oliver Wolcott, Secretary of the Treasury. 2 vols. New York: 1846.

GOODNOW, FRANK J.: *The Principles of the Administrative Law of the United States.* New York: 1905.

GREATHOUSE, CHARLES H., comp.: *A Historical Sketch of the U. S. Department of Agriculture;* its Objects and Present Organization. Revised ed. Issued as Bulletin 3, Division of Publications. Washington: 1907.

GREENE, EVARTS B.: *Provincial America: 1690-1740.* New York: 1905. The Amer. Nation. vi.
The Provincial Governor in the English Colonies of North America. New York: 1898. Harv. Hist. Studies. vii.

GREVILLE, CHARLES C. F.: *Memoirs;* a Journal of the Reigns of King George IV, and King William IV. Ed. by Henry Reeve. 3d ed. 3 vols. London: 1875.

GREY, ANCHITELL, comp.: *Debates of the House of Commons from 1667 to 1694.* 10 vols. London: 1763.

GREY, EARL: *Parliamentary Government considered with Reference to a Reform of Parliament.* London: 1858.

GUGGENHEIMER, JAY C.: "The Development of the Executive Departments, 1775-1789." In *Essays in the Constitutional History of the United States in the Formative Period.* Ed. by J. Franklin Jameson. Boston: 1889. Pp. 116-185.

HALL, CAPTAIN BASIL: *Travels in North America, in the Years 1827 and 1828.* 2 vols. Philadelphia: 1829.

HALLAM, HENRY: *Constitutional History of England from the Accession of Henry VII to the Death of George II.* 3 vols. Paris: 1827.

HAMILTON, ALEXANDER: *Complete Works.* Ed. by Henry Cabot Lodge. 9 vols. New York: 1885-1886.

HAMILTON, ALLAN McL.: *The Intimate Life of Alexander Hamilton* .... based chiefly upon original Family Letters and other Documents, etc. New York: 1910.

HAMILTON, JOHN C.: *History of the Republic of the United States,* as traced in the Writings of Alexander Hamilton and of his Contemporaries. 7 vols. New York: 1857-1864.

[HAMILTON, THOMAS]: *Men and Manners in America.* By the Author of Cyril Thornton. 2d Amer. ed. 2 vols. Philadelphia: 1833.

HARDWICKE PAPERS: *Miscellaneous State Papers.* From 1501 to 1726. 2 vols. London: 1778.

HATCH, LOUIS C.: *The Administration of the American Revolutionary Army.* New York: 1904. Harv. Hist. Studies. x.

HATSELL, JOHN: *Precedents of Proceedings in the House of Commons.* 2d ed. 3 vols. in two. London: 1785.

HEARN, WILLIAM E.: *The Government of England:* its Structure and its Development. 2d ed. London: 1886.

HENING, WILLIAM W., ed.; *The Statutes at Large:* being a Collection of all the Laws of Virginia, from the first Session of the Legislature, in the Year 1619. 13 vols. Richmond: 1819-1823.

HINSDALE, MARY L.: "The Cabinet and Congress: an historical Inquiry." In *Proceedings of the Amer. Pol. Science Association* (1905), ii, 127-135. "The Cabinet of the United States." In *The Americana:* a universal reference Library. New York: [1907-1908]. xv.

HOAR, GEORGE F.: *Autobiography of Seventy Years.* 2 vols. New York: 1903.

HOLST, HERMANN E. VON: *Constitutional and Political History of the United States.* Trans. by John J. Lalor *et al.* 8 vols. Chicago: 1877-1892.

HOUGH, F. B., ed.: *Proceedings of a Convention of Delegates from several of the New England States,* held at Boston, August 3-9, 1780. Albany: 1867.

HUNT, GAILLARD: *The Department of State of the United States:* its History and Functions. Washington: 1893. "The History of the Department of State." In *The Amer. Journal of International Law* as follows:

October, 1907, i, 867-890.	April, 1910, iv, 384-403.
July, 1908, ii, 591-606.	July, 1910, iv, 596-611.
January, 1909, iii, 137-162.	January, 1911, v, 118-143.
October, 1909, iii. 909-927.	April, 1911, v, 414-432.

INDUSTRIAL COMMISSION: *Report.* 19 vols. Washington: 1900-1902.

IREDELL, JAMES: "Answers to Mr. Mason's Objections to the New Constitution recommended by the late Convention at Philadelphia. By Marcus" [Dated January 8, 1788]. Reprinted in Griffith J. McRee's *Life and Correspondence of James Iredell* (2 vols. New York: 1857-1858), ii, 197 ff.

JAMESON, J. FRANKLIN: "Studies in the History of the Federal Convention of 1787." In the *Annual Report* of the Amer. Hist. Association for 1902. i, 89-167.

JANET, PAUL: *Histoire de la Science Politique* dans ses Rapports avec la Morale. 3e éd. 2 vols. Paris: 1887.

JAY, JOHN: *Correspondence and Public Papers.* Ed. by Henry P. Johnston. 4 vols. New York: 1890-1893.

JAY, WILLIAM: *The Life of John Jay* . . . . with Selections from his Correspondence and Miscellaneous Papers. 2 vols. New York: 1833.

JEFFERSON, THOMAS: *Memoir, Correspondence, and Miscellanies from the Papers of* . . . . Ed. by T. J. Randolph. 4 vols. Charlottesville: 1829. *Writings* . . . . being his Autobiography, Correspondence . . . . and other Writings. Ed. by H. A. Washington. 9 vols. Washington: 1853-1854. *Writings.* Ed. by Paul Leicester Ford. 10 vols. New York: 1892-1899.

JENKINS, JOHN S.: *Lives of the Governors of the State of New York.* Auburn: 1851.
Useful for the sketch of John Jay, pp. 74-131.

JENKS, EDWARD: *Parliamentary England, the Evolution of the Cabinet System.* New York: 1903. Story of the Nations.
The Constitutional Experiments of the Commonwealth. Cambridge Hist. Essays, No. III. Cambridge: 1890.

JOHNSON, SAMUEL: *Dictionary.* London: 1755. 2d ed. London: 1755. 3d ed. London: 1765. Revised 4th ed. London: 1773.

JONES, JOSEPH: *Letters,* 1777-1787. Ed. by W. C. Ford. Washington: 1889.

JOYCE, HERBERT: *The History of the Post-Office from its Establishment down to 1836.* London: 1893.
See especially Chapter viii, 110-116, ''American Posts, 1692-1707.''

Kalendar, The Royal: or, complete and correct Annual Register [1808-1837]. 30 vols. London: 1809 ff.

KENDALL, AMOS: *Autobiography.* Ed. by his Son-in-Law, William Stickney. Boston: 1872.

KENNEDY, JOHN P.: *Memoirs of the Life of William Wirt.* 2 vols. Philadelphia: 1849.
For comments on this work, see the *Monthly Law Reporter* (Boston), December, 1850, xiii, 373-379.

KING, RUFUS: *Life and Correspondence.* Ed. by Charles R. King. 6 vols. New York: 1894-1900.

LANMAN, CHARLES: *Biographical Annals of the Civil Government of the United States, during its First Century.* Washington: 1876.

LA ROCHEFOUCAULD-LIANCOURT, DUC DE: *Travels through the United States of North America in the Years 1795, 1796, and 1797.* 2 vols. London: 1799.

LEARNED, HENRY B.: ''Origin of the Title Superintendent of Finance.'' In *Amer. Hist. Review,* April, 1905. x, 565-573. ''The Origin and Creation of the President's Cabinet, 1781-1793.'' In *Yale Review,* August, 1906, xv, 160-194. ''Qualifications of Cabinet Officers.'' In *Nation*

(New York), February 20, 1908. lxxxvi, 169. "The Cabinet." In *Hartford Courant*, March 19, 1908. "Historical Significance of the Term 'Cabinet' in England and the United States." In *Am. Pol. Science Review*, August, 1909. iii, 329-346. "The Attorney-General and the Cabinet." In *Pol. Science Quarterly*, September, 1909. xxiv, 444-467. "The Diary of Gideon Welles." In *Nation*, May 12, 1910. xc, 480. "The Attorney-General and the Cabinet." In *Nation*, September 22, 1910. xci, 260-261. "The Hon. Charles Pinckney, LL. D." In *Nation*, August 24, 1911. xciii, 164. "The Postmaster-General." In *Yale Review*, October, 1911. i (n.s.), 99-118.

LECKY, WILLIAM E. H.: *A History of England in the Eighteenth Century.* 8 vols. London: 1883-1890.

LEE, RICHARD H.: "Letter to Edmond Randolph, esq." In Carey's *American Museum*, December, 1787. ii, 553-558.

LEFTWICH, GEORGE J.: "Robert J. Walker." In *Green Bag* (Boston), March, 1903. xv, 101-106.

LISTER, T. H.: *Life and Administration of Edward, First Earl of Clarendon.* 3 vols. London: 1837-1838.

LODGE, HENRY C.: *A Frontier Town and other Essays.* New York: 1906.
    Contains an essay on "The Senate of the United States," pp. 56-85.
Life and Letters of George Cabot. 2d ed. Boston: 1878.

LOW, SIDNEY: *The Governance of England.* New York: 1904.

LOWELL, A. LAWRENCE: *Essays on Government.* Boston: 1889.
    See Essay I, "Cabinet Responsibility and the Constitution," pp. 20-59.
The Government of England. 2 vols. New York: 1908.

MACAULAY, THOMAS B.: *The History of England from the Accession of James the Second.* 5 vols. Boston: 1901.

McCARTY, DWIGHT G.: *The Territorial Governors of the Old Northwest.* A Study in Territorial Administration.

Iowa City: 1910. Publications of the State Historical Society of Iowa.
Glimpses of Judge A. B. Woodward.

McCONACHIE, LAUROS G.: *Congressional Committees:* a Study of the Origin and Development of our National and Local Legislative Methods. New York: 1898.

[McLAUGHLIN, ANDREW C.] : "Sketch of Pinckney's Plan for a Constitution, 1787." In *Amer. Hist. Review,* July, 1904. ix, 735-747.

MACLAY, WILLIAM: *Journal.* Ed. by Edgar S. Maclay. New York: 1890.

McLEAN, JOHN: See D. W. Clark, Edward Everett, W. B. Sprague.

MADISON, JAMES: *Letters and other Writings.* Ed. by W. C. Rives. 4 vols. Philadelphia: 1865. *Papers* . . . . purchased by Order of Congress; being his Correspondence and Reports of Debates during the Congress of the Confederation. . . . . Ed. by Henry D. Gilpin. 3 vols. Washington: 1840. *Writings* . . . . comprising his Public Papers and his Private Correspondence. . . . . Ed. by Gaillard Hunt. 9 vols. New York: 1906-1910.

MAGIE, DAVID: *Life of Garret Augustus Hobart.* New York: 1910.

MASSON, DAVID: *The Life of John Milton:* narrated in Connexion with the Political, Ecclesiastical, and Literary History of his Time. 7 vols. London: 1877-1896.

MEIGS, WILLIAM M.: *The Growth of the Constitution in the Federal Convention of 1787,* an Effort to trace the Origin and Development of each separate Clause from its first Suggestion in that Body, etc. 2d ed. Philadelphia: 1900.

MERENESS, NEWTON D.: *Maryland as a Proprietary Province.* New York: 1901.

MILES, PLINY: *Postal Reform:* its urgent Necessity and Practicability. New York: 1855.

MILLER, ELMER I.: "The Legislature of the Province of Virginia." New York: 1907. *Columbia Univ. Studies.* xxviii.

418 THE PRESIDENT'S CABINET

MONTESQUIEU, C. DE S., BARON DE: *The Spirit of Laws.* Trans. by T. Nugent. 2 vols. Cincinnati: 1873.

MOORE, CHARLES: *Governor, Judge, and Priest: Detroit, 1805-1815.* A Paper read before the Witenagemote on Friday Evening, October the Second, 1891. New York: [1891]. The "Judge" was Judge A. B. Woodward (c. 1775-1827).

MORLEY, JOHN: *Burke.* New York: 1879. Eng. Men of Letters.
Walpole. London: 1889. Twelve Eng. Statesmen.

MORRIS, GOUVERNEUR: *Diary and Letters.* Ed. by Anne C. Morris. 2 vols. New York: 1888. "Observations on the Finances of the United States, in 1789." In Jared Sparks, *Life of G. Morris,* q. v.

MOSHER, ROBERT B., comp.: *Executive Register of the United States, 1789-1902.* Baltimore: [1903].

MURAT, ACHILLE: *A Moral and Political Sketch of the United States of North America.* London: 1833.

MURRAY, JAMES A. H., and HENRY BRADLEY: *A New English Dictionary on Historical Principles.* Oxford: 1888 ff.

NEWSPAPERS: Where it has seemed advisable, newspapers have been consulted. But any mere list of such material is likely to be misleading. I have used the files of the following papers:
Pennsylvania Gazette, Philadelphia: 1779-1781.
Pennsylvania Packet, Philadelphia: 1779-1781.
Pennsylvania Packet and Daily Advertiser, Philadelphia: 1787.
American Mercury, Hartford, Conn.: 1789-1801.
National Intelligencer, Washington, D. C.: 1800 ff.
Niles's Register, Baltimore, Md.: 1811 ff.
National Journal, Washington, D. C.: 1824.
American Athenaeum, New York: 1825.
The Nation, New York: 1865 ff.
New York Times.
The Sun, New York.
The Hartford Courant.

Citations have been made from the following:

Maryland Gazette, 1747.

Connecticut Courant, 1787.

New York Journal, 1787.

United States Telegraph, 1829.

Cincinnati Gazette, 1841.

Louisville Courier-Journal, 1881.

The Commoner, Lincoln, Neb., 1901.

NICOLAS, SIR HARRIS, ed. See *Privy Council of England.*

NORTH, ROGER: *The Lives of the Right Hon. Francis North, Baron Guilford . . . . Hon. Sir Dudley North . . . . and Rev. Dr. John North.* 3 vols. London: 1826.

O'NEALL, JOHN B.: *Biographical Sketches of the Bench and Bar of South Carolina.* 2 vols. Charleston, S. C.: 1859. Useful for a sketch of Charles Pinckney.

OSGOOD, HERBERT L.: *The American Colonies in the Seventeenth Century.* 3 vols. 1904-1907.

Parliamentary History of England. Vols. v-vi [1688-1714]; xxx (1792-1794); clvi (26 April-10 May, 1906), 4th Series. London.

PAULLIN, CHARLES O.: "Early Naval Administration under the Constitution." In *Proceedings of the United States Naval Institute,* September, 1906. xxxii, 1001-1030.
The Navy of the American Revolution: its Administration, its Policy, and its Achievements. Cleveland: 1906.

PEPYS, SAMUEL: *Diary.* Ed. by H. B. Wheatley. 8 vols. London: 1893.

PERCY, LORD EUSTACE: *The Privy Council under the Tudors.* Stanhope Prize Essay, 1907. Oxford: 1907.

PICKERING, OCTAVIUS, and CHARLES W. UPHAM: *Life of Timothy Pickering.* 4 vols. Boston: 1867-1873.

PIERCE, MAJOR WILLIAM: "Notes . . . . on the Federal Convention of 1787." In *Amer. Hist. Review,* January, 1898. iii, 310-334.

PIKE, LUKE O.: *The Public Records and the Constitution.* A Lecture delivered at All Souls College, Oxford, at the

Request of the Regius Professors of Civil Law and
Modern History. . . . . With Plan of Evolution of the
chief Courts and Departments of the Government. London: 1907.

PINCKNEY, CHARLES: *Observations on the Plan of Govern-
ment submitted to the Federal Convention, in Philadel-
phia, on the 28th of May, 1787.* By the Hon. Charles
Pinckney, Esq., L. L. D., Delegate from the State of
South Carolina. . . . . New York: Printed by Francis
Childs. (No date.) Pp. 27.

For comment on this pamphlet, see *Nation*, August 24, 1911, xciii,
164. It has been recently reprinted in Farrand, *Records of the
Federal Convention* (1911), III, Appendix A, cxxix, 106-123.

POLK, JAMES K.: *The Diary of* . . . . *during his Presidency,
1845 to 1849.* Now first printed from the original Manuscript in the Collections of the Chicago Historical Society. Ed. by Milo Milton Quaife. 4 vols. Chicago:
1910.

POORE, BEN: P., ed.: *The Federal and State Constitutions,
Colonial Charters, and other Organic Laws.* Parts I and
II. 2 vols. 2d ed. Washington: 1878.

"Post Office Department." In *Collections of the Mass. Hist.
Society,* vii, 3d ser. Boston: 1838. Pp. 48-89.

A useful variety of materials from the sources, 1639-1775.

PRIVY COUNCIL OF ENGLAND: *Proceedings and Ordinances*
[1386-1542]. Ed. by Harris Nicolas. Record Commission. 7 vols. [London:] 1834-1837.

Acts of the Privy Council. Ed. by J. H. Dasent. Vols.
i-xxxii [1542-1604]. Rolls Series. London: 1890-1907.

PROTHERO, GEORGE W., ed.: *Select Statutes and other Constitutional Documents illustrative of the Reigns of Eliza-
beth and James I* [1559-1625]. Oxford: 1894.

QUINCY, JOSIAH: *Speeches delivered in the Congress of the
United States* . . . . *1805-1813.* Ed. by his Son, Edmund
Quincy. Boston: 1874.

RANDALL, HENRY S.: *The Life of Thomas Jefferson.* 3 vols.
New York: 1858.

REDLICH, JOSEF: *The Procedure of the House of Commons;* a Study of its History and present Form. Trans. by A. E. Steinthal. Introd. and Supplementary Chapter by Sir Courtenay Ilbert. 3 vols. London: 1908.

REED, WILLIAM B.: *Life and Correspondence of Joseph Reed.* 2 vols. Philadelphia: 1847.

RERESBY, SIR JOHN: *Memoirs. . . . .* Written by Himself. Ed. by James J. Cartwright. London: 1875.

RHEES, WILLIAM J., ed. and comp.: *The Smithsonian Institution:* Documents relative to its Origin and History [1835-1899]. 2 vols. Washington: 1901.

RHODES, JAMES F.: *History of the United States from the Compromise of 1850* [1850-1877]. 7 vols. New York: 1892-1906.

RICHARDSON, JAMES D., *et al.*, eds.: *A Compilation of the Messages and Papers of the Presidents* [1789-1905]. 13 vols. Washington: 1896-1906.

RIVES, WILLIAM C.: *History of the Life and Times of James Madison.* 3 vols. Boston: 1859-1868.

ROBINSON, WILLIAM C.: *The Law of Patents for Useful Inventions.* 3 vols. Boston: 1890.

ROWLAND, KATE M.: *The Life of George Mason, 1725-1792.* Including his Opinions, Public Papers, and Correspondence. 2 vols. New York: 1892.

RUSH, RICHARD: *Memoranda of a Residence at the Court of London.* 2d ed. Philadelphia: 1833.

RUSHWORTH, JOHN: *Historical Collections,* 1618-1648. 8 vols. London: 1721.

SALMON, LUCY M.: "History of the Appointing Power of the President." In *Papers of the Amer. Hist. Association.* New York: 1886. i, No. 5, pp. 291-419.

SARGENT, NATHAN: *Public Men and Events* from the Commencement of Mr. Monroe's Administration in 1817, to the Close of Mr. Fillmore's Administration, in 1853. 2 vols. Philadelphia: 1875.

SCHOULER, JAMES: *History of the United States of America under the Constitution.* [1783-1865.]   Rev. ed.   6 vols. New York: 1894-1899.

SIDGWICK, HENRY: *The Development of European Polity.* London: 1903.

SINCLAIR, JOHN: *The Correspondence of the Right Honourable Sir John Sinclair, Bart.*   2 vols.   London: 1831.
See *Dictionary of National Biography*, lii, 301-305, for article on Sinclair.

SMITH, W. ROY: *South Carolina as a Royal Province, 1719-1776.*   New York: 1903.

SOUTHARD, SAMUEL L.: *A Discourse on the professional Character and Virtues of the late William Wirt.*   Delivered in the Hall of the House of Representatives, March 18, 1834. Washington: 1834.

SPARKS, JARED: *The Life of Gouverneur Morris.*   3 vols.   Boston: 1832.

SPEED, JOHN: *History of Great Britain,* etc.   London: 1611.

SPRAGUE, WILLIAM B.: *A Discourse delivered Sunday Morning, April 7, 1861, in the Second Presbyterian Church, Albany, in Commemoration of the late Hon. John McLean, LL. D.*   Albany: 1861.

STANWOOD, EDWARD: *A History of the Presidency.*   Boston: 1898.

Statutes at Large, The.   London: 1763.   iv, 434-445 for the Act of 1710 regarding the Post-Office.

STEINER, BERNARD C.: *Life and Correspondence of James McHenry.*   Cleveland: 1907.

STEPHEN, LESLIE: *The English Utilitarians.*   3 vols.   New York: 1900.

STUART, JAMES: *Three Years in North America.*   2d ed.   2 vols.   Edinburgh: 1833.

STUBBS, WILLIAM: *The Constitutional History of England in its Origin and Development.*   3 vols.   Oxford: 1896-1903.

SULLIVAN, WILLIAM: *The Political Class Book.*   New ed.   Boston: 1831.

SUMNER, WILLIAM G.: *The Financier and the Finances of the American Revolution.* 2 vols. New York: 1891.

SWANK, JAMES M.: *The Department of Agriculture: its History and Objects.* Washington: 1872.

SWIFT, JONATHAN: *Prose Works.* Ed. by Temple Scott. 12 vols. London: 1897 ff.
See especially vols. ii, v, and x.

TANNER, EDWIN P.: "The Province of New Jersey, 1664-1738." New York: 1908. *Columbia Univ. Studies.* xxx.

TAUSSIG, FRANK W.: *The Tariff History of the United States.* 5th ed. New York: 1898.

THAYER, JAMES B., ed: *Cases on Constitutional Law.* With Notes. 2 vols. Cambridge: 1895.
John Marshall. Boston: 1901. Riverside Biographical Ser., No. 9.
Legal Essays. Boston: 1908.

TILDEN, SAMUEL J.: *Writings and Speeches.* Ed. by John Bigelow. 2 vols. New York: 1885.

TODD, ALPHEUS: *On Parliamentary Government in England: its Origin, Development, and Practical Operation.* 2 vols. London: 1867-1869.
Edited and much abbreviated by Sir Spencer Walpole. 2 vols. London: 1892.

TOWNSEND, WILLIAM K.: "Patents: 1701-1901." In *Two Centuries' Growth of American Law, 1701-1901.* By Members of the Faculty of the Yale Law School. New York: 1901. Pp. 392 ff.

TRENCHARD, THOMAS [i.e. JOHN]: *A Short History of Standing Armies in England.* London: 1698.
Important for remarks on the Privy Council in relation to the Cabinet. For the proper name of the author—John and not Thomas—see *Dictionary of National Biography* sub "John Trenchard."

TROLLOPE, MRS. [FRANCES M.]: *Domestic Manners of the Americans.* 2 vols. in one. London: 1832.

TRUMBULL, JOHN: *Autobiography, Reminiscences, and Letters, from 1756 to 1841.* New York: 1841.

TUCKER, GEORGE: *Life of Thomas Jefferson.* 2 vols. Philadelphia: 1837.

TUCKER, GILBERT M.: *American Agricultural Periodicals:* an Historical Sketch. Privately printed. Albany: 1909.

TURNER, FREDERICK J.: "Social Forces in American History." In *Amer. Hist. Review,* January, 1911. xvi, 217-233.

UNITED STATES:

CONGRESS—PROCEEDINGS:

Journals of Congress [1774-1788]. 13 vols. Philadelphia: 1800-1801.

The Secret Journals of the Acts and Proceedings of Congress. 4 vols. Boston: 1821-1823.

Journals of the Continental Congress, 1774-1789. Ed. from the Original Records by Worthington C. Ford (15 vols. [1774-1779]. Washington: 1904-1909) and Gaillard Hunt (vols. 16-18 [1780] thus far issued. Washington: 1910).

Annals of Congress: Debates and Proceedings in Congress. 42 vols. Washington: 1834-1856.

Register of Debates in Congress, 1824-1837. 29 vols. Washington: 1825-1837.

Congressional Globe, 1834-1873. 108 vols. Washington: 1834-1873.

Congressional Record, 1873 ff. Washington: 1873 ff.

CONGRESS—MISCELLANY:

American State Papers. Documents, Legislative and Executive. 38 vols. Washington: 1832-1861.

The Revolutionary Diplomatic Correspondence. Ed. by Francis Wharton. 6 vols. Washington: 1889.

Executive Journals of the Senate: 1789-1891. 27 vols. Washington: 1829-1901.

Vols. 28-32 are now (October, 1911) printed, covering the years 1891-1901, but they have not been distributed.

Senate Manual. Ed. of February 8, 1905. Washington: 1905.

LAWS, ETC.:

The Public Statutes at Large (1789-1911). 36 vols.

Revised Statutes. (1st ed.) Washington: 1875. 2d ed. Washington: 1878.

Official Opinions of the Attorneys-General. 27 vols. [1852-1909].

The first collection of these Opinions was made and issued in 1841. See Chapter vii of this volume. They were arranged for serial publication and issued in 1852 ff.

United States Circuit Court of the District of Columbia, Reports of Cases, Civil and Criminal, in the (1836-1841). Ed. by William Cranch. 5 vols. Boston: 1853.

United States Supreme Court Reports: 1 Cranch, 2d ed. New York: 1812. Pp. 165 ff. [*Marbury* vs. *Madison.*] 167 *Reports*, pp. 324-344. [*Parsons* vs. *United States.*] Discussion of legislative and judicial history of the President's power of removal.

UNITED STATES AGRICULTURAL SOCIETY: A list of the Publications, with comment, has already been printed as Note 3 to Chapter xi of these Studies, *supra,* pp. 343-345.

VALOIS, NOEL: *Le Conseil du Roi aux xive, xve, et xvie Siècles.* Paris: 1888.

VAN TYNE, CLAUDE H., and WALDO G. LELAND: *Guide to the Archives of the United States in Washington.* 2d ed. revised and enlarged by W. G. Leland. Washington: 1907.

VARNUM, JUDGE JAMES M.: "Oration delivered July 4, 1788, at Marietta, Ohio." In Carey's *American Museum,* May, 1789, v, 453-455.

Contemporary estimate by Judge (or General) Varnum of Knox, Secretary at War.

"Walker, Robert J." In *Democratic Review.* February, 1845. xvi, 157-164.

WASHINGTON, GEORGE: *Diary . . . . from 1789 to 1791.* Ed. by Benson J. Lossing. Richmond: 1861.

Writings. Collected and ed. by Worthington C. Ford. 14 vols. New York: 1889-1893.

Writings, with Life by Jared Sparks. 12 vols. Boston: 1837.

WATSON, ELKANAH: *History of the Rise, Progress, and Existing Condition of the Western Canals in the State of New York . . . . together with the Rise, Progress, and Existing State of Modern Agricultural Societies, on the Berkshire System.* Albany: 1820.

WEBSTER, DANIEL: *Letters . . . .* from Documents owned principally by the New Hampshire Historical Society. Ed. by Claude H. Van Tyne. New York: 1902.
Works. 6 vols. Boston: 1851.

WEBSTER, NOAH: *Sketches of American Policy.* Hartford: 1785.

WEBSTER, PELATIAH: *Political Essays on the Nature and Operation of Money, Public Finance, and other Subjects.* Philadelphia: 1791.

WELLES, GIDEON: "Diary." In *Atlantic Monthly,* February-November, 1909. ciii-civ. *Ibid.,* February, 1910-January, 1911. cv-cvii.
The work, presumably amplified, is about to appear as *The Diary of Gideon Welles.* Introd. by John T. Morse, Jr. 3 vols. Boston: 1911.

WHARTON, FRANCIS, ed.: See United States: Congress—Miscellany.

WILSON, WILLIAM L.: "The American Post-Office." In *The Ship of State,* by Those at the Helm. Boston: 1903.

WILSON, WOODROW: *Congressional Government:* a Study in American Politics. 13th ed. Boston: 1898.
Chapter v, 242-293. "The Executive."

WOODWARD, AUGUSTUS B.: *Considerations on the Executive Government of the United States of America.* Flatbush, N. Y.: 1809.
The Presidency of the United States. New York: 1825.
The material for this latter pamphlet was first issued in installments in the *National Journal* of Washington, D. C., between April 24 and August 31, 1824. For further comment see Note 1 to Chapter x.

WOOLLEY, MARY E.: "The Early History of the American
Post-Office." In *Papers from the Historical Seminary
of Brown University,* ed. by J. Franklin Jameson. No.
2, pp. 33. Providence: 1894.

WRIGHT, FRANCES: *Views of Society and Manners in America*
(1818-1820). 2d ed. London: 1822.

YONGE, WALTER: *Diary* . . . . *from 1604 to 1628.* Camden
Society. London: 1848.

INDEX

son (1816) urges new executive department on, 161 ff.; provision (1818-1819) for Attorney-General's Office, 169; authorizes *Official Opinions* (1841) issued, 171; alterations (1830) in Attorney-Generalship, 173-175, 273; disregards Polk's suggestions (1845), 176; favors bill for Department of Justice (1870), 191; provides for fleet (1794), 207-209; authorizes J. Adams to employ vessels, 212; attitude toward postal arrangements (1789 ff.), 230-231; forced, after 1865, to reorganize Post-Office, 234-235; raises salary (1827) of Postmaster-General, 240; recognizes need for Interior Department, 253, 275, 276-287, *passim;* against separating Home Department (1789) from Foreign Affairs, 255; Madison's special message to, on burdens of secretariat (1812), 257; declares war (1812), 257; no action on Home Department project (1825-1826), 271-272; favors similar project (1830), 273; aroused to need of Agricultural Department, 294-295, 334, 374; opposes increase of administrative machinery (1817), 307-308; creates committee on agriculture (1820), 309, note 30, 322, 324; first appropriation (1839) for agriculture, 311; tables petition of Agricultural Society of the U. S. (1842), 311; Taylor's suggestion of agricultural bureau to (1849), 314; appropriations for agriculture (1850 ff.), 321, 326, 340-341; memorialized by U. S. Agricultural Society for a Department

of Agriculture, 324; freedom from extremists (1862), 331; petitions before, for Secretaryship of Agriculture, 334-335; charters U. S. Agricultural Society (1860), 341-342; power to regulate commerce, 350; development of standing committees, 350-351; influence of President Roosevelt on (1901), 357; effort to establish ninth Department in, 358-365; indisposed unduly to enlarge Cabinet, 363. *See* House of Representatives, and Senate, *infra.*

Considerations on the Executive Government of the U. S. (1809), by A. B. Woodward, cited and quoted, 142 ff., 288.

Constellation (frigate), 208, 212.

Constitution (frigate), 208, 212.

Constitution of the United States: imposes responsibility on President, 4, 98, 379 ff.; helped to predetermine advisory council, 5, 86, 379, 390 ff.; contemplated principal officers, 5, 92, 97; allowed discretion to President, 6, 86, 140 ff., 379 ff.; ''opinions in writing,'' 5, 87-88, 120, 143, 383 ff.; change of government (1789) accomplished by, 59; opposition to (1787), 73; final draft of, 85; no provision for council to President in, 88, 91, 119, 139, 144, 149, 151, 153, 369; C. Pinckney doubtful about advisability of having recognition of council in, 91; tenure of office of secretariat unprovided by, 97; appointing power arranged by, 101; attempts to amend, in order to give Congress appointment of Secretary of the Treas-

178; favors Department of the Interior (1849) as Senator, 281, 283, 284, 287.

Dayton, Jonathan: youngest member of Philadelphia Convention (1787), 91, note [61].

De Bow, James D. B.: his *Commercial Review* cited, 313; member of U. S. Agricultural Society, 320.

Delano, Columbus: 404.

De Lolme, Jean L.: influence of, over J. Bentham, A. Hamilton and others through his *Constitution de l'Angleterre* (1771), 28; influence of Montesquieu on, 28-29; analysis of work of, 29-31; estimate of, 31-32, note [44], 35; quoted by Hamilton (1788) on unity of executive, 380.

"Department": as applied to U. S. Post-Office, 231, note [21], 232, 373.

Department of the Productive Arts: 329.

Departments: contemplated in Constitution, 5, 92, 97, 119; movement toward, in Revolution, 52 ff., 201 ff.; five, in G. Morris's plan for council (1787), 76; four, in C. Pinckney's plan, 91; debates in 1789 on, 97-100; "executive" as applied to, 100 ff., 372 ff.; committee (1789) on, 109; rank of, 144; suggestion that Attorney-General (1830) be raised to head of one of, 173; relation of President to the, 182; minor changes in (1812), 257; lack of proper differentiation of tasks in, 273 ff.; comments on, 333; trend of efforts (1865 ff.) for, 351 ff. *See* Principal Officers, *infra*.

Dexter, Samuel: 217.

Diary of James K. Polk: cited, 177, 182, 285, 383, 385.

Diary of Gideon Welles: cited, 182, 383, note [30].

Dicey, Professor Albert V.: estimate by, of Bagehot and W. E. Hearn, 41; peculiarity of English cabinet history, 42; general obligation to, 404.

Dickinson, Hon. Jacob M.: authority (1911) for practice of written opinions under President Taft, 384, note [33].

Dickinson, John: 71.

Diocletian: 2.

Dissertation on the Political Union and Constitution of the Thirteen United States (1783), by Pelatiah Webster: cited, 62, note [35], 254.

District Attorneys: 185, 188.

Domestic Affairs. *See* Home Department; Interior Department, *infra*.

Dongan, Governor Thomas: 222.

Douglas, Stephen A.: member of U. S. Agricultural Society, 320; opposed to either Bureau or Department of Agriculture, 324.

Downing Street: 153.

Dred Scott case: 237.

Duane, James: favors single heads (1780), 50 ff.

Duane, William J.: removal of, commented on, 103 ff., 381-382.

Eaton, John H.: Secretary of War, 247.

Edward VI (1547-1553): Privy Council under, 20.

Elgin, Earl of: 252.

Ellsworth, Henry L.: Commissioner of Patents (1836-1845), 309, 331 sketch of, 310 ff.; recommends agricultural bureau (1843), 311; comments of J. Q. Adams (1845) on, 311-312; accomplishments of, 312-313; interest in Smithson bequest, 311, 316.

Ellsworth, Oliver: favors Madison's idea for a council of revision (1787), 69; plan for advisory council, 75; influence of, on G. Morris's revised plan of advisory council, 77; wishes principal officers to give advice, 86-87; chairman of committee in Senate (1789) to arrange judicial establishment, 105; probable author of Judiciary Act, 106; his son, Henry L., 309.

Estates-General: similarity to Congress of Confederation, 49-50.

Evarts, William M.: fees of, for legal services, 185; cited on legal aspect of presidential power of removal, 381, note [29].

Evelyn, John (1620-1706): cited on usage of "cabinet," 15; characterized Thomas Neale in his *Diary*, 223.

Everett, Edward: J. McLean's idea of Cabinet conveyed to, 150, 242; Representative from Massachusetts, 220; remarks of, on office of Postmaster-General (1828), 220; impressions of J. McLean, 238, 242, 244, 249; addressed U. S. Agricultural Society (1855), 320.

Ewing, Thomas: remarks on incongruity in title of Department of Interior (1849), 281, 289-290.

Examiner of Claims (State Department): 190.

Executive, American: unity of the, 3, 50 ff., 66, 67, 69, 70, 72, 75, 76, 85, 97, 98, 102 ff., 110, 119, 120, 122 ff., 135, 140, 163, 169, 172, 179, 182, 189-190, 200-201, 235, 240, 242, 250, 260, 280, 371, 373-374, 378 ff., 388, 392; responsibility of the, 4, 7, 67, 73, 77, 84, 87, 98 ff., 154, 182, 379 ff., 387, 391, 392; discretion of the, 48, 75 ff., 83, 86 ff., 99, 119, 126, 136, 139 ff., 149-150, 156, 179, 188, 217, 233 ff., 369, 379 ff., 388, 390, 392; fear of the, 49, 80, 233; independence of the, 49, 62, 66 ff., 73, 74, 83, 84, 126 ff., 170, 172; single form of, approved by the Philadelphia Convention (1787), 52, 75, 380, note [25]; theories of, before the Convention, 66-68; a directory, 141, 142, 149-150; stability of, doubted, 142-143; travellers' comments on the, 150 ff.

Fairs: nature of, in colonial and Revolutionary times, 304, 306; in Wethersfield, Conn. (1784), Washington, D. C. (1804 ff.), 306; "Arlington Sheep-Shearing," 306; of the U. S. Agricultural Society (1853 ff.), 320.

Farrand, Max: comment on his *Records of the Federal Convention* (1911), 348, note [3].

Federalist, The: clue to possible authorship of No. 50 of, 162, note [7]; reveals interest of authors in general problems of commerce regulation, 348; quotation from, on unity of the executive, 380, note [24].

Fessenden, William Pitt: member of U. S. Agricultural Society, 320.

FILLMORE, MILLARD (1850-

of the ideals of the office of, 392-393; salary of the, 396 (Table A.); perquisites of the, 398-399. *See* Executive, American, *supra.*

Presidency of the United States (The), by A. B. Woodward: quoted, 146-147; cited, 288.

Preston, Senator W. C.: theory (1842) of presidential office, 67, note [2].

Price, Dr. Richard: 56.

Prime Minister: functions of, 3, 36; modern conception of, 31; usage of phrase (1878), and recognition of, in order of precedence (1906), 158, note [60].

Principal Officers: considered as "constitutional advisers," 5, 140, 379, 389 ff.; ideal of, as assistants, 47-48, 78, 85 ff., 107, 110, 118 ff., 122, 125 ff., 378, 392; should assist in appointments, 62, 86; appointed by President, 68-69; advisory functions of, 75 ff.; Iredell's view (1788) of, 87-88; G. Mason and G. Clinton (1787) predict council of state from combination of, 89-90; C. Pinckney's prediction and views of a Cabinet Council of, 90-94, 136, 370; assumed by Constitution, 92, 119; should be in Cabinet (1787), 93, note [65]; tenure of office of, 97; removal of, 98, 140, 381, note [29], 382, 391 ff.; confidence between, and President, 98-99, 135, 140, 182, 378, 387, 391 ff.; four (1789) provided, 97 ff.; Washington's principles in appointing, 110-111; factors making for combination of, 119 ff.; qualifications of, 144-145, 214; suggestion that

they sit either in H. of R. or Senate, 153, 154; salaries (1907) of, 157; (1853), 163, 178; (*See* Table A, Appendix, 396); sense of subordination to President, 182, 378; burdensome duties of, 256-260, *passim;* joint plan (1816) of, for Home Department, 261; letter of, to W. Lowndes quoted, 262; states from which choice of, has been made (1789-1909), 399 ff. *See* under titles of various departments and headships.

Privy Council (American): ideals (1787) of an, 72-73, 88; revised title of G. Morris's council of state, 77; historic usage and significance of phrase, 78 ff., 82, 92-93, 95-96, 369; advisory body to colonial and state governors, 79 ff.; modes of selection of, 80; composition of, doubtful, 81; unlike English institution, 81-82.

Privy Council (British): origins of, 2, 11 ff.; its effectiveness under Tudors (1485-1603), 11, 19-20; predecessor of modern English Cabinet, 11; differentiated from Cabinet Council, 16, 17; Roger North's explanation of relation of, to Cabinet Council, 18-19; divisions of, under Edward VI and successors, 20, 21; unmanageable under Charles II, 21-22; attempt to revive authority of, under Anne, 25; Hallam on, 36-37; Sir W. Temple's scheme (1679) for, 22, 45; belated institution (1787), 93; Wedderburn's invective before committee of the, 226.

Proceedings of the 29th Annual Meeting of the U. S. Agricul-